KU-594-358

OXFORD WORLD'S CLASSICS

===

ALEXANDER POPE

Selected Poetry

===

Edited with an Introduction and Notes by
PAT ROGERS

OXFORD
UNIVERSITY PRESS

OXFORD
UNIVERSITY PRESS

Great Clarendon Street, Oxford OX2 6DP

Oxford University Press is a department of the University of Oxford.
It furthers the University's objective of excellence in research, scholarship,
and education by publishing worldwide in

Oxford New York

Athens Auckland Bangkok Bogotá Buenos Aires Calcutta
Cape Town Chennai Dar es Salaam Delhi Florence Hong Kong Istanbul
Karachi Kuala Lumpur Madrid Melbourne Mexico City Mumbai
Nairobi Paris São Paulo Singapore Taipei Tokyo Toronto Warsaw

with associated companies in Berlin Ibadan

Oxford is a registered trade mark of Oxford University Press
in the UK and in certain other countries

Published in the United States
by Oxford University Press Inc., New York

Introduction and editorial matter © Pat Rogers 1994

The moral rights of the author have been asserted

Database right Oxford University Press (maker)

First published as a World's Classics paperback 1996
Reissued as an Oxford World's Classics paperback 1998

All rights reserved. No part of this publication may be reproduced,
stored in a retrieval system, or transmitted, in any form or by any means,
without the prior permission in writing of Oxford University Press,
or as expressly permitted by law, or under terms agreed with the appropriate
reprographics rights organizations. Enquiries concerning reproduction
outside the scope of the above should be sent to the Rights Department,
Oxford University Press, at the address above

You must not circulate this book in any other binding or cover
and you must impose this same condition on any acquire

British Library Cataloguing in Publication Data

Data available

Library of Congress Cataloging in Publication Data

Data available

ISBN 0–19–283494–0

3 5 7 9 10 8 6 4

Printed in Great Britain by
Cox & Wyman Ltd.
Reading, Berkshire

for Donald and Susan Nichol

Contents

Introduction

In a famous passage E. M. Forster remarked that 'Scott is a novelist over whom we shall violently divide.' Walter Scott appears to have lost that battle in the history of taste, at least for the present, but we continue to take sides over Pope. In fact, Alexander Pope has been dividing the literary world for more than two centuries. He has had a host of distinguished admirers, from Byron and Lamb through to W. H. Auden; practising writers such as Peter Porter still testify to his enduring stature. But he has also been among the most actively disliked of major poets, and it is worth asking why this should be so.

At one time Pope was disparaged for failing to touch the deepest strings of human aspiration—for lacking a soul. This line of attack started with Joseph Warton in the second half of the eighteenth century, and the campaign was intensified by Matthew Arnold a hundred years later. Warton could only assail Pope for not being Homer or Shakespeare; Arnold had been given a new touchstone by the Romantic movement, and could point up Pope's deficiencies by showing he was not Wordsworth or Shelley either. More commonly, the Victorians disliked Pope because he seemed malicious, 'the wasp of Twickenham'—a prejudice based on their ranking of satire low among the literary kinds, permitting a sort of genre-ism to determine Pope's historical position. When the *Golden Treasury* was compiled in 1861, a canon of English literature was inscribed in the consciousness of readers everywhere, according to which lyric, elegiac, and pastoral-ruminative verse was ranged above discursive and didactic poetry. Pope would not go away, but the official manuals portrayed him as less lofty in his aims and less delightful in his effects than any number of nineteenth-century versifiers.

He had acquired the reputation of being a poet of the home counties. In a literal sense this is true: Pope never went abroad, and never travelled further north than the gentle landscapes of the Yorkshire Wolds. But the implication lay deeper: Pope's cosy environment precluded him, so it was suggested, from attaining the sublimity of the Lake poets. Whether the Cumberland hills, or even the Alps, come all that close to the universal may be doubted. But the more serious point is that this geographical prejudice closed many minds to Pope's achievement. Most of his poetry concerns people rather than places: that was part of the trouble, when poetry was identified with the description of natural sublimity. In his own area of subject matter—which dominates much traditional literature, from the ancients onward—Pope displays astonishing human insight, extraordinary sympathy, and unrivalled powers of social observation—witness the 'epistles' to his friends and *The Rape of the Lock*. The truth is that we cannot accurately place Pope's special gifts if we adopt a wholly post-Romantic conceptual framework. He is in many ways the last of the great Renaissance writers: *Windsor Forest* harks back to the river poems of Spenser and Drayton, the *Rape* itself draws heavily on the fantasy of enchantment within *A Midsummer Night's Dream*, and *The Dunciad* transposes the forms and methods of Renaissance scholarship to create a kind of pseudo-antiquarian artefact. There was no need to stand on a mountain-top in Snowdonia to reimagine a pagan or Druidic past. Pope could do that very well in Twickenham, which was incidentally not then a straggling piece of outer London but a delightful riverside village, where Pope could feel safely removed from the city. It was not in other words, 'suburban', an epithet that does not tell us much that is useful about Pope or his age.

In the present century Pope has enjoyed a considerable revival, but niggling doubts remain in some quarters. Partly this has to do with his unprecedented success as a commercial poet: unprecedented and certainly unrepeatable in the modern world. He failed to be wiped out by the South Sea Bubble; he made a profit of £10,000 from his Homer translations, and he reached the head of his profession without an Arts Council grant, subsidies from a university, or even a literary agent. He was the first writer to grasp the potential opened up by the Copyright Act of 1710, a measure which largely served, in intention and in reality, the needs of the book trade. Pope became his own publisher, managed his rights with care, manipulated the booksellers, and planned his own career with the cunning of—well, of a modern writer. He did not even owe his financial independence to land-deals or investment, as was the case with Voltaire. All he did was to write the most accomplished poems of his age, arrange for their publication at the most advantageous juncture, and harvest the returns carefully. It is enough to make enemies of the entire book trade, not to mention less successful rivals, romantic visionaries, and people who hate capitalism most of all when it works to the benefit of the talented.

Alexander Pope was born on 21 May 1688, the only child of the
marriage between Alexander Pope senior (1646–1717) and Edith
Turner Pope (1643–1733). He had a half-sister Magdalen by his
father's first marriage: she was several years older and the two were
not especially close, but the poet was devoted to his parents. The
family belonged to the Roman Catholic faith, and within months
of the boy's arrival in the world came the departure from the British
throne of the last Catholic monarch, James II, ousted in a palace
revolution in favour of his daughter Mary and her husband William
of Orange. The birth had taken place in the heart of the City of
London, where Pope's father had been in the linen business. But
soon afterwards he retired to Hammersmith, then a village a few
miles outside the city limits to the west, and subsequently further
out to Binfield, in Windsor Forest, only about thirty miles from the
capital—but a wholly rural environment in those days, with the
forest still technically an area preserved for royal hunting. It was
a spot with numerous literary and historical associations, proudly
chronicled in the poem *Windsor Forest* (1713), and it was dominated
by Windsor Castle on the banks of the Thames, not just a seat of
chivalry but an administrative headquarters of the monarchy. Later
in life, the poet's family was to run foul of the Windsor establish-
ment, even though the poet's friend Lord Cobham held the office
of Constable of the Castle.

The move to Binfield had been motivated in the first place by
anti-Catholic legislation, introduced during William's reign, which
prevented Catholics from living in the environs of the city. But a
subsidiary purpose became that of bringing up the young Alexander
in a healthier location, since he soon fell victim to Pott's disease, a
result of drinking infected milk, which left him with severe curva-
ture of the spine and retarded his growth. He survived into middle
age, but never reached more than a puny stature, and had to settle
for an invalid's condition for the rest of his life. It is not surprising
that he acquired an irritable streak and a thin skin so far as personal
criticism was concerned. Tiny, misshapen, racked with pain,
sexually frustrated, house-bound, he set up a classic defence mech-
anism—he became a creature of the mind and the soul rather than
the body, a poet, an omnivorous reader, a devotee of the fine arts,
a platonic admirer of women, a closet rake, and a dreamer of fan-
tasies, gothic, surreal, or exotic.

The young Pope quickly acquired a retinue of elderly patrons,
first in Berkshire—notably a retired diplomat, Sir William Trum-

bull—and then in London, where he started to become known in his teens. The first location brought him the friendship of leading Berkshire gentry, especially the Catholic squirearchy. It was in this way that he got to know the Blount family of Mapledurham, just up the Thames from Reading: in their fine Elizabethan house, set in a pleasant woodland above the river, and surviving until today, lived the sisters Teresa, pert and coquettish, and Martha, quieter, moody, and literary. They were to be the poet's closest women friends in his formative years, and Martha was to retain a deep hold on him for the rest of his life—she was his residuary legatee. In London Pope made the acquaintance of what had been Dryden's circle, before the old man's death when his successor was no more than 12. These included the superannuated playwright William Wycherley; the minor poet, minor politician, and minor gentleman William Walsh; and the flashy rake Henry Cromwell. Before long the set extended to include major patrons like Lord Somers and Lord Halifax, and the physician-poet Samuel Garth, author of the first important mock-heroic in English, *The Dispensary* (1699). As time went on, the roles reversed. It was the older generation who had turned into an aged fan-club, and young Pope who shone as the new star in the literary firmament. When the *Pastorals* appeared in 1709, a brilliant diploma-piece supposed to have been written mainly in his teens, Pope bestowed generous compliments on his admirers; but the truth was clear to all. In future it would be an honour for them to be noticed by Pope, not the other way round. And when *Windsor Forest* came out in 1713 (again there is earlier work embedded), the dedicatee was Lord Lansdowne, a poet, a politician recently elevated to the peerage, and a member of the Tory government—but who has heard of Lansdowne today?

As well as patrons, Pope had made contact with the major publishers. The *Pastorals* were brought out in a miscellany by Jacob Tonson, the unofficial president of the English book trade, whose list was based around authors such as Shakespeare, Milton, and Dryden. It was in this very same year, 1709, that Tonson issued the first serious attempt at a critical edition of Shakespeare, prepared by Nicholas Rowe, soon to become poet laureate. The edition is defective, naturally by modern standards, and even by the standards of the later eighteenth century, when editors from Johnson and Capell to Steevens and Malone gradually advanced the quality of their performance. Nevertheless, the fact that Pope had joined Tonson's team was significant in more than one way. It gave him an outlet for his work; it introduced him to the commercial side of book production, and no lesson of this kind was ever lost on Pope; it suggested Shakespeare as a possible topic for endeavour, with the result that Pope himself occupied his middle years with 'the dull duty of an editor'; and it brought him into the orbit of the distinguished authors who wrote for Tonson. Rowe himself, a successful dramatist, a translator, and a fluent practitioner in light verse especially, held a more important place in Pope's development than has generally been recognized.

Thus launched, Pope's career took over with remarkable *élan*. Nothing could stop him now. *An Essay on Criticism* (1711) was quite simply the most brilliant, audacious, and witty art of poetry that England had ever seen—perhaps it still is. The ideas scud off the page, as the marvellously engineered couplets illustrate the very poetic of controlled energy which the work defends. This is high Augustanism at its youthful, cocky prime; nobody who reads the poem with attention can go away with Victorian prejudices intact, so blithe, vigorous, and *engagé* are its accents. A century later readers tended to identify 'poetic' qualities with the vague, the evanescent, the impalpable, the yearning, the atmospheric. As a matter of fact, Pope was capable of most of these things. But in the reckless confidence of his youth, he aimed for directly opposite qualities—here, for hard precision and definition, firmness of outline, clarity, gusto. The *Essay* breathes the air not of twilight musings of a solitary walker, rather the combative atmosphere of a coffee-house exchange, a bluestocking salon or even at times a bar-room brawl. Its mode is not private but social. We can still accept a badminton rally of witticisms in plays like *The Importance of Being Earnest*, or in novels like *Point Counterpoint*. Wit, indeed, is the largest single feature in Joyce's linguistic register. But poetically we still live in the gloaming of the Romantic movement, and neither modernism nor postmodernism has overcome all our prejudices in this regard.

Just as glittering in technique, but with a greater human depth, *The Rape of the Lock* burst before the world in 1712. This was a short version in two cantos, again literally a 'miscellany piece' in a collection put out by another prominent publisher, Bernard Lintot. Two years later Pope substituted an expanded version in five cantos, more or less the poem we know today. His great innovation lay in the 'machinery' of sylphs and gnomes, elemental spirits who attempt to direct the fate of the heroine Belinda, and who represent conflicting human (and particularly female) urges in the *psychomachia* of the poem. It was styled 'an heroi-comical poem', and it is in its subtle traffic with traditional epic that some of the most delicate humour is found—echoes of the story of the Fall in *Paradise Lost* are especially prominent. Mock-heroic is a mode of satire which operates at once by belittlement and aggrandizement. The big deeds of epic are scaled down, but trivial actions are granted the dignity of big words. The *Rape* boils a full-dress epic down to a comically shrivelled miniature. At the same time it reduces the cosmos of epic adventures to a tiny domestic frame. Instead of the fabled plains of Ilium, a young lady's boudoir; instead of the wine-dark Aegean, girded with the islands of myth, a short stretch of polluted urban waterway (the cognomen, 'silver Thames', at the start of Canto II, has some heavy ironical undertones.) Specific bits of the standard epic narrative are parodied (see notes below, p. 186). A wonderful double-edged meaning, to match the fatal shears which enact the rape in Canto III, inheres in almost every part, one might say every statement, of the poem. At the heart is Belinda, at once silly young miss and preposterously inflated demi-goddess. Are her sins venial? Or, if her offences are as dire in their way as the Baron's, as some have thought, then can we blame that on her upbringing, instructed as she was in rolling her eyes and taught as she was to blush prettily at the sight of a beau? All this comes not in shallow *vers de société*, but expressed in a language daring in its allusive scope, which can flit from sophisticated courtly language to the rites and spells of traditional folk belief. The *Rape* is in my belief Pope's greatest poem with its formal perfection, its imaginative density, its shimmering verse textures, and its wonderfully controlled moods. It should not surprise us that it remains a controversial work, with feminist critics now teasing out veiled implications (intended or otherwise) in Pope's bland-looking text. If it ever exhausts its power to challenge us, then Mozart's piano concertos will also have given up all their meaning—at a date which used to be identified as the Greek Kalends.

By the time that the expanded *Rape* appeared, Pope was already accepted as a worthy member of the literary élite of the nation. He had met the essayists Joseph Addison and Richard Steele, and contributed to a successor to the *Spectator* known as the *Guardian*. More importantly, he had joined the most talented coterie of that age, arguably of any other—the group of Tory satirists which included Jonathan Swift, John Gay, John Arbuthnot, and Thomas Parnell, along with a politician, Robert Harley, the Lord Treasurer.

He also knew the other prime figure in the ministry, Henry St John, later Lord Bolingbroke; as well as writers outside the *Spectator* and Scriblerus networks, notably the philosopher George Berkeley, the poet Matthew Prior, and the gifted writer Lady Mary Wortley Montagu. The centre of his operations for a while lay in the Scriblerian club, who combined convivial meetings with hilarious attacks on pedantry and misplaced learning. Here were the roots of *Gulliver's Travels* and *The Dunciad*. It was a more coherent group than the Bloomsbury set, with a wider range of literary abilities and a closer feel for the popular culture of the day. Meanwhile Pope had embarked on his translation of the *Iliad*, completed in 1720, the basis of his financial and social independence.

This initial phase of his career was celebrated with the appearance of Pope's *Works* in a handsome volume (1717), shortly before he attained his thirtieth birthday. Again it is hard to think of a comparable retrospective volume by an English poet, up to this date, which contains so many outstanding items. As well as the poems already mentioned, Pope could now include his Chaucerian dream poem, *The Temple of Fame*; some splendid shorter poems, for example the epistle to Teresa Blount after the coronation of George I, one of Pope's most characteristic works; the 'sacred eclogue' *Messiah*; and two considerable new poems, *Eloisa to Abelard* and the *Elegy to the Memory of an Unfortunate Lady*, both revealing a more dramatic and more sensationalist aspect to the poet than he had revealed before. There were changes to the *Rape* and to *Windsor Forest*. As Vincent Caretta has shown, the entire volume was planned to underline Pope's claims as a moral and prophetic writer. About a year later, Pope's settled position was further emphasized when he moved to Twickenham, his base for the rest of his life.

The 1720s saw something of a halt to this amazing progress. Pope was bogged down in translating the *Odyssey*, on which he needed the well-concealed assistance of two collaborators, Elijah Fenton and William Broome, and on the edition of Shakespeare. The latter was perhaps a mistake; Pope's failings as a scholar of Jacobean drama were easily exposed by the critic Lewis Theobald, and despite the eloquence of the Preface it might have been better for Pope's reputation if he had declined this task, which did not bring him very much money from Tonson. At the same time he found himself locked into minor projects—editions of the poems of his friend Parnell, and of the Duke of Buckingham, one of the early group of older writers who had supported him at the start of his career. He was drawn into a national political issue when his friend Francis Atterbury, Bishop of Rochester, was implicated in a Jacobite conspiracy in 1723 and exiled. A further proof that anti-Catholicism was still a force came when his brother-in-law Charles Rackett was picked up as a poacher in the royal forest of Windsor, during attempts to reassert Whig control in the face of alleged Jacobite plots to organize crime. But Pope shook himself free of this apparent writer's block—it may have been the visit of Swift to England in 1726, after twelve years' exile in Dublin, which stimulated his return to creative work. *Gulliver's Travels* led to a renewed burst of Scriblerian publication, including Gay's *Beggar's Opera*, the wickedly precise manual of bad writing, *Peri Bathous*, and finally *The Dunciad*. By the age of 40 Pope was back in full flow.

The Dunciad is less like an ordinary reading experience than a tour of some museum of early Hanoverian culture and its teeming library. One way of explaining this bizarre mixture of parody, prophecy, and hoax is to say that it is not so much a mock-epic as a mock-forgery. That is, the poem from 1729 presents itself as a kind of *objet trouvé*, a manuscript allegedly 'restored' as the classical scholar Richard Bentley was about to restore *Paradise Lost*: it is a thing, a lump of text, which has been pored over by an army of critics, whose activities parallel the inept bookmaking of the legion of dunces within the poem. In this, it resembles the forgeries and pseudepigraphia of ancient times, which the developing science of philology was helping to detect—Bentley's role in this had been singled out by Swift in his *Battle of the Books*. There was a growing anxiety about 'authenticity', and its presumed link with authorship, something that in medieval and Renaissance literature had mattered a good deal less. In his book *Forgers and Critics*, Anthony Grafton points out that genuine works were styled by the ancient Greeks 'legitimate' (as used for children), while forgeries were termed 'bastard'. This fear of unlawful progeny runs right through *The Dunciad*, with images of mixed marriages, aborted progeny, and incest everywhere. In its own condition as a well got-up fake, then, the poem embodies Augustan terror of a world where the old literary categories were breaking down; its anomalous textual condition (the poem almost strangled by notes and appendices, safely removed from this edition) suggests the threats to high culture posed by the new race of duncely authors, makers of books which are not really books, fabricators of sprawling textual lumps which may engulf real literature.

Thus renewed, and in his characteristic way lent new confidence by the sight of his enemies ranged against him, Pope entered the 1730s in better heart. His friend Swift was back in Ireland, his mother was now sick and declining, and his own health deteriorated still further. But he kept up a running assault on the dominant figures and institutions of the time through his ambitious updatings of Horace, his familiar epistles to friends like the Earl of Burlington and Martha Blount (one would rather be the recipient of these epistles than those on the end of their less than friendly barbs—Pope's enemies must have thought he was all too 'familiar' with their weaknesses), and even in the *Essay on Man* (1733–4), though this is formally a work of philosophical apologetics. By now Pope's muse was politicized to the extent that a poem which begins by confronting basic metaphysical questions turns to social and consti-tutional issues by its end. Pope addresses 'the science of human nature', and this turns out to mean as much what we should call psychology as it does pure metaphysical enquiry. By this date he was revelling in his command of a free-spoken, racy idiom which allowed him to cast his satiric eye on almost every facet of Eng-land—in the *Epistle to Bathurst* it is the economic and human conse-quences of the South Sea Bubble, while in the first satire of Horace's second book it is the rule of law. The *Epistle to Arbuthnot* incorporates a defiant autobiography and a view of the poet's role within society.

The 1730s, then, had been a decade of splendid achievement. But by their end Pope was entering his own fifties, and his compli-cated disorders were combining to shorten his life. Gay and Arbuth-not had gone before him, Swift was lapsing into senility in Ireland, and the long campaign against Walpole's ministry lost its focus and idealism as the great man's fall became imminent. There was time for a few more salvos. The *Memoirs of Scriblerus*, a last remnant of the old parodic fun, emerged in 1741; and the next year came a new fourth book to *The Dunciad*, underlining its vision of national crisis with a disparate array of new characters and new themes, ranging from opera and butterfly-collecting to the Grand Tour and deistic free thinking. After that, silence: Pope was not able to carry through any of his other grand designs, including a serious epic on the legendary founder of the British nation, Brut. He tinkered with the text of his earlier poems, with the help of his literary executor William Warburton; it is the version which Warburton ultimately produced which has been used as the basis of the text in this edition.

Pope died on 30 May 1744, just after his fifty-sixth birthday. Martha Blount survived him but most of his other friends were dead or, in the case of Swift, as good as dead.

In the same year, Samuel Johnson produced his first major work, and it was the life of a poet who had shared many of the dunces' hard days in Grub Street—Richard Savage. But Johnson's book is a study in sympathy, despite some harsh moral judgements, and that is something which could not be said of *The Dunciad*. A new era in literature was dawning, where satire would be ousted by sentiment, and where the novel would wrest primacy from the older literary forms. Partly as a consequence, Pope began to lose ground, and to give up the automatic rank in the order of poetic precedence he had attained. As we saw at the outset, critics like Joseph Warton started to dislodge him in the eighteenth century; but it was the prestige of the great Romantic poets which emboldened the carpers. Pope was still one of the most quoted poets in the language, a position he has not entirely lost. In the twentieth century the critical debates have gone on, and the revaluations of Pope's historical place will outlast our own time. He has left his mark on our language, and liked or disliked, he continues to hang around our literary consciousness.

The interested reader may wish to follow Pope beyond the limits of this selection. Luckily there is an abundance of distinguished scholarship and criticism which will illuminate the poet and his work. The fullest and most searching biography is that of Maynard Mack, *Alexander Pope: A Life* (1985). For the ways in which Pope promoted his own career and fashioned his identity as a poet, see David Foxon, *Pope and the Early Eighteenth-Century Book Trade* (1991). For glimpses of Pope's personal views and private life, collected by a friend, see *Observations, Anecdotes and Characters* by Joseph Spence, ed. J. M. Osborn (1966). Naturally, the best place to go is to the works themselves; here we have the splendid Twickenham edition of the poems, ed. John Butt *et al.* (1939–69), and the outstandingly interesting *Correspondence*, ed. George Sherburn (1956). Pope's later *Prose Works* have been edited by Rosemary Cowler (1986). A wide selection of poetry, prose, and correspondence is provided in my edition, *Pope*, in the Oxford Authors series (1993). Those who want to trace the exacting methods by which the poems evolved from early draft into the finished work of art should consult Maynard Mack, *The Last and Greatest Art: Some Unpublished Poetical Manuscripts of Alexander Pope*

(1984). The critical history can be followed in *Pope: The Critical Heritage*, ed. John Barnard (1973). A good way to learn about Pope's many connections with arts other than literature—especially landscape gardening and architecture—is to look at Morris Brownell, *Alexander Pope and the Arts of Georgian England* (1978). Pope's chequered health and his relation to the science of his day are described in Marjorie Hope Nicolson and G. S. Rousseau, *'This Long Disease my Life'* (1968). We still do not have a comprehensive survey of the world in which Pope operated, but relevant contexts (the classics, the economic background, society, the fine arts, etc.) are treated in *Writers and their Background: Alexander Pope*, ed. P. Dixon (1972).

Finally, something should be said about the scope of this edition and about the editorial procedures. As to the first, it is impossible to display the whole of Pope's art in a volume of this kind. He was a poet of consistent imaginative invention, and almost all his works, from his youth onwards, reach at the least a high level of competence. Those readers who aim to get a full sense of his achievement will wish to look at the *Pastorals*, *The Temple of Fame*, the *Essay on Man*, the entire series of imitations of Horace and the *Epistle to Cobham*, not to mention a number of squibs, ballads, and shorter items for which there is no room here. I particularly regret the omission of the version of Horace's *Epistle* II. ii, a remarkable and somewhat neglected item. It should also be pointed out that *The Dunciad* has had to be shorn of its elaborate mock-scholarly apparatus, including Pope's own elaborate notes—these would require further editorial gloss, and that would make it indigestible reading in a volume of this size. But one need not be too apologetic about all this. The major poems of a great writer are present in full, and that should be enough. Those who do not find anything to their taste here must be hard to please, and they are unlikely to find it in Pope's other works. Those who do will be able to track down elsewhere the less celebrated portions of his *œuvre*.

As for editorial procedures, it should be stated that this is a modernized text, with spelling and (where obscurity might result) punctuation and presentation brought into line with today's usage. In most cases the text is based on William Warburton's edition of 1751, which in turn was largely based on versions to which Pope had given his approval in his last years. In general this means that we have the state of the text towards which Pope inclined by the end of his life. Some of Pope's notes have been removed where they relate to the buried archaeology of composition. The notes supplied by the present editor are limited to matters affecting the meaning and drift of the verse: see p. 175 for the principles underlying the annotation. Poems are printed in chronological order of their composition.

Chronology

1688	21 May, P born in London.
1688–9	Protestant Revolution: James II forced to abdicate in favour of William and Mary.
c.1700	P's family moves from London to Binfield, in Windsor Forest.
1702	Queen Anne succeeds to throne.
1704	Swift, *A Tale of a Tub*.
1709	P's first published works, including his *Pastorals*, appear in a London miscellany.
1710	Formation of Tory Government led by Harley and St John (Bolingbroke), later close friend of P.
1711	P's *Essay on Criticism* brings him fame; Addison and Steele launch the *Spectator* (P and Swift occasional contributions).
1712	20 May, first appearance of *Rape of the Lock* (two-canto version).
1713	7 March, *Windsor Forest* published; P writes essays for Steele's journal the *Guardian*. Scriblerus Club becomes active, with P, Swift, Gay, Arbuthnot, Parnell, and Harley (now Lord Oxford) members.
1714	4 March, five-canto version of *Rape of the Lock* published. 1 August, death of Queen Anne and accession of first Hanoverian king, George I. Tories out of office for the remainder of P's life. Swift settled in Dublin as Dean of St Patrick's.
1715	1 February, *The Temple of Fame*; 6 June, first instalment of P's *Iliad* translation. Jacobite rising in Scotland in support of the Old Pretender, put down with relative ease. Anti-Catholic legislation limits P's personal liberties.
1716	P's family moves to Chiswick on outskirts of London. P attacks the bookseller Curll in prose pamphlets.
1716–20	Remaining volumes of *Iliad* translation published.
1717	P, Gay, and Arbuthnot collaborate in farce *Three Hours after Marriage*. P's father dies. 3 June, P's first major collection of *Works* published, including new poems such as *Eloisa to Abelard*.
1718	Death of Parnell. P moves to Twickenham.
1719	Death of Addison. Defoe, *Robinson Crusoe*, admired by P.

1720   South Sea Bubble.

1721   Walpole comes to power.

1722   P edits Parnell's poems. P's friend Atterbury implicated in Jacobite plot (exiled 1723).

1723   P edits works of Duke of Buckingham. P's brother-in-law arrested for deer-stealing in the 'Windsor Blacks' affair, involving a series of anti-Jacobite measures.

1724   Swift, *Drapier's Letters*, attacking English Government's treatment of Ireland.

1725   March, P's subscription edition of Shakespeare published. April, first instalment of P's translation of *Odyssey* published.

1726   Remaining volumes of *Odyssey* published. Swift visits England for publication of *Gulliver's Travels*.

1727   First two volumes of Pope–Swift *Miscellanies* published. Swift visits England for last time.

1728   7 March, third volume of *Miscellanies* including *Peri Bathous*. May, first version of *The Dunciad* in three books. Gay, *Beggar's Opera*, premiered with great success.

1729   April, *Dunciad Variorum* adds extensive apparatus and notes. Swift, *A Modest Proposal*.

1730   Fielding, *The Author's Farce*.

1731   14 December, *Epistle to Burlington*. Death of Defoe.

1732   Further volume of *Miscellanies*. Death of Gay.

1733   15 January, *Epistle to Bathurst*; 20 February, *Essay on Man*, i–iii. First in the series of *Imitations of Horace* appear. Death of P's mother.

1734   2 January, *Epistle to Cobham*; 24 January, *Essay on Man*, iv. Further Horatian imitations published.

1735   2 January, *Epistle to Arbuthnot*; 8 February, *Epistle to a Lady*. Second volume of P's *Works*. Death of Arbuthnot. P engineers publication of his letters.

1737   Authorized edition of P's letters. Death of Queen Caroline. Theatrical Licensing Act imposed restraints on new plays.

1738   Series of imitations of Horace culminate in *Epilogue to Satires*. Samuel Johnson's *London*, admired by P.

1740   Richardson, *Pamela*, i.

1741   *Memoirs of Scriblerus* published, largely written in years of Scriblerus Club activity and edited by P.

1742   March, new fourth book of *The Dunciad*. Fielding, *Joseph*

Andrews. Swift officially declared of unsound mind. Handel, *The Messiah*.

1743   October, revised *Dunciad in Four Books*.

1744   Important quarto editions of several poems by P. 30 May, P dies. Johnson, *Life of Savage*.

1745   19 October, Swift dies in Dublin.

AN
ESSAY
ON
CRITICISM

—Si quid novisti rectius istis,
Candidus imperti; si non, his utere mecum.

HORACE.

'Tis hard to say, if greater want of skill   1
Appear in writing or in judging ill;
But, of the two, less dangerous is th' offence
To tire our patience, than mislead our sense.
Some few in that, but numbers err in this,
Ten censure wrong for one who writes amiss;
A fool might once himself alone expose,
Now one in verse makes many more in prose.
 'Tis with our judgments as our watches, none
Go just alike, yet each believes his own.   10
In poets as true genius is but rare,
True taste as seldom is the critic's share;
Both must alike from Heaven derive their light,
These born to judge, as well as those to write.
Let such teach others who themselves excel,
And censure freely who have written well.
Authors are partial to their wit, 'tis true,
But are not critics to their judgment too?
 Yet if we look more closely, we shall find
Most have the seeds of judgment in their mind: 20
Nature affords at least a glimmering light;
The lines, though touched but faintly, are drawn right.
But as the slightest sketch, if justly traced,
Is by ill-colouring but the more disgraced,
So by false learning is good sense defaced:
Some are bewildered in the maze of schools,
And some made coxcombs Nature meant but fools.
In search of wit these lose their common sense,
And then turn critics in their own defence:
Each burns alike, who can, or cannot write,   30

Or with a rival's, or an eunuch's spite.
All fools have still an itching to deride,
And fain would be upon the laughing side.
If Maevius scribble in Apollo's spite,
There are, who judge still worse than he can write.
   Some have at first for wits, then poets passed,
Turned critics next, and proved plain fools at last.
Some neither can for wits nor critics pass,
As heavy mules are neither horse nor ass.
Those half-learned witlings, numerous in our isle,   40
As half-formed insects on the banks of Nile;
Unfinished things, one knows not what to call,
Their generation's so equivocal:
To tell 'em, would a hundred tongues require,
Or one vain wit's, that might a hundred tire.
   But you who seek to give and merit fame,
And justly bear a critic's noble name,
Be sure yourself and your own reach to know,
How far your genius, taste, and learning go;
Launch not beyond your depth, but be discreet,   50
And mark that point where sense and dullness meet.
   Nature to all things fixed the limits fit,
And wisely curbed proud man's pretending wit.
As on the land while here the ocean gains,
In other parts it leaves wide sandy plains;
Thus in the soul while memory prevails,
The solid power of understanding fails;
Where beams of warm imagination play,
The memory's soft figures melt away.
One science only will one genius fit;   60
So vast is art, so narrow human wit:
Not only bounded to peculiar arts,
But oft in those confined to single parts.
Like kings we lose the conquests gained before,
By vain ambition still to make them more;
Each might his several province well command,
Would all but stoop to what they understand.
   First follow *Nature*, and your judgment frame
By her just standard, which is still the same:
Unerring NATURE, still divinely bright,   70
One clear, unchanged, and universal light,

Life, force, and beauty, must to all impart,
At once the source, and end, and test of art.
Art from that fund each just supply provides,
Works without show, and without pomp presides:
In some fair body thus th' informing soul
With spirits feeds, with vigour fills the whole,
Each motion guides, and every nerve sustains;
Itself unseen, but in th' effects, remains.
Some, to whom Heaven in wit has been profuse,   80
Want as much more, to turn it to its use;
For wit and judgment often are at strife,
Though meant each other's aid like man and wife.
'Tis more to guide, than spur the Muse's steed;
Restrain his fury, than provoke his speed;
The winged courser, like a generous horse,
Shows most true mettle when you check his course.
   Those RULES of old discovered, not devised,
Are Nature still, but Nature methodized;
Nature, like liberty, is but restrained   90
By the same laws which first herself ordained.
   Hear how learned Greece her useful rules indites,
When to repress, and when indulge our flights:
High on Parnassus' top her sons she showed,
And pointed out those arduous paths they trod;
Held from afar, aloft, th' immortal prize,
And urged the rest by equal steps to rise.
Just precepts thus from great examples given,
She drew from them what they derived from Heaven.
The generous critic fanned the poet's fire,   100
And taught the world with reason to admire.
Then criticism the Muse's handmaid proved,
To dress her charms, and make her more beloved:
But following wits from that intention strayed,
Who could not win the mistress, wooed the maid;
Against the poets their own arms they turned,
Sure to hate most the men from whom they learned.
So modern 'pothecaries, taught the art
By doctor's bills to play the doctor's part,
Bold in the practice of mistaken rules,   110
Prescribe, apply, and call their masters fools.
Some on the leaves of ancient authors prey,

Nor time nor moths e'er spoiled so much as they.
Some drily plain, without invention's aid,
Write dull receipts how poems may be made.
These leave the sense, their learning to display,
And those explain the meaning quite away.
    You then whose judgment the right course would steer,
Know well each ANCIENT's proper character;
His fable, subject, scope in every page;   120
Religion, country, genius of his age:
Without all these at once before your eyes,
Cavil you may, but never criticize.
Be Homer's works your study, and delight,
Read them by day, and meditate by night;
Thence form your judgment, thence your maxims bring,
And trace the Muses upward to their spring.
Still with itself compared, his text peruse;
And let your comment be the Mantuan Muse.
    When first young Maro in his boundless mind   130
A work t'outlast immortal Rome designed,
Perhaps he seemed above the critic's law,
And but from Nature's fountains scorned to draw:
But when t'examine every part he came,
Nature and Homer were, he found, the same.
Convinced, amazed, he checks the bold design; ⎫
And rules as strict his laboured work confine, ⎬
As if the Stagyrite o'erlooked each line.   ⎭
Learn hence for ancient rules a just esteem;
To copy nature is to copy them.   140
    Some beauties yet no precepts can declare,
For there's a happiness as well as care.
Music resembles poetry, in each   ⎫
Are nameless graces which no methods teach, ⎬
And which a master-hand alone can reach.   ⎭
If, where the rules not far enough extend,
(Since rules were made but to promote their end)
Some lucky licence answers to the full
Th'intent proposed, that licence is a rule.
Thus Pegasus, a nearer way to take,   150
May boldly deviate from the common track.
Great wits sometimes may gloriously offend,
And rise to faults true critics dare not mend;

From vulgar bounds with brave disorder part,
And snatch a grace beyond the reach of art,
Which without passing through the judgment, gains
The heart, and all its end at once attains.
In prospects thus, some objects please our eyes, ⎫
Which out of nature's common order rise,   ⎬
The shapeless rock, or hanging precipice.   ⎭   160
But though the Ancients thus their rules invade,
(As kings dispense with laws themselves have made)
Moderns, beware! or if you must offend
Against the precept, ne'er transgress its end;
Let it be seldom, and compelled by need;
And have, at least, their precedent to plead.
The critic else proceeds without remorse,
Seizes your fame, and puts his laws in force.
  I know there are, to whose presumptuous thoughts
Those freer beauties, ev'n in them, seem faults.   170
Some figures monstrous and mis-shaped appear,
Considered singly, or beheld too near,
Which, but proportioned to their light, or place,
Due distance reconciles to form and grace.
A prudent chief not always must display
His powers in equal ranks, and fair array,
But with th'occasion and the place comply,
Conceal his force, nay seem sometimes to fly.
Those oft are stratagems which errors seem,
Nor is it Homer nods, but we that dream.   180
  Still green with bays each ancient altar stands,
Above the reach of sacrilegious hands;
Secure from flames, from envy's fiercer rage,
Destructive war, and all-involving age.
See, from each clime the learned their incense bring!
Hear, in all tongues consenting paeans ring!
In praise so just let every voice be joined,
And fill the general chorus of mankind.
Hail, bards triumphant! born in happier days;
Immortal heirs of universal praise!   190
Whose honours with increase of ages grow,
As streams roll down, enlarging as they flow;
Nations unborn your mighty names shall sound,
And worlds applaud that must not yet be found!

Oh may some spark of your celestial fire,
The last, the meanest of your sons inspire,
(That on weak wings, from far, pursues your flights;
Glows while he reads, but trembles as he writes)
To teach vain wits a science little known,
T'admire superior sense, and doubt their own!   200

Of all the causes which conspire to blind
Man's erring judgment, and misguide the mind
What the weak head with strongest bias rules,
Is *pride*, the never-failing vice of fools.
Whatever Nature has in worth deny'd,
She gives in large recruits of needful pride;
For as in bodies, thus in souls, we find
What wants in blood and spirits, swelled with wind:
Pride, where wit fails, steps in to our defence,
And fills up all the mighty void of sense.   210
If once right reason drives that cloud away,
Truth breaks upon us with resistless day.
Trust not yourself; but your defects to know,
Make use of every friend—and every foe.
A *little learning* is a dangerous thing;
Drink deep, or taste not the Pierian spring:
There shallow draughts intoxicate the brain,
And drinking largely sobers us again.
Fired at first sight with what the Muse imparts,
In fearless youth we tempt the heights of arts,   220
While from the bounded level of our mind,
Short views we take, nor see the lengths behind;
But, more advanced, behold with strange surprise
New distant scenes of endless science rise!
So pleased at first the towering Alps we try,
Mount o'er the vales, and seem to tread the sky,
Th' eternal snows appear already past,
And the first clouds and mountains seem the last:
But, those attained, we tremble to survey
The growing labours of the lengthened way,   230
Th' increasing prospect tires our wandering eyes,
Hills peep o'er hills, and Alps on Alps arise!
A perfect judge will read each work of wit
With the same spirit that its author writ:

Survey the WHOLE, nor seek slight faults to find
Where nature moves, and rapture warms the mind;
Nor lose, for that malignant dull delight,
The generous pleasure to be charmed with wit.
But in such lays as neither ebb, nor flow,
Correct cold, and regularly low,   240
That shunning faults, one quiet tenor keep;
We cannot blame indeed—but we may sleep.
In wit, as nature, what affects our hearts
Is not th' exactness of peculiar parts;
'Tis not a lip, or eye, we beauty call,
But the joint force and full result of all.
Thus when we view some well-proportioned dome,
(The world's just wonder, and ev'n thine, O Rome!)
No single parts unequally surprise,
All comes united to th' admiring eyes;   250
No monstrous height, or breadth, or length appear;
The whole at once is bold, and regular.
  Whoever thinks a faultless piece to see,
Thinks what ne'er was, nor is, nor e'er shall be.
In every work regard the writer's end,
Since none can compass more than they intend;
And if the means be just, the conduct true,
Applause, in spite of trivial faults, is due.
As men of breeding, sometimes men of wit,
T' avoid great errors, must the less commit: 260
Neglect the rules each verbal critic lays,
For not to know some trifles, is a praise.
Most critics, fond of some subservient art,
Still make the whole depend upon a part:
They talk of principles, but notions prize,
And all to one loved folly sacrifice.
  Once on a time, La Mancha's knight, they say,
A certain bard encountering on the way,
Discoursed in terms as just, with looks as sage,
As e'er could Dennis, of the Grecian stage;   270
Concluding all were desperate sots and fools,
Who durst depart from Aristotle's rules.
Our author, happy in a judge so nice,
Produced his play, and begged the knight's advice;
Made him observe the subject, and the plot,

The manners, passions, unities; what not?
All which, exact to rule, were brought about,
Were but a combat in the lists left out.
'What! leave the combat out?' exclaims the knight;
Yes, or we must renounce the Stagyrite.   280
'Not so by Heaven', he answers in a rage,
'Knights, squires, and steeds, must enter on the stage.'
So vast a throng the stage can ne'er contain.
'Then build a new, or act it in a plain.'
      Thus critics, of less judgment than caprice,
Curious not knowing, not exact but nice,
Form short ideas; and offend in arts
(As most in manners) by a love to parts.
      Some to *conceit* alone their taste confine,
And glittering thoughts struck out at every line;   290
Pleased with a work where nothing's just or fit;
One glaring chaos and wild heap of wit.
Poets like painters, thus, unskilled to trace
The naked nature and the living grace,
With gold and jewels cover every part,
And hide with ornaments their want of art.
True wit is nature to advantage dressed,
What oft was thought, but ne'er so well expressed;
Something, whose truth convinced at sight we find,
That gives us back the image of our mind.   300
As shades more sweetly recommend the light,
So modest plainness sets off sprightly wit.
For works may have more wit than does 'em good,
As bodies perish through excess of blood.
      Others for *language* all their care express,
And value books, as women men, for dress:
Their praise is still,—the style is excellent:
The sense, they humbly take upon content.
Words are like leaves; and where they most abound,
Much fruit of sense beneath is rarely found.   310
False eloquence, like the prismatic glass,
Its gaudy colours spreads on every place;
The face of nature we no more survey,
All glares alike, without distinction gay:
But true expression, like th' unchanging sun,
Clears, and improves whate'er it shines upon,

It gilds all objects, but it alters none.
Expression is the dress of thought, and still
Appears more decent, as more suitable;
A vile conceit in pompous words expressed,   320
Is like a clown in regal purple dressed:
For different styles with different subjects sort,
As several garbs with country, town, and court.
Some by old words to fame have made pretence,
Ancients in phrase, mere moderns in their sense:
Such laboured nothings, in so strange a style,
Amaze th' unlearned, and make the learned smile.
Unlucky, as Fungoso in the Play,   ⎫
These sparks with awkward vanity display   ⎬
What the fine gentleman wore yesterday;   ⎭   330
And but so mimic ancient wits at best,
As apes our grandsires, in their doublets dressed.
In words, as fashions, the same rule will hold;
Alike fantastic, if too new, or old;
Be not the first by whom the new are tried,
Nor yet the last to lay the old aside.
    But most by numbers judge a poet's song,
And smooth or rough, with them, is right or wrong;
In the bright Muse though thousand charms conspire,
Her voice is all these tuneful fools admire;   340
Who haunt Parnassus but to please their ear,   ⎫
Not mend their minds; as some to church repair, ⎬
Not for the doctrine, but the music there.   ⎭
These equal syllables alone require,
Though oft the ear the open vowels tire;
While expletives their feeble aid do join;
And ten low words oft creep in one dull line;
While they ring round the same unvaried chimes,
With sure returns of still expected rhymes.
Where-e'er you find 'the cooling western breeze,'   350
In the next line, it 'whispers through the trees;'
If crystal streams 'with pleasing murmurs creep,'
The reader's threatened (not in vain) with 'sleep.'
Then, at the last and only couplet fraught
With some unmeaning thing they call a thought,

328. See Ben Jonson's *Every Man in* [rather, *out of*] *his Humour.*

A needless Alexandrine ends the song,
That, like a wounded snake, drags its slow length along.
Leave such to tune their own dull rhymes, and know
What's roundly smooth, or languishingly slow;
And praise the easy vigour of a line,   360
Where Denham's strength, and Waller's sweetness join.
True ease in writing comes from art, not chance,
As those move easiest who have learned to dance.
'Tis not enough no harshness gives offence,
The sound must seem an echo to the sense:
Soft is the strain when Zephyr gently blows,
And the smooth stream in smoother numbers flows;
But when loud surges lash the sounding shore,
The hoarse, rough verse should like the torrent roar.
When Ajax strives, some rock's vast weight to throw,   370
The line too labours, and the words move slow;
Not so, when swift Camilla scours the plain,
Flies o'er th' unbending corn, and skims along the main.
Hear how Timotheus' varied lays surprise,
And bid alternate passions fall and rise!
While, at each change, the son of Libyan Jove
Now burns with glory, and then melts with love;
Now his fierce eyes with sparkling fury glow,
Now sighs steal out, and tears begin to flow:
Persians and Greeks like turns of nature found,   380
And the world's victor stood subdued by sound!
The power of music all our hearts allow,
And what Timotheus was, is DRYDEN now.

    Avoid *extremes*; and shun the fault of such,
Who still are pleased too little or too much.
At every trifle scorn to take offence,
That always shows great pride, or little sense;
Those heads, as stomachs, are not sure the best,
Which nauseate all, and nothing can digest.
Yet let not each gay turn thy rapture move,   390
For fools admire, but men of sense approve:
As things seem large which we through mists descry,
Dulness is ever apt to magnify.
    Some foreign writers, some our own despise;

374. See *Alexander's Feast*, or *the Power of Music*, an ode by Mr Dryden.

The Ancients only, or the Moderns prize.
Thus wit, like faith, by each man is applied
To one small sect, and all are damned beside.
Meanly they seek the blessing to confine,
And force that sun but on a part to shine,
Which not alone the southern wit sublimes,   400
But ripens spirits in cold northern climes;
Which from the first has shone on ages past,
Enlights the present, and shall warm the last:
Though each may feel increases and decays,
And see now clearer and now darker days.
Regard not then if wit be old or new,
But blame the false, and value still the true.
   Some ne'er advance a judgment of their own,
But catch the spreading notion of the town;
They reason and conclude by precedent,   410
And own stale nonsense which they ne'er invent.
Some judge of authors' names, not works, and then
Nor praise nor blame the writings, but the men.
Of all this servile herd, the worst is he
That in proud dulness joins with quality.
A constant critic at the great man's board,
To fetch and carry nonsense for my Lord.
What woeful stuff this madrigal would be,
In some starved hackney sonneteer, or me?
But let a lord once own the happy lines,   420
How the wit brightens! how the style refines!
Before his sacred name flies every fault,
And each exalted stanza teems with thought!
   The vulgar thus through imitation err;
As oft the learned by being singular;
So much they scorn the crowd, that if the throng
By chance go right, they purposely go wrong:
So schismatics the plain believers quit,
And are but damned for having too much wit.
   Some praise at morning what they blame at night;   430
But always think the last opinion right.
A Muse by these is like a mistress used,
This hour she's idolized, the next abused;
While their weak heads, like towns unfortified,
'Twixt sense and nonsense daily change their side.

Ask them the cause; they're wiser still, they say;
And still tomorrow's wiser than today.
We think our fathers fools, so wise we grow;
Our wiser sons, no doubt, will think us so.
Once school-divines this zealous isle o'er-spread;   440
Who knew most sentences, was deepest read;
Faith, gospel, all, seemed made to be disputed,
And none had sense enough to be confuted:
Scotists and Thomists, now, in peace remain,
Amidst their kindred cobwebs in Duck Lane.
If faith itself has different dresses worn,
What wonder modes in wit should take their turn?
Oft, leaving what is natural and fit,
The current folly proves the ready wit;
And authors think their reputation safe,   450
Which lives as long as fools are pleased to laugh.
   Some valuing those of their own side or mind,
Still make themselves the measure of mankind:
Fondly we think we honour merit then,
When we but praise ourselves in other men.
Parties in wit attend on those of state,
And public faction doubles private hate.
Pride, Malice, Folly, against Dryden rose,
In various shapes of parsons, critics, beaux;
But sense survived, when merry jests were past;   460
For rising merit will buoy up at last.
Might he return, and bless once more our eyes,
New Blackmores and new Milbournes must arise:
Nay should great Homer lift his awful head,
Zoilus again would start up from the dead.
Envy will merit, as its shade, pursue;
But like a shadow, proves the substance true;
For envied wit, like Sol eclipsed, makes known
Th' opposing body's grossness, not its own.
When first that sun too powerful beams displays,   470
It draws up vapours which obscure its rays;
But ev'n those clouds at last adorn its way,
Reflect new glories, and augment the day.

445. A place where old and second-hand books were sold formerly, near Smithfield.

Be thou the first true merit to befriend;
His praise is lost, who stays till all commend.
Short is the date, alas, of modern rhymes,
And 'tis but just to let them live betimes.
No longer now that golden age appears,
When patriarch-wits survived a thousand years:
Now length of fame (our second life) is lost,   480
And bare threescore is all ev'n that can boast;
Our sons their fathers failing language see,
And such as Chaucer is, shall Dryden be.
So when the faithful pencil has designed
Some bright idea of the master's mind,
Where a new world leaps out at his command,
And ready Nature waits upon his hand;
When the ripe colours soften and unite,
And sweetly melt into just shade and light,
When mellowing years their full perfection give,   490
And each bold figure just begins to live;
The treacherous colours the fair art betray,
And all the bright creation fades away!
　　Unhappy wit, like most mistaken things,
Atones not for that envy which it brings.
In youth alone its empty praise we boast,
But soon the short-lived vanity is lost:
Like some fair flower the early spring supplies,
That gaily blooms, but ev'n in blooming dies.
What is this wit, which must our cares employ?   500
The owner's wife, that other men enjoy;
Then most our trouble still when more admired,
And still the more we give, the more required;
Whose fame with pains we guard, but lose with ease,
Sure some to vex, but never all to please;
'Tis what the vicious fear, the virtuous shun,
By fools 'tis hated, and by knaves undone!
　　If wit so much from ignorance undergo,
Ah let not learning too commence its foe!
Of old, those met rewards who could excel,   510
And such were praised who but endeavoured well:
Though triumphs were to generals only due,
Crowns were reserved to grace the soldiers too.
Now, they who reach Parnassus' lofty crown,

Employ their pains to spurn some others down;
And while self-love each jealous writer rules,
Contending wits become the sport of fools:
But still the worst with most regret commend,
For each ill author is as bad a friend.
To what base ends, and by what abject ways,   520
Are mortals urged through sacred lust of praise!
Ah ne'er so dire a thirst of glory boast,
Nor in the critic let the man be lost.
Good nature and good sense must ever join;
To err is human, to forgive, divine.
   But if in noble minds some dregs remain
Not yet purged off, of spleen and sour disdain;
Discharge that rage on more provoking crimes,
Nor fear a dearth in these flagitious times.
No pardon vile obscenity should find,   530
Though wit and art conspire to move your mind;
But dulness with obscenity must prove
As shameful sure as impotence in love.
In the fat age of pleasure, wealth, and ease,
Sprung the rank weed, and thrived with large increase;
When love was all an easy monarch's care;
Seldom at council, never in a war:
Jilts ruled the state, and statesmen farces writ;
Nay wits had pensions, and young lords had wit:
The fair sate panting at a courtier's play,   540
And not a mask went unimproved away:
The modest fan was lifted up no more,
And virgins smiled at what they blushed before.
The following licence of a foreign reign
Did all the dregs of bold Socinus drain;
Then unbelieving priests reformed the nation,
And taught more pleasant methods of salvation;
Where Heaven's free subjects might their rights dispute,
Lest God himself should seem too absolute:
Pulpits their sacred satire learned to spare,   550
And vice admired to find a flatterer there!
Encouraged thus, wit's Titans braved the skies,
And the press groaned with licensed blasphemies.
These monsters, critics! with your darts engage,
Here point your thunder, and exhaust your rage!

Yet shun their fault, who, scandalously nice,
Will needs mistake an author into vice;
All seems infected that th' infected spy,
As all looks yellow to the jaundiced eye.

LEARN then what MORALS critics ought to show,   560
For 'tis but half a judge's task, to know.
'Tis not enough, taste, judgment, learning, join;
In all you speak, let truth and candour shine:
That not alone what to your sense is due
All may allow; but seek your friendship too.

Be silent always when you doubt your sense;
And speak, though sure, with seeming diffidence:
Some positive, persisting fops we know,
Who, if once wrong, will needs be always so;
But you, with pleasure own your errors past,   570
And make each day a critic on the last.

'Tis not enough, your counsel still be true;
Blunt truths more mischief than nice falsehoods do;
Men must be taught as if you taught them not,
And things unknown proposed as things forgot.
Without good breeding, truth is disapproved;
That only makes superior sense beloved.

Be niggards of advice on no pretence;
For the worst avarice is that of sense.
With mean complacence ne'er betray your trust,   580
Nor be so civil as to prove unjust.
Fear not the anger of the wise to raise;
Those best can bear reproof, who merit praise.

'Twere well might critics still this freedom take;
But Appius reddens at each word you speak,
And stares, tremendous, with a threatening eye,
Like some fierce tyrant in old tapestry.
Fear most to tax an honourable fool,
Whose right it is, uncensured to be dull;
Such, without wit, are poets when they please,   590
As without learning they can take degrees.

586. This picture was taken to himself by John Dennis, a furious old critic by profession, who, upon no other provocation, wrote against this *Essay* and its author, in a manner perfectly lunatic: for, as to the mention made of him in v. 270, he took it as a compliment, and said it was treacherously meant to cause him to overlook this *abuse* of his *person*.

Leave dangerous truths to unsuccessful satires,
And flattery to fulsome dedicators,
Whom, when they praise, the world believes no more,
Than when they promise to give scribbling o'er.
'Tis best sometimes your censure to restrain,
And charitably let the dull be vain:
Your silence there is better than your spite,
For who can rail so long as they can write?
Still humming on, their drowsy course they keep,   600
And lashed so long, like tops, are lashed asleep.
False steps but help them to renew the race,
As, after stumbling, jades will mend their pace.
What crowds of these, impenitently bold,
In sounds and jingling syllables grown old,
Still run on poets, in a raging vein,
Ev'n to the dregs and squeezings of the brain,
Strain out the last dull droppings of their sense,
And rhyme with all the rage of impotence.
    Such shameless bards we have, and yet 'tis true,   610
There are as mad, abandoned critics too.
The bookful blockhead, ignorantly read,
With loads of learnèd lumber in his head,
With his own tongue still edifies his ears,
And always listening to himself appears.
All books he reads, and all he reads assails,
From Dryden's fables down to Durfey's tales.
With him, most authors steal their works, or buy;
Garth did not write his own *Dispensary*.
Name a new play, and he's the poet's friend,   620
Nay showed his faults—but when would poets mend?
No place so sacred from such fops is barred,
Nor is Paul's church more safe than Paul's church yard:
Nay, fly to altars; there they'll talk you dead:
For fools rush in where angels fear to tread.
Distrustful sense with modest caution speaks,   ⎫
It still looks home, and short excursions makes;   ⎬
But rattling nonsense in full volleys breaks,   ⎭

---

619. A common slander at that time in prejudice of that deserving author. Our poet did him this justice, when that slander most prevailed; and it is now (perhaps the sooner for this very verse) dead and forgotten.

And never shocked, and never turned aside,
Bursts out, resistless, with a thundering tide.   630
   But where's the man, who counsel can bestow,
Still pleased to teach, and yet not proud to know?
Unbiassed, or by favour, or by spite:
Not dully prepossessed, nor blindly right;
Though learned, well-bred; and though well-bred, sincere;
Modestly bold, and humanly severe:
Who to a friend his faults can freely show,
And gladly praise the merit of a foe?
Blessed with a taste exact, yet unconfined;
A knowledge both of books and human kind;   640
Generous converse; a soul exempt from pride;
And love to praise, with reason on his side?
   Such once were critics; such the happy few,
Athens and Rome in better ages knew.
The mighty Stagyrite first left the shore,
Spread all his sails, and durst the deeps explore;
He steered securely, and discovered far,
Led by the light of the Maeonian star.
Poets, a race long unconfined, and free,
Still fond and proud of savage liberty,   650
Received his laws; and stood convinced 'twas fit,
Who conquered nature, should preside o'er wit.
   Horace still charms with graceful negligence,
And without method talks us into sense,
Will, like a friend, familiarly convey
The truest notions in the easiest way.
He, who supreme in judgment, as in wit,
Might boldly censure, as he boldly writ,
Yet judged with coolness, though he sung with fire,
His precepts teach but what his works inspire.   660
Our critics take a contrary extreme,
They judge with fury, but they write with phlegm.
Nor suffers Horace more in wrong translations
By wits, than critics in as wrong quotations.
   See Dionysius Homer's thoughts refine,
And call new beauties forth from every line!
   Fancy and art in gay Petronius please,

665. *Dionysius*] Of Halicarnassus.

The scholar's learning, with the courtier's ease.
In grave Quintilian's copious work, we find
The justest rules, and clearest method joined: 670
Thus useful arms in magazines we place,
All ranged in order, and disposed with grace,
But less to please the eye, than arm the hand,
Still fit for use, and ready at command.
Thee, bold Longinus! all the Nine inspire,
And bless their critic with a poet's fire.
An ardent judge, who zealous in his trust,
With warmth gives sentence, yet is always just;
Whose own example strengthens all his laws,
And is himself that great sublime he draws.   680
Thus long succeeding critics justly reigned,
Licence repressed, and useful laws ordained.
Learning and Rome alike in empire grew;
And arts still followed where her eagles flew:
From the same foes, at last, both felt their doom,
And the same age saw learning fall, and Rome.
With tyranny, then superstition joined,
As that the body, this enslaved the mind;
Much was believed, but little understood,
And to be dull was construed to be good;   690
A second deluge learning thus o'er-run,
And the monks finished what the Goths begun.
At length Erasmus, that great, injured name,
(The glory of the priesthood, and the shame!)
Stemmed the wild torrent of a barbarous age,
And drove those holy vandals off the stage.
But see! each Muse, in LEO's golden days,
Starts from her trance, and trims her withered bays!
Rome's ancient Genius, o'er its ruins spread,
Shakes off the dust, and rears his reverend head.   700
Then sculpture and her sister-arts revive;
Stones leaped to form, and rocks began to live;
With sweeter notes each rising temple rung;
A Raphael painted, and a Vida sung.
Immortal Vida: on whose honoured brow

705. M. Hieronymus Vida, an excellent Latin poet, who wrote an *Art of Poetry* in verse. He flourished in the time of Leo the Tenth.

The poet's bays and critics ivy grow:
Cremona now shall ever boast thy name,
As next in place to Mantua, next in fame!
  But soon by impious arms from Latium chased,
Their ancient bounds the banished Muses passed;   710
Thence arts o'er all the northern world advance,
But critic-learning flourished most in France:
The rules a nation, born to serve, obeys;
And Boileau still in right of Horace sways.
But we, brave Britons, foreign laws despised,
And kept unconquered, and uncivilized;
Fierce for the liberties of wit, and bold,
We still defied the Romans, as of old.
Yet some there were, among the sounder few
Of those who less presumed, and better knew,   720
Who durst assert the juster ancient cause,
And here restored wit's fundamental laws.
Such was the Muse, whose rules and practice tell,
'Nature's chief masterpiece is writing well.'
Such was Roscommon, not more learned than good,
With manners generous as his noble blood;
To him the wit of Greece and Rome was known,

---

723. *Essay on Poetry* by the Duke of Buckingham. Our poet is not the only one of his time who complimented this *Essay*, and its noble author. Mr Dryden had done it very largely in the Dedication to his translation of the *Aeneid*; and Dr Garth in the first edition of his *Dispensary* says,

> *The Tiber now no courtly Gallus sees,*
> *But smiling Thames enjoys his Normanbys.*

Though afterwards omitted, when parties were carried so high in the reign of Queen Anne, as to allow no commendation to an opposite in politics. The Duke was all his life a steady adherent to the Church of England party, yet an enemy to the extravagant measures of the court in the reign of Charles II. On which account after having strongly patronized Mr Dryden, a coolness succeeded between them on that poet's absolute attachment to the court, which carried him some lengths beyond what the Duke could approve of. This nobleman's true character had been very well marked by Mr Dryden before,

> *the Muse's friend,*
> *Himself a Muse. In Sanadrin's debate*
> *True to his prince, but not a slave of state.*
>
> *Absalom and Achitophel.*

Our author was more happy, he was honoured very young with his friendship, and it continued till his death in all the circumstances of a familiar esteem.

And every author's merit, but his own.
Such late was Walsh—the Muse's judge and friend,
Who justly knew to blame or to commend;   730
To failings mild, but zealous for desert;
The clearest head, and the sincerest heart.
This humble praise, lamented shade! receive,
This praise at least a grateful Muse may give:
The Muse, whose early voice you taught to sing,
Prescribed her heights, and pruned her tender wing,
(Her guide now lost) no more attempts to rise,
But in low numbers short excursions tries:
Content, if hence th' unlearned their wants may view,
The learned reflect on what before they knew: 740
Careless of censure, nor too fond of fame;
Still pleased to praise, yet not afraid to blame;
Averse alike to flatter, or offend;
Not free from faults, nor yet too vain to mend.

WINDSOR FOREST

To the Right Honourable
GEORGE Lord LANSDOWNE

Non injussa cano: Te nostrae, *Vare*, myricae,
Te *Nemus* omne canet; nec Phoebo gratior ulla est
Quam sibi quae *Vari* praescripsit pagina nomen.

VIRGIL.

Thy forests, Windsor! and thy green retreats,   1
At once the monarch's and the muse's seats,
Invite my lays. Be present, sylvan maids!
Unlock your springs, and open all your shades.
GRANVILLE commands; your aid, O muses, bring!
What muse for GRANVILLE can refuse to sing?
   The groves of Eden, vanished now so long,
Live in description, and look green in song:
These, were my breast inspired with equal flame,
Like them in beauty, should be like in fame.   10
Here hills and vales, the woodland and the plain,

Here earth and water seem to strive again,
Not chaos-like together crushed and bruised,
But, as the world, harmoniously confused:
Where order in variety we see,
And where, though all things differ, all agree.
Here waving groves a chequered scene display,
And part admit, and part exclude the day;
As some coy nymph her lover's warm address
Nor quite indulges, nor can quite repress.   20
There, interspersed in lawns and opening glades,
Thin trees arise that shun each other's shades.
Here in full light the russet plains extend:
There wrapped in clouds the blueish hills ascend.
Ev'n the wild heath displays her purple dyes,
And 'midst the desert fruitful fields arise,
That crowned with tufted trees and springing corn,
Like verdant isles the sable waste adorn.
Let India boast her plants, nor envy we
The weeping amber or the balmy tree,   30
While by our oaks the precious loads are born,
And realms commanded which those trees adorn.
Not proud Olympus yields a nobler sight,
Though Gods assembled grace his towering height,
Than what more humble mountains offer here,
Where, in their blessings, all those Gods appear.
See Pan with flocks, with fruits Pomona crowned,
Here blushing Flora paints th'enamelled ground,
Here Ceres' gifts in waving prospect stand,
And nodding tempt the joyful reaper's hand;   40
Rich Industry sits smiling on the plains,
And peace and plenty tell, a STUART reigns.
   Not thus the land appeared in ages past,
A dreary desert, and a gloomy waste,
To savage beasts and savage laws a prey,
And kings more furious and severe than they;
Who claimed the skies, dispeopled air and floods,
The lonely lords of empty wilds and woods:
Cities laid waste, they stormed the dens and caves,
(For wiser brutes were backward to be slaves.)   50

45. *savage laws*] The forest laws.

What could be free, when lawless beasts obeyed,
And ev'n the elements a tyrant swayed?
In vain kind seasons swelled the teeming grain,
Soft showers distilled, and suns grew warm in vain;
The swain with tears his frustrate labour yields,
And famished dies amidst his ripened fields.
What wonder then, a beast or subject slain
Were equal crimes in a despotic reign?
Both doomed alike, for sportive tyrants bled,
But while the subject starved, the beast was fed.   60
Proud Nimrod first the bloody chase began,
A mighty hunter, and his prey was man:
Our haughty Norman boasts that barbarous name,
And makes his trembling slaves the royal game.
The fields are ravished from th'industrious swains,
From men their cities, and from Gods their fanes:
The levelled towns with weeds lie covered o'er;
The hollow winds through naked temples roar;
Round broken columns clasping ivy twined;
O'er heaps of ruin stalked the stately hind;   70
The fox obscene to gaping tombs retires,
And savage howlings fill the sacred quires.
Awed by his nobles, by his commons cursed,
Th'oppressor ruled tyrannic where he durst,
Stretched o'er the poor and church his iron rod,
And served alike his vassals and his God.
Whom ev'n the Saxon spared and bloody Dane,
The wanton victims of his sport remain.
But see, the man who spacious regions gave
A waste for beasts, himself denied a grave!   80
Stretched on the lawn his second hope survey,

65. Alluding to the destruction made in the New Forest, and the tyrannies exercised there by William I.

65, 66. Translated from

> Templa adimit divis, fora civibus, arva colonis,

by an old monkish writer, I forget who.

72.   And wolves with howling fill, etc.

The author thought this an error, wolves not being common in England at the time of the Conqueror.

81. second hope] Richard, second son of William the Conqueror.

At once the chaser, and at once the prey:
Lo Rufus, tugging at the deadly dart,
Bleeds in the forest, like a wounded hart.
Succeeding monarchs heard the subjects' cries,
Nor saw displeased the peaceful cottage rise.
Then gathering flocks on unknown mountains fed,
O'er sandy wilds were yellow harvests spread,
The forests wondered at th' unusual grain,
And secret transport touched the conscious swain.   90
Fair Liberty, Britannia's Goddess, rears
Her cheerful head, and leads the golden years.

Ye vigorous swains! while youth ferments your blood,
And purer spirits swell the sprightly flood,
Now range the hills, the gameful woods beset,
Wind the shrill horn, or spread the waving net.
When milder autumn summer's heat succeeds,
And in the new-shorn field the partridge feeds,
Before his lord the ready spaniel bounds,
Panting with hope, he tries the furrowed grounds;   100
But when the tainted gales the game betray,
Couched close he lies, and meditates the prey:
Secure they trust th' unfaithful field, beset,
Till hovering o'er 'em sweeps the swelling net.
Thus (if small things we may with great compare)
When Albion sends her eager sons to war,
Some thoughtless town, with ease and plenty blessed,
Near, and more near, the closing lines invest;
Sudden they seize th' amazed, defenceless prize,
And high in air Britannia's standard flies.   110

See! from the brake the whirring pheasant springs,
And mounts exulting on triumphant wings:
Short is his joy; he feels the fiery wound,
Flutters in blood, and panting beats the ground.
Ah! what avail his glossy, varying dyes,
His purple crest, and scarlet-circled eyes,
The vivid green his shining plumes unfold,
His painted wings, and breast that flames with gold?

Nor yet, when moist Arcturus clouds the sky,
The woods and fields their pleasing toils deny.   120
To plains with well-breathed beagles we repair,

And trace the mazes of the circling hare:
(Beasts, urged by us, their fellow-beasts pursue,
And learn of man each other to undo.)
With slaughtering guns th' unwearied fowler roves,
When frosts have whitened all the naked groves;
Where doves in flocks the leafless trees o'ershade,
And lonely woodcocks haunt the watery glade.
He lifts the tube, and levels with his eye;
Straight a short thunder breaks the frozen sky.   130
Oft, as in airy rings they skim the heath,
The clamorous lapwings feel the leaden death:
Oft, as the mounting larks their notes prepare,
They fall, and leave their little lives in air.

  In genial spring, beneath the quivering shade,
Where cooling vapours breathe along the mead,
The patient fisher takes his silent stand,
Intent, his angle trembling in his hand;
With looks unmoved, he hopes the scaly breed,
And eyes the dancing cork, and bending reed.   140
Our plenteous streams a various race supply,
The bright-eyed perch with fins of Tyrian dye,
The silver eel, in shining volumes rolled,
The yellow carp, in scales bedropped with gold,
Swift trouts, diversified with crimson stains,
And pikes, the tyrants of the watery plains.

  Now Cancer glows with Phoebus' fiery car:
The youth rush eager to the sylvan war,
Swarm o'er the lawns, the forest walks surround,
Rouse the fleet hart, and cheer the opening hound.   150
Th' impatient courser pants in every vein,
And pawing, seems to beat the distant plain:
Hills, vales, and floods appear already crossed,
And e'er he starts, a thousand steps are lost.
See the bold youth strain up the threatening steep,
Rush through the thickets, down the valleys sweep,
Hang o'er their coursers heads with eager speed,
And earth rolls back beneath the flying steed.
Let old Arcadia boast her ample plain,
Th' immortal huntress, and her virgin-train;   160
Nor envy, Windsor! since thy shades have seen
As bright a Goddess, and as chaste a QUEEN;

Whose care, like hers, protects the sylvan reign,
The earth's fair light, and empress of the main.
　Here too, 'tis sung, of old Diana strayed,
And Cynthus' top forsook for Windsor shade;
Here was she seen o'er airy wastes to rove,
Seek the clear spring, or haunt the pathless grove;
Here armed with silver bows, in early dawn,
Her buskined virgins traced the dewy lawn.　　　　　　　170
　Above the rest a rural nymph was famed,
Thy offspring, Thames! the fair Lodona named;
(Lodona's fate, in long oblivion cast,
The Muse shall sing, and what she sings shall last.)
Scarce could the Goddess from her nymph be known,
But by the crescent and the golden zone:
She scorned the praise of beauty, and the care;
A belt her waist, a fillet binds her hair;
A painted quiver on her shoulder sounds,
And with her dart the flying deer she wounds.　　　　　180
It chanced, as eager of the chase the maid
Beyond the forest's verdant limits strayed,
Pan saw and loved, and burning with desire
Pursued her flight, her flight increased his fire.
Not half so swift the trembling doves can fly,
When the fierce eagle cleaves the liquid sky;
Not half so swiftly the fierce eagle moves,
When through the clouds he drives the trembling doves;
As from the God she flew with furious pace,
Or as the God, more furious, urged the chase.　　　　　190
Now fainting, sinking, pale, the nymph appears;
Now close behind his sounding steps she hears;
And now his shadow reached her as she run,
(His shadow lengthened by the setting sun)
And now his shorter breath, with sultry air,
Pants on her neck, and fans her parting hair.
In vain on Father Thames she calls for aid,
Nor could Diana help her injured maid.
Faint, breathless, thus she prayed, nor prayed in vain;
'Ah Cynthia! ah—though banished from thy train,　　　　200
Let me, O let me, to the shades repair,
My native shades—there weep, and murmur there.'
She said, and melting as in tears she lay,

In a soft, silver stream dissolved away.
The silver stream her virgin coldness keeps,
For ever murmurs, and for ever weeps;
She still bears the name the hapless virgin bore,
And bathes the forest where she ranged before.
In her chaste current oft the Goddess laves,
And with celestial tears augments the waves.   210
Oft in her glass the musing shepherd spies
The headlong mountains and the downward skies.
The watery landskip of the pendant woods,
And absent trees that tremble in the floods;
In the clear azure gleam the flocks are seen,
And floating forests paint the waves with green.
Through the fair scene roll slow the lingering streams,
Then foaming pour along, and rush into the Thames.
        Thou too, great father of the British floods!
With joyful pride surveyst our lofty woods;   220
Where towering oaks their growing honours rear,
And future navies on thy shores appear.
Not Neptune's self from all her streams receives
A wealthier tribute, than to thine he gives.
No seas so rich, so gay no banks appear,
No lake so gentle, and no spring so clear.
Nor Po so swells the fabling poet's lays,
While led along the skies his current strays,
As thine, which visits Windsor's famed abodes,
To grace the mansion of our earthly Gods: 230
Nor all his stars above a lustre show,
Like the bright beauties on thy banks below;
Where Jove, subdued by mortal passion still,
Might change Olympus for a nobler hill.
        Happy the man whom this bright court approves,
His sovereign favours, and his country loves:
Happy next him, who to these shades retires,
Whom nature charms, and whom the Muse inspires:
Whom humbler joys of home-felt quiet please,
Successive study, exercise, and ease.   240
He gathers health from herbs the forest yields,
And of their fragrant physic spoils the fields:

207. The River Loddon.

With chymic art exalts the mineral powers,
And draws the aromatic souls of flowers:
Now marks the course of rolling orbs on high;
O'er figured worlds now travels with his eye;
Of ancient writ unlocks the learned store,
Consults the dead, and lives past ages o'er:
Or wandering thoughtful in the silent wood,
Attends the duties of the wise and good, 250
T'observe a mean, be to himself a friend,
To follow nature, and regard his end;
Or looks on heaven with more than mortal eyes,
Bids his free soul expatiate in the skies,
Amid her kindred stars familiar roam,
Survey the region, and confess her home!
Such was the life great Scipio once admired,
Thus Atticus, and TRUMBULL thus retired.
 Ye sacred Nine! that all my soul possess,
Whose raptures fire me, and whole visions bless, 260
Bear me, oh bear me to sequestered scenes,
The bowery mazes, and surrounding greens:
To Thames's banks which fragrant breezes fill,
Or where ye Muses sport on COOPER's HILL.
(On COOPER's HILL eternal wreaths shall grow,
While lasts the mountain, or while Thames shall flow)
I seem through consecrated walks to rove,
I hear soft music die along the grove:
Led by the sound, I roam from shade to shade,
By god-like poets venerable made: 270
Here his first lays majestic DENHAM sung;
There the last numbers flowed from COWLEY's tongue.
O early lost! what tears the river shed,
When the sad pomp along his banks was led?
His drooping swans on every note expire,
And on his willows hung each Muse's lyre.
 Since fate relentless stopped their heavenly voice,
No more the forests ring, or groves rejoice;
Who now shall charm the shades, where COWLEY strung
His living harp, and lofty DENHAM sung? 280

272. Mr Cowley died at Chertsey, on the borders of the Forest, and was from thence conveyed to Westminster.

But hark! the groves rejoice, the forest rings!
Are these revived? or is it GRANVILLE sings?
'Tis yours, my lord, to bless our soft retreats,
And call the Muses to their ancient seats;
To paint anew the flowery sylvan scenes,
To crown the forests with immortal greens,
Make Windsor hills in lofty numbers rise,
And lift her turrets nearer to the skies;
To sing those honours you deserve to wear,
And add new lustre to her silver star.   290

  Here noble SURREY felt the sacred rage,
SURREY, the GRANVILLE of a former age:
Matchless his pen, victorious was his lance,
Bold in the lists, and graceful in the dance:
In the same shades the Cupids tuned his lyre,
To the same notes, of love, and soft desire:
Fair Geraldine, bright object of his vow,
Then filled the groves, as heavenly Myra now.

  Oh wouldst thou sing what heroes Windsor bore,
What kings first breathed upon her winding shore,   300
Or raise old warriors, whose adored remains
In weeping vaults her hallowed earth contains!
With Edward's acts adorn the shining page,
Stretch his long triumphs down through every age,
Draw monarchs chained, and Cressi's glorious field,
The lilies blazing on the regal shield:
Then, from her roofs when Verrio's colours fall,
And leave inanimate the naked wall,
Still in thy song should vanquished France appear,
And bleed for ever under Britain's spear.   310

  Let softer strains ill-fated Henry mourn,
And palms eternal flourish round his urn.
Here o'er the Martyr-King the marble weeps,
And fast beside him, once-feared Edward sleeps:
Whom not th' extended Albion could contain,

291. Henry Howard, Earl of Surrey, one of the first refiners of the English poetry
who flourished in the time of Henry VIII.

303. Edward III born here.

311. Henry VI.

314. Edward IV.

From old Belerium to the northern main,
The grave unites; where ev'n the great find rest,
And blended lie th' oppressor and th' oppressed!
　　Make sacred Charles's tomb for ever known,
(Obscure the place, and un-inscribed the stone)   320
Oh fact accursed! what tears has Albion shed,
Heavens, what new wounds! and how her old have bled?
She saw her sons with purple deaths expire,
Her sacred domes involved in rolling fire,
A dreadful series of intestine wars,
Inglorious triumphs and dishonest scars,
At length great ANNA said—'Let Discord cease!'
She said, the world obeyed, and all was peace!
　　In that blessed moment from his oozy bed
Old Father Thames advanced his reverend head.   330
His tresses dropped with dews, and o'er the stream
His shining horns diffused a golden gleam:
Graved on his urn appeared the moon, that guides
His swelling waters, and alternate tides;
The figured streams in waves of silver rolled,
And on their banks Augusta rose in gold.
Around his throne the sea-born brothers stood,
Who swell with tributary urns his flood;
First the famed authors of his ancient name,
The winding Isis and the fruitful Thame: 340
The Kennet swift, for silver eels renowned;
The Loddon slow, with verdant alders crowned;
Cole, whose dark streams his flowery islands lave;
And chalky Wey, that rolls a milky wave:
The blue, transparent Vandalis appears;
The gulphy Lea his sedgy tresses rears;
And sullen Mole, that hides his diving flood;
And silent Darent, stained with Danish blood.
　　High in the midst, upon his urn reclined,
(His sea-green mantle waving with the wind)   350
The God appeared: he turned his azure eyes
Where Windsor domes and pompous turrets rise;
Then bowed and spoke; the winds forget to roar,
And the hushed waves glide softly to the shore.
　　Hail, sacred Peace! hail long-expected days,
That Thames's glory to the stars shall raise!

Though Tiber's streams immortal Rome behold,
Though foaming Hermus swells with tides of gold,
From heaven itself though seven-fold Nilus flows,
And harvests on a hundred realms bestows;   360
These now no more shall be the Muse's themes,
Lost in my fame, as in the sea their streams.
Let Volga's banks with iron squadrons shine,
And groves of lances glitter on the Rhine,
Let barbarous Ganges arm a servile train;
Be mine the blessings of a peaceful reign.
No more my sons shall dye with British blood
Red Iber's sands, or Ister's foaming flood:
Safe on my shore each unmolested swain
Shall tend the flocks, or reap the bearded grain;   370
The shady empire shall retain no trace
Of war or blood, but in the sylvan chase;
The trumpets sleep, while cheerful horns are blown,
And arms employed on birds and beasts alone.
Behold! th' ascending villas on my side,
Project long shadows o'er the crystal tide.
Behold! Augusta's glittering spires increase,
And temples rise, the beauteous works of peace.
I see, I see where two fair cities bend
Their ample bow, a new Whitehall ascend!   380
There mighty nations shall enquire their doom,
The world's great oracle in times to come;
There kings shall sue, and suppliant states be seen
Once more to bend before a BRITISH QUEEN.
   Thy trees, fair Windsor! now shall leave their woods,
And half thy forests rush into my floods,
Bear Britain's thunder, and her cross display,
To the bright regions of the rising day;
Tempt icy seas, where scarce the waters roll,
Where clearer flames glow round the frozen pole;   390
Or under southern skies exalt their sails,
Led by new stars, and borne by spicy gales!
For me the balm shall bleed, and amber flow,
The coral redden, and the ruby glow,
The pearly shell its lucid globe infold,

378. The fifty new churches.

And Phoebus warm the ripening ore to gold.
The time shall come, when free as seas or wind
Unbounded Thames shall flow for all mankind,
Whole nations enter with each swelling tide,
And seas but join the regions they divide;   400
Earth's distant ends our glory shall behold,
And the new world launch forth to seek the old.
Then ships of uncouth form shall stem the tide,
And feathered people crowd my wealthy side,
And naked youths and painted chiefs admire
Our speech, our colour, and our strange attire!
Oh stretch thy reign, fair Peace! from shore to shore,
Till conquest cease, and slavery be no more;
Till the freed Indians in their native groves
Reap their own fruits, and woo their sable loves,   410
Peru once more a race of kings behold,
And other Mexicos be roofed with gold.
Exiled by thee from earth to deepest hell,
In brazen bonds shall barbarous Discord dwell;
Gigantic Pride, pale Terror, gloomy Care,
And mad Ambition shall attend her there:
There purple Vengeance bathed in gore retires,
Her weapons blunted, and extinct her fires:
There hateful Envy her own snakes shall feel,
And Persecution mourn her broken wheel: 420
There Faction roar, Rebellion bite her chain,
And gasping Furies thirst for blood in vain.
   Here cease thy flight, nor with unhallowed lays
Touch the fair fame of Albion's golden days:
The thoughts of Gods let GRANVILLE's verse recite,
And bring the scenes of opening fate to light.
My humble Muse, in unambitious strains,
Paints the green forests and the flowery plains,
Where Peace descending bids her olives spring,
And scatters blessings from her dove-like wing.   430
Ev'n I more sweetly pass my careless days,
Pleased in the silent shade with empty praise;
Enough for me, that to the listening swains
First in these fields I sung the sylvan strains.

398. A wish that London may be made a free port.

THE
RAPE of the LOCK
AN
HEROI-COMICAL
POEM
Written in the Year MDCCXII

TO
Mrs ARABELLA FERMOR

MADAM,

It will be in vain to deny that I have some regard for this piece, since I dedicate it to you. Yet you may bear me witness, it was intended only to divert a few young ladies, who have good sense and good humour enough to laugh not only at their sex's little unguarded follies, but at their own. But as it was communicated with the air of a secret, it soon found its way into the world. An imperfect copy having been offered to a bookseller, you had the good nature for my sake to consent to the publication of one more correct: this I was forced to, before I had executed half my design, for the machinery was entirely wanting to complete it.

The machinery, Madam, is a term invented by the critics, to signify that part which the deities, angels, or daemons are made to act in a poem: for the ancient poets are in one respect like many modern ladies; let an action be never so trivial in itself, they always make it appear of the utmost importance. These machines I determined to raise on a very new and odd foundation, the Rosicrucian doctrine of spirits.

I know how disagreeable it is to make use of hard words before a lady; but 'tis so much the concern of a poet to have his works understood, and particularly by your sex, that you must give me leave to explain two or three difficult terms.

The Rosicrucians are a people I must bring you acquainted with. The best account I know of them is in a French book called *Le Comte de Gabalis*, which both in its title and size is so like a novel, that many of the fair sex have read it for one by mistake. According to these gentlemen, the four elements are inhabited by spirits, which they call sylphs, gnomes, nymphs, and salamanders. The gnomes or daemons of earth delight in mischief; but the sylphs, whose habitation is in the air, are the best conditioned creatures imaginable. For they say, any mortals may enjoy the most intimate familiarities with these gentle spirits, upon a condition very easy to all true adepts, an inviolate preservation of chastity.

As to the following cantos, all the passages of them are as fabulous, as the vision at the beginning, or the transformation at the end (except the loss of your hair, which I always mention with reverence.) The human persons are as fictitious as the airy ones; and the character of Belinda, as it is now managed, resembles you in nothing but in beauty.

If this poem had as many graces as there are in your person, or in your mind, yet I could never hope it should pass through the world half so uncensured as you have done. But let its fortune be what it will, mine is happy enough, to have given me this occasion of assuring you that I am, with the truest esteem,

MADAM,
Your most obedient, humble servant,

A. POPE.

Nolueram, Belinda, tuos violare capillos;
Sed juvat, hoc precibus me tribuisse tuis.

MARTIAL.

CANTO I

What dire offence from amorous causes springs,   1
What mighty contests rise from trivial things,
I sing—This verse to CARYLL, Muse! is due:
This, ev'n Belinda may vouchsafe to view:
Slight is the subject, but not so the praise,
If She inspire, and He approve my lays.
Say what strange motive, Goddess! could compel
A well-bred lord t'assault a gentle belle?
Oh say what stranger cause, yet unexplored,
Could make a gentle belle reject a lord?   10
In tasks so bold, can little men engage,
And in soft bosoms dwells such mighty rage?
Sol through white curtains shot a timorous ray,
And oped those eyes that must eclipse the day:
Now lapdogs give themselves the rousing shake,
And sleepless lovers, just at twelve, awake:
Thrice rung the bell, the slipper knocked the ground,
And the pressed watch returned a silver sound.
Belinda still her downy pillow pressed,
Her guardian SYLPH prolonged the balmy rest: 20

'Twas he had summoned to her silent bed
The morning-dream that hovered o'er her head.
A youth more glittering than a birth-night beau,
(That ev'n in slumber caused her cheek to glow)
Seemed to her ear his winning lips to lay,
And thus in whispers said, or seemed to say:
  'Fairest of mortals, thou distinguished care
Of thousand bright inhabitants of air!
If e'er one vision touched thy infant thought,
Of all the nurse and all the priest have taught;   30
Of airy elves by moonlight shadows seen,
The silver token, and the circled green,
Or virgins visited by angel-powers,
With golden crowns and wreaths of heavenly flowers;
Hear and believe! thy own importance know,
Nor bound thy narrow views to things below.
Some secret truths, from learned pride concealed,
To maids alone and children are revealed:
What though no credit doubting wits may give?
The fair and innocent shall still believe.   40
Know then, unnumbered spirits round thee fly,
The light militia of the lower sky;
These, though unseen, are ever on the wing,
Hang o'er the box, and hover round the ring:
Think what an equipage thou hast in air,
And view with scorn two pages and a chair.
As now your own, our beings were of old,
And once enclosed in woman's beauteous mould;
Thence, by a soft transition, we repair
From earthly vehicles to these of air.   50
Think not, when woman's transient breath is fled,
That all her vanities at once are dead;
Succeeding vanities she still regards,
And though she plays no more, o'erlooks the cards.
Her joy in gilded chariots, when alive,
And love of ombre, after death survive.
For when the fair in all their pride expire,
To their first elements their souls retire:
The sprites of fiery termagants in flame
Mount up, and take a salamander's name.   60
Soft yielding minds to water glide away,

And sip, with nymphs, their elemental tea.
The graver prude sinks downward to a gnome,
In search of mischief still on earth to roam.
The light coquettes in sylphs aloft repair,
And sport and flutter in the fields of air.
  Know farther yet; whoever fair and chaste
Rejects mankind, is by some sylph embraced:
For spirits, freed from mortal laws, with ease
Assume what sexes and what shapes they please.   70
What guards the purity of melting maids,
In courtly balls, and midnight masquerades,
Safe from the treacherous friend, the daring spark,
The glance by day, the whisper in the dark,
When kind occasion prompts their warm desires,
When music softens, and when dancing fires?
'Tis but their sylph, the wise celestials know,
Though honour is the word with men below.
  Some nymphs there are, too conscious of their face,
For life predestined to the gnomes' embrace.   80
These swell their prospects and exalt their pride,
When offers are disdained, and love denied.
Then gay ideas crowd the vacant brain,
While peers and dukes, and all their sweeping train,
And garters, stars, and coronets appear,
And in soft sounds, 'Your Grace' salutes their ear.
'Tis these that early taint the female soul,
Instruct the eyes of young coquettes to roll,
Teach infant-cheeks a bidden blush to know,
And little hearts to flutter at a beau.   90
  Oft, when the world imagine women stray,
The sylphs through mystic mazes guide their way,
Through all the giddy circle they pursue,
And old impertinence expel by new.
What tender maid but must a victim fall
To one man's treat, but for another's ball?
When Florio speaks, what virgin could withstand,
If gentle Damon did not squeeze her hand?
With varying vanities, from every part,
They shift the moving toyshop of their heart;   100
Where wigs with wigs, with sword-knots sword-knots strive,
Beaux banish beaux, and coaches coaches drive.

This erring mortals levity may call,
Oh blind to truth! the sylphs contrive it all.
    Of these am I, who thy protection claim,
A watchful sprite, and Ariel is my name.
Late, as I ranged the crystal wilds of air,
In the clear mirror of thy ruling star
I saw, alas! some dread event impend,
Ere to the main this morning sun descend,   110
But heaven reveals not what, or how, or where:
Warned by the sylph, oh pious maid, beware!
This to disclose is all thy guardian can:
Beware of all, but most beware of man!'
    He said; when Shock, who thought she slept too long,
Leaped up, and waked his mistress with his tongue.
'Twas then Belinda, if report say true,
Thy eyes first opened on a billet-doux;
Wounds, charms, and ardours, were no sooner read,
But all the vision vanished from thy head.   120
    And now, unveiled, the toilet stands displayed,
Each silver vase in mystic order laid.
First, robed in white, the nymph intent adores,
With head uncovered, the cosmetic powers.
A heavenly image in the glass appears,
To that she bends, to that her eyes she rears;
Th' inferior priestess, at her altar's side,
Trembling, begins the sacred rites of pride.
Unnumbered treasures ope at once, and here
The various offerings of the world appear;   130
From each she nicely culls with curious toil,
And decks the goddess with the glittering spoil.
This casket India's glowing gems unlocks,
And all Arabia breathes from yonder box.
The tortoise here and elephant unite,
Transformed to combs, the speckled, and the white.
Here files of pins extend their shining rows,
Puffs, powders, patches, bibles, billet-doux.
Now awful beauty puts on all its arms;
The fair each moment rises in her charms,   140

108. The language of the Platonists, the writers of the intelligible world of spirits, etc.

Repairs her smiles, awakens every grace,
And calls forth all the wonders of her face;
Sees by degrees a purer blush arise,
And keener lightnings quicken in her eyes.
The busy sylphs surround their darling care,
These set the head, and those divide the hair,
Some fold the sleeve, whilst others plait the gown;
And Betty's praised for labours not her own.

CANTO II

Not with more glories, in th' ethereal plain,   I
The sun first rises o'er the purpled main,
Than, issuing forth, the rival of his beams
Launched on the bosom of the silver Thames.
Fair nymphs, and well-dressed youths around her shone,
But every eye was fixed on her alone.
On her white breast a sparkling cross she wore,
Which Jews might kiss, and infidels adore.
Her lively looks a sprightly mind disclose,
Quick as her eyes, and as unfixed as those: 10
Favours to none, to all she smiles extends;
Oft she rejects, but never once offends.
Bright as the sun, her eyes the gazers strike,
And, like the sun, they shine on all alike.
Yet graceful ease, and sweetness void of pride
Might hide her faults, if belles had faults to hide:
If to her share some female errors fall,
Look on her face, and you'll forget 'em all.

This nymph, to the destruction of mankind,
Nourished two locks, which graceful hung behind   20
In equal curls, and well conspired to deck
With shining ringlets her smooth ivory neck.
Love in these labyrinths his slaves detains,
And mighty hearts are held in slender chains.
With hairy springes we the birds betray,

145. Ancient traditions of the Rabbis relate, that several of the fallen angels became amorous of women, and particularize some; among the rest Asael, who lay with Naamah, the wife of Noah, or of Ham; and who continuing impenitent, still presides over the women's toilets. Bereshi Rabbi in Genes. vi. 2.

Slight lines of hair surprise the finny prey,
Fair tresses man's imperial race ensnare,
And beauty draws us with a single hair.
   Th' adventurous Baron the bright locks admired;
He saw, he wished, and to the prize aspired.   30
Resolved to win, he meditates the way,
By force to ravish, or by fraud betray;
For when success a lover's toil attends,
Few ask, if fraud or force attained his ends.
   For this, ere Phoebus rose, he had implored
Propitious heaven, and every power adored,
But chiefly love—to love an altar built,
Of twelve vast French romances, neatly gilt.
There lay three garters, half a pair of gloves;
And all the trophies of his former loves;   40
With tender billet-doux he lights the pyre,
And breathes three amorous sighs to raise the fire.
Then prostrate falls, and begs with ardent eyes
Soon to obtain, and long possess the prize:
The powers gave ear, and granted half his prayer,
The rest, the winds dispersed in empty air.
   But now secure the painted vessel glides,
The sunbeams trembling on the floating tides;
While melting music steals upon the sky,
And softened sounds along the waters die;   50
Smooth flow the waves, the zephyrs gently play,
Belinda smiled, and all the world was gay.
All but the sylph—with careful thoughts oppressed,
Th' impending woe sat heavy on his breast.
He summons straight his denizens of air;
The lucid squadrons round the sails repair:
Soft o'er the shrouds aërial whispers breathe,
That seemed but zephyrs to the train beneath.
Some to the sun their insect-wings unfold,
Waft on the breeze, or sink in clouds of gold;   60
Transparent forms, too fine for mortal sight,
Their fluid bodies half dissolved in light.
Loose to the wind their airy garments flew,
Thin glittering textures of the filmy dew,
Dipped in the richest tincture of the skies,
Where light disports in ever-mingling dyes,

While every beam new transient colours flings,
Colours that change whene'er they wave their wings.
Amid the circle, on the gilded mast,
Superior by the head, was Ariel placed;   70
His purple pinions opening to the sun,
He raised his azure wand, and thus begun:
'Ye sylphs and sylphids, to your chief give ear,
Fays, fairies, genii, elves, and daemons hear!
Ye know the spheres and various talks assigned
By laws eternal to th' aërial kind.
Some in the fields of purest ether play,
And bask and whiten in the blaze of day.
Some guide the course of wandering orbs on high,
Or roll the planets through the boundless sky.   80
Some less refined, beneath the moon's pale light
Pursue the stars that shoot athwart the night,
Or suck the mists in grosser air below,
Or dip their pinions in the painted bow,
Or brew fierce tempests on the wintry main,
Or o'er the glebe distil the kindly rain.
Others on earth o'er human race preside,
Watch all their ways, and all their actions guide:
Of these the chief the care of nations own,
And guard with arms divine the British throne.   90
    Our humbler province is to tend the fair,
Not a less pleasing, though less glorious care;
To save the powder from too rude a gale,
Nor let th' imprisoned essences exhale;
To draw fresh colours from the vernal flowers;
To steal from rainbows e'er they drop in showers
A brighter wash; to curl their waving hairs,
Assist their blushes, and inspire their airs;
Nay oft, in dreams, invention we bestow,
To change a flounce, or add a furbelow.   100
    This day, black omens threat the brightest fair
That e'er deserved a watchful spirit's care;
Some dire disaster, or by force, or slight;
But what, or where, the fates have wrapped in night.
Whether the nymph shall break Diana's law,
Or some frail china jar receive a flaw;
Or stain her honour, or her new brocade;

Forget her prayers, or miss a masquerade;
Or lose her heart, or necklace, at a ball;
Or whether Heaven has doomed that Shock must fall.   110
Haste then, ye spirits! to your charge repair:
The fluttering fan be Zephyretta's care;
The drops to thee, Brillante, we consign;
And, Momentilla, let the watch be thine;
Do thou, Crispissa, tend her favourite lock;
Ariel himself shall be the guard of Shock.

   To fifty chosen sylphs, of special note,
We trust th' important charge, the petticoat:
Oft have we known that seven-fold fence to fail,
Though stiff with hoops, and armed with ribs of whale;   120
Form a strong line about the silver bound,
And guard the wide circumference around.

   Whatever spirit, careless of his charge,
His post neglects, or leaves the fair at large,
Shall feel sharp vengeance soon o'ertake his sins,
Be stopped in vials, or transfixed with pins;
Or plunged in lakes of bitter washes lie,
Or wedged whole ages in a bodkin's eye:
Gums and pomatums shall his flight restrain,
While clogged he beats his silken wings in vain;   130
Or alum styptics with contracting power
Shrink his thin essence like a rivelled flower:
Or, as Ixion fixed, the wretch shall feel
The giddy motion of the whirling mill,
In fumes of burning chocolate shall glow,
And tremble at the sea that froths below!'

   He spoke; the spirits from the sails descend;
Some, orb in orb, around the nymph extend,
Some thread the mazy ringlets of her hair,
Some hang upon the pendants of her ear;   140
With beating hearts the dire event they wait,
Anxious, and trembling for the birth of fate.

CANTO III

Close by those meads, for ever crowned with flowers,   1
Where Thames with pride surveys his rising towers,
There stands a structure of majestic frame,
Which from the neighbouring Hampton takes its name.
Here Britain's statesmen oft the fall foredoom
Of foreign tyrants, and of nymphs at home;
Here thou, great ANNA! whom three realms obey,
Dost sometimes counsel take—and sometimes tea.
   Hither the heroes and the nymphs resort,
To taste awhile the pleasures of a court;   10
In various talk th' instructive hours they passed,
Who gave the ball, or paid the visit last:
One speaks the glory of the British Queen,
And one describes a charming Indian screen;
A third interprets motions, looks, and eyes;
At every word a reputation dies.
Snuff, or the fan, supply each pause of chat,
With singing, laughing, ogling, and all that.
   Meanwhile, declining from the noon of day,
The sun obliquely shoots his burning ray;   20
The hungry judges soon the sentence sign,
And wretches hang that jurymen may dine;
The merchant from th'Exchange returns in peace,
And the long labours of the toilet cease.
Belinda now, whom thirst of fame invites,
Burns to encounter two adventurous knights,
At ombre singly to decide their doom;
And swells her breast with conquests yet to come.
Straight the three bands prepare in arms to join,
Each band the number of the sacred nine.   30
Soon as she spreads her hand, th' aërial guard
Descend, and sit on each important card:
First Ariel perched upon a matadore,
Then each, according to the rank they bore;
For sylphs, yet mindful of their ancient race,
Are, as when women, wondrous fond of place.
   Behold, four kings in majesty revered,
With hoary whiskers and a forky beard;

And four fair queens whose hands sustain a flower,
Th' expressive emblem of their softer power;   40
Four knaves in garbs succinct, a trusty band,
Caps on their heads, and halberts in their hand;
And particoloured troops, a shining train,
Draw forth to combat on the velvet plain.
  The skilful nymph reviews her force with care:
'Let spades be trumps!' she said, and trumps they were.
  Now move to war her sable matadores,
In show like leaders of the swarthy Moors.
Spadillio first, unconquerable lord!
Led off two captive trumps, and swept the board.   50
As many more Manillio forced to yield,
And marched a victor from the verdant field.
Him Basto followed, but his fate more hard
Gained but one trump and one plebeian card.
With his broad sabre next, a chief in years,
The hoary majesty of spades appears,
Puts forth one manly leg, to sight revealed,
The rest, his many-coloured robe concealed.
The rebel knave, who dares his prince engage,
Proves the just victim of his royal rage.   60
Ev'n mighty Pam, that kings and queens o'erthrew
And mowed down armies in the fights of lu,
Sad chance of war! now destitute of aid,
Falls undistinguished by the victor spade!
  Thus far both armies to Belinda yield;
Now to the Baron fate inclines the field.
His warlike Amazon her host invades,
Th' imperial consort of the crown of spades.
The club's black tyrant first her victim died,
Spite of his haughty mien, and barbarous pride: 70
What boots the regal circle on his head,
His giant limbs, in state unwieldy spread;
That long behind he trails his pompous robe,
And, of all monarchs, only grasps the globe?
  The Baron now his diamonds pours apace;
Th' embroidered king who shows but half his face,
And his refulgent queen, with powers combined,
Of broken troops an easy conquest find.
Clubs, diamonds, hearts, in wild disorder seen,

With throngs promiscuous strow the level green.   80
Thus when dispersed a routed army runs,
Of Asia's troops, and Afric's sable sons,
With like confusion different nations fly,
Of various habit, and of various dye,
The pierced battalions disunited fall,
In heaps on heaps; one fate o'erwhelms them all.
　　The knave of diamonds tries his wily arts,
And wins (oh shameful chance!) the queen of hearts.
At this, the blood the virgin's cheek forsook,
A livid paleness spreads o'er all her look;   90
She sees, and trembles at th' approaching ill,
Just in the jaws of ruin, and codille.
And now, (as oft in some distempered state)
On one nice trick depends the general fate.
An ace of hearts steps forth: the king unseen
Lurked in her hand, and mourned his captive queen:
He springs to vengeance with an eager pace,
And falls like thunder on the prostrate ace.
The nymph exulting fills with shouts the sky;
The walls, the woods, and long canals reply.   100
　　Oh thoughtless mortals! ever blind to fate,
Too soon dejected, and too soon elate.
Sudden, these honours shall be snatched away,
And cursed for ever this victorious day.
　　For lo! the board with cups and spoons is crowned,
The berries crackle, and the mill turns round;
On shining altars of Japan they raise
The silver lamp; the fiery spirits blaze:
From silver spouts the grateful liquors glide,
While China's earth receives the smoking tide: 110
At once they gratify their scent and taste,
And frequent cups prolong the rich repast.
Straight hover round the fair her airy band;
Some, as she sipped, the fuming liquor fanned,
Some o'er her lap their careful plumes displayed,
Trembling, and conscious of the rich brocade.
Coffee (which makes the politician wise,
And see through all things with his half-shut eyes)
Sent up in vapours to the Baron's brain
New stratagems, the radiant lock to gain.   120

Ah cease, rash youth! desist ere 'tis too late,
Fear the just gods, and think of Scylla's fate!
Changed to a bird, and sent to flit in air,
She dearly pays for Nisus' injured hair!

But when to mischief mortals bend their will,
How soon they find fit instruments of ill?
Just then, Clarissa drew with tempting grace
A two-edged weapon from her shining case:
So ladies in romance assist their knight,
Present the spear, and arm him for the fight.   130
He takes the gift with reverence, and extends
The little engine on his finger's ends;
This just behind Belinda's neck he spread,
As o'er the fragrant steams she bends her head.
Swift to the lock a thousand sprites repair,
A thousand wings, by turns, blow back the hair;
And thrice they twitched the diamond in her ear;
Thrice she looked back, and thrice the foe drew near.
Just in that instant, anxious Ariel sought
The close recesses of the virgin's thought;   140
As on the nosegay in her breast reclined,
He watched th' ideas rising in her mind,
Sudden he viewed, in spite of all her art,
An earthly lover lurking at her heart.
Amazed, confused, he found his power expired,
Resigned to fate, and with a sigh retired.

The peer now spreads the glittering forfex wide,
T' enclose the lock; now joins it, to divide.
Ev'n then, before the fatal engine closed,
A wretched sylph too fondly interposed;   150
Fate urged the shears, and cut the sylph in twain,
(But airy substance soon unites again)
The meeting points the sacred hair dissever
From the fair head, for ever, and for ever!

Then flashed the living lightning from her eyes,
And screams of horror rend th' affrighted skies.
Not louder shrieks to pitying heaven are cast,
When husbands, or when lapdogs breathe their last,
Or when rich china vessels, fallen from high,

152. See Milton, [*Paradise Lost*,] lib. vi. of Satan cut asunder by the angel Michael.

In glittering dust, and painted fragments lie! 160
  'Let wreaths of triumph now my temples twine,'
The victor cried, 'the glorious prize is mine!
While fish in streams, or birds delight in air,
Or in a coach and six the British fair,
As long as *Atalantis* shall be read,
Or the small pillow grace a lady's bed,
While visits shall be paid on solemn days,
When numerous wax-lights in bright order blaze,
While nymphs take treats, or assignations give,
So long my honour, name, and praise shall live! 170
What time would spare, from steel receives its date,
And monuments, like men, submit to fate!
Steel could the labour of the Gods destroy,
And strike to dust th' imperial towers of Troy;
Steel could the works of mortal pride confound,
And hew triumphal arches to the ground.
What wonder then, fair nymph! thy hairs should feel
The conquering force of unresisted steel?'

CANTO IV

  But anxious cares the pensive nymph oppressed, 1
And secret passions laboured in her breast.
Not youthful kings in battle seized alive,
Not scornful virgins who their charms survive,
Not ardent lovers robbed of all their bliss,
Not ancient ladies when refused a kiss,
Not tyrants fierce than unrepenting die,
Not Cynthia when her manteau's pinned awry,
E'er felt such rage, resentment, and despair,
As thou, sad virgin! for thy ravished hair. 10
  For, that sad moment, when the sylphs withdrew,
And Ariel weeping from Belinda flew,
Umbriel, a dusky, melancholy sprite,
As ever sullied the fair face of light,
Down to the central earth, his proper scene,
Repaired to search the gloomy Cave of Spleen.
  Swift on his sooty pinions flits the gnome,
And in a vapour reached the dismal dome.

No cheerful breeze this sullen region knows,
The dreaded east is all the wind that blows.   20
Here in a grotto, sheltered close from air,
And screened in shades from day's detested glare,
She sighs for ever on her pensive bed,
Pain at her side, and megrim at her head.

    Two handmaids wait the throne: alike in place,
But differing far in figure and in face.
Here stood Ill-nature like an ancient maid,
Her wrinkled form in black and white arrayed;
With store of prayers, for mornings, nights, and noons,
Her hand is filled; her bosom with lampoons.   30

    There Affectation, with a sickly mien,
Shows in her cheek the roses of eighteen,
Practised to lisp, and hang the head aside,
Faints into airs, and languishes with pride,
On the rich quilt sinks with becoming woe,
Wrapped in a gown, for sickness, and for show.
The fair ones feel such maladies as these,
When each new nightdress gives a new disease.

    A constant vapour o'er the palace flies;
Strange phantoms rising as the mists arise;   40
Dreadful, as hermit's dreams in haunted shades,
Or bright, as visions of expiring maids.
Now glaring fiends, and snakes on rolling spires,
Pale spectres, gaping tombs, and purple fires:
Now lakes of liquid gold, Elysian scenes,
And crystal domes, and angels in machines.

    Unnumbered throngs on every side are seen,
Of bodies changed to various forms by spleen.
Here living teapots stand, one arm held out,
One bent; the handle this, and that the spout: 50
A pipkin there like Homer's tripod walks;
Here sighs a jar, and there a goose-pie talks;
Men prove with child, as powerful fancy works,
And maids turned bottles, call aloud for corks.

    Safe passed the gnome through this fantastic band,
A branch of healing spleenwort in his hand.

---

52. *and there a goose-pie talks*] Alludes to a real fact, a lady of distinction imagined herself in this condition.

Then thus addressed the power: 'Hail wayward Queen!
Who rule the sex to fifty from fifteen:
Parent of vapours and of female wit,
Who give th' hysteric, or poetic fit,   60
On various tempers act by various ways,
Make some take physic, others scribble plays;
Who cause the proud their visits to delay,
And send the godly in a pet to pray.
A nymph there is, that all thy power disdains,
And thousands more in equal mirth maintains.
But oh! if e'er thy gnome could spoil a grace,
Or raise a pimple on a beauteous face,
Like citron-waters matrons cheeks inflame,
Or change complexions at a losing game;   70
If e'er with airy horns I planted heads,
Or rumpled petticoats, or tumbled beds,
Or caused suspicion when no soul was rude,
Or discomposed the head-dress of a prude,
Or e'er to costive lap-dog gave disease,
Which not the tears of brightest eyes could ease:
Hear me, and touch Belinda with chagrin;
That single act gives half the world the spleen.'
    The goddess with a discontented air
Seems to reject him, though she grants his prayer.   80
A wondrous bag with both her hands she binds,
Like that where once Ulysses held the winds;
There she collects the force of female lungs,
Sighs, sobs, and passions, and the war of tongues.
A vial next she fills with fainting fears,
Soft sorrows, melting griefs, and flowing tears.
The gnome rejoicing bears her gifts away,
Spreads his black wings, and slowly mounts to day.
    Sunk in Thalestris' arms the nymph he found,
Her eyes dejected and her hair unbound.   90
Full o'er their heads the swelling bag he rent,
And all the furies issued at the vent.
Belinda burns with more than mortal ire,
And fierce Thalestris fans the rising fire.
'O wretched maid!' she spread her hands, and cried,
(While Hampton's echoes, 'wretched maid!' replied)
'Was it for this you took such constant care

The bodkin, comb, and essence to prepare?
For this your locks in paper durance bound,
For this with torturing irons wreathed around?   100
For this with fillets strained your tender head,
And bravely bore the double loads of lead?
Gods! shall the ravisher display your hair,
While the fops envy, and the ladies stare!
Honour forbid! at whose unrivalled shrine
Ease, pleasure, virtue, all, our sex resign.
Methinks already I your tears survey,
Already hear the horrid things they say,
Already see you a degraded toast,
And all your honour in a whisper lost!   110
How shall I, then, your helpless fame defend?
'Twill then be infamy to seem your friend!
And shall this prize, th' inestimable prize,
Exposed through crystal to the gazing eyes,
And heightened by the diamond's circling rays,
On that rapacious hand for ever blaze?
Sooner shall grass in Hyde Park Circus grow,
And wits take lodgings in the sound of Bow;
Sooner let earth, air, sea, to chaos fall,
Men, monkeys, lapdogs, parrots, perish all!'   120
    She said; then raging to Sir Plume repairs,
And bids her beau demand the precious hairs:
(Sir Plume of amber snuff-box justly vain,
And the nice conduct of a clouded cane)
With earnest eyes, and round unthinking face,
He first the snuff-box opened, then the case,
And thus broke out—'My Lord, why, what the devil?
Z—ds! damn the lock! 'fore Gad, you must be civil!
Plague on't! 'tis past a jest—nay prithee, pox!
Give her the hair'—he spoke, and rapped his box.   130
    'It grieves me much,' replied the peer again,
'Who speaks so well should ever speak in vain.
But by this lock, this sacred lock I swear,
(Which never more shall join its parted hair;
Which never more its honours shall renew,
Clipped from the lovely head where late it grew)
That while my nostrils draw the vital air,
This hand, which won it, shall for ever wear.'

He spoke, and speaking, in proud triumph spread
The long-contended honours of her head.　140
　　But Umbriel, hateful gnome! forbears not so;
He breaks the vial whence the sorrows flow.
Then see! the nymph in beauteous grief appears,
Her eyes half-languishing, half-drowned in tears;
On her heaved bosom hung her drooping head,
Which, with a sigh, she raised, and thus she said:
　　'For ever cursed be this detested day,
Which snatched my best, my favourite curl away!
Happy! ah ten times happy had I been,
If Hampton Court these eyes had never seen!　150
Yet am not I the first mistaken maid,
By love of courts to numerous ills betrayed.
Oh had I rather un-admired remained
In some lone isle, or distant northern land;
Where the gilt chariot never marks the way,
Where none learn ombre, none e'er taste bohea!
There kept my charms concealed from mortal eye,
Like roses that in deserts bloom and die.
What moved my mind with youthful lords to roam?
Oh had I stayed, and said my prayers at home!　160
'Twas this, the morning omens seemed to tell;
Thrice from my trembling hand the patch-box fell;
The tottering china shook without a wind,
Nay Poll sat mute, and Shock was most unkind!
A sylph too warned me of the threats of fate,
In mystic visions, now believed too late!
See the poor remnants of these slighted hairs!
My hands shall rend what ev'n thy rapine spares:
These in two sable ringlets taught to break
Once gave new beauties to the snowy neck;　170
The sister-lock now sits uncouth, alone,
And in its fellow's fate foresees its own;
Uncurled it hangs, the fatal shears demands,
And tempts once more thy sacrilegious hands.
Oh hadst thou, cruel! been content to seize
Hairs less in sight, or any hairs but these!'

CANTO V

She said: the pitying audience melt in tears.   1
But Fate and Jove had stopped the Baron's ears.
In vain Thalestris with reproach assails,
For who can move when fair Belinda fails?
Not half so fixed the Trojan could remain,
While Anna begged and Dido raged in vain.
Then grave Clarissa graceful waved her fan;
Silence ensued, and thus the nymph began:
   'Say why are beauties praised and honoured most,
The wise man's passion, and the vain man's toast?   10
Why decked with all that land and sea afford,
Why angels called, and angel-like adored?
Why round our coaches crowd the white-gloved beaux,
Why bows the side-box from its inmost rows?
How vain are all these glories, all our pains,
Unless good sense preserve what beauty gains:
That men may say, when we the front-box grace,
Behold the first in virtue as in face!
Oh! if to dance all night, and dress all day,
Charmed the smallpox, or chased old age away;   20
Who would not scorn what housewife's cares produce,
Or who would learn one earthly thing of use?
To patch, nay ogle, might become a saint,
Nor could it sure be such a sin to paint.
But since, alas! frail beauty must decay,
Curled or uncurled, since locks will turn to grey;
Since painted, or not painted, all shall fade,
And she who scorns a man, must die a maid;
What then remains but well our power to use,
And keep good-humour still whate'er we lose?   30
And trust me, dear! good-humour can prevail,
When airs, and flights, and screams, and scolding fail.
Beauties in vain their pretty eyes may roll;
Charms strike the sight, but merit wins the soul.'

---

7. *Clarissa*] A new character introduced in the subsequent editions, to open more clearly the MORAL of the poem, in a parody of the speech of Sarpedon to Glaucus in Homer.

So spoke the dame, but no applause ensued;
Belinda frowned, Thalestris called her prude.
'To arms, to arms!' the fierce virago cries,
And swift as lightning to the combat flies.
All side in parties and begin th' attack;
Fans clap, silks rustle and tough whalebones crack;   40
Heroes' and heroines' shouts confusedly rise,
And bass and treble voices strike the skies.
No common weapons in their hands are found,
Like gods they fight, nor dread a mortal wound.

So when bold Homer makes the gods engage,
And heavenly breasts with human passions rage;
'Gainst Pallas, Mars; Latona, Hermes arms;
And all Olympus rings with loud alarms:
Jove's thunder roars, heaven trembles all around,
Blue Neptune storms, the bellowing deeps resound: 50
Earth shakes her nodding towers, the ground gives way,
And the pale ghosts start at the flash of day!

Triumphant Umbriel on a sconce's height
Clapped his glad wings, and sate to view the fight:
Propped on their bodkin spears, the sprites survey
The growing combat, or assist the fray.

While through the press enraged Thalestris flies,
And scatters deaths around from both her eyes,
A beau and witling perished in the throng,
One died in metaphor, and one in song.   60
'O cruel nymph! a living death I bear,'
Cried Dapperwit, and sunk beside his chair.
A mournful glance Sir Fopling upwards cast,
'Those eyes are made so killing'—was his last.
Thus on Maeander's flowery margin lies
Th' expiring swan, and as he sings he dies.

When bold Sir Plume had drawn Clarissa down,
Chloe stepped in, and killed him with a frown;
She smiled to see the doughty hero slain,
But, at her smile, the beau revived again.   70

Now Jove suspends his golden scales in air,
Weighs the men's wits against the lady's hair;
The doubtful beam long nods from side to side;
At length the wits mount up, the hairs subside.

See fierce Belinda on the Baron flies,

With more than usual lightning in her eyes:
Nor feared the chief th' unequal fight to try,
Who sought no more than on his foe to die.
But this bold lord with manly strength endued,
She with one finger and a thumb subdued: 80
Just where the breath of life his nostrils drew,
A charge of snuff the wily virgin threw;
The gnomes direct, to every atom just,
The pungent grains of titillating dust.
Sudden, with starting tears each eye o'erflows,
And the high dome re-echoes to his nose.
    'Now meet thy fate,' incensed Belinda cried,
And drew a deadly bodkin from her side.
(The same, his ancient personage to deck,
Her great great grandsire wore about his neck   90
In three seal-rings; which after, melted down,
Formed a vast buckle for his widow's gown:
Her infant grandame's whistle next it grew,
The bells she jingled, and the whistle blew;
Then in a bodkin graced her mother's hairs,
Which long she wore, and now Belinda wears.)
    'Boast not my fall,' he cried, 'insulting foe!
Thou by some other shalt be laid as low.
Nor think, to die dejects my lofty mind:
All that I dread is leaving you behind!   100
Rather than so, ah let me still survive,
And burn in Cupid's flames,—but burn alive.'
    'Restore the lock!' she cries; and all around
'Restore the lock!' the vaulted roofs rebound.
Not fierce Othello in so loud a strain
Roared for the handkerchief that caused his pain.
But see how oft ambitious aims are crossed,
And chiefs contend till all the prize is lost!
The lock, obtained with guilt, and kept with pain,
In every place is sought, but sought in vain: 110
With such a prize no mortal must be blessed,
So heaven decrees! with heaven who can contest?
    Some thought it mounted to the lunar sphere,
Since all things lost on earth are treasured there.
There heroes' wits are kept in ponderous vases,
And beaux' in snuff-boxes and tweezer-cases.

There broken vows, and death-bed alms are found,
And lovers' hearts with ends of ribband bound,
The courtier's promises, and sick man's prayers,
The smiles of harlots, and the tears of heirs,   120
Cages for gnats, and chains to yoke a flea,
Dried butterflies, and tomes of casuistry.
    But trust the Muse—she saw it upward rise,
Though marked by none but quick, poetic eyes:
(So Rome's great founder to the heavens withdrew,
To Proculus alone confessed in view)
A sudden star, it shot through liquid air,
And drew behind a radiant trail of hair.
Not Berenice's locks first rose so bright,
The heavens bespangling with dishevelled light.   130
The sylphs behold it kindling as it flies,
And pleased pursue its progress through the skies.
    This the beau monde shall from the Mall survey,
And hail with music its propitious ray.
This the blessed lover shall for Venus take,
And send up vows from Rosamonda's lake.
This Partridge soon shall view in cloudless skies,
When next he looks through Galileo's eyes;
And hence th' egregious wizard shall foredoom
The fate of Louis, and the fall of Rome.   140
    Then cease, bright nymph! to mourn thy ravished hair,
Which adds new glory to the shining sphere!
Not all the tresses that fair head can boast,
Shall draw such envy as the lock you lost.
For, after all the murders of your eye,
When, after millions slain, yourself shall die;
When those fair suns shall set, as set they must,
And all those tresses shall be laid in dust;
This lock, the Muse shall consecrate to fame,
And 'midst the stars inscribe Belinda's name.   150

EPISTLE
To Miss BLOUNT

On her leaving the Town after the CORONATION

As some fond virgin, whom her mother's care   1
Drags from the town to wholesome country air,
Just when she learns to roll a melting eye,
And hear a spark, yet think no danger nigh;
From the dear man unwilling she must sever,
Yet takes one kiss before she parts for ever:
Thus from the world fair Zephalinda flew,
Saw others happy, and with sighs withdrew;
Not that their pleasures caused her discontent,
She sighed not that They stayed, but that She went.   10

She went, to plain-work, and to purling brooks,
Old-fashioned halls, dull aunts, and croaking rooks:
She went from opera, park, assembly, play,
To morning-walks, and prayers three hours a day;
To part her time 'twixt reading and bohea,
To muse, and spill her solitary tea,
Or o'er cold coffee trifle with the spoon,
Count the slow clock, and dine exact at noon;
Divert her eyes with pictures in the fire,
Hum half a tune, tell stories to the squire;   20
Up to her godly garret after seven,
There starve and pray, for that's the way to heaven.

Some squire, perhaps, you take delight to rack;
Whose game is whisk, whose treat a toast in sack;
Who visits with a gun, presents you birds,
Then gives a smacking buss, and cries,—'No words!'
Or with his hound comes hallowing from the stable,
Makes love with nods, and knees beneath a table;
Whose laughs are hearty, though his jests are coarse,
And loves you best of all things—but his horse.   30

In some fair evening, on your elbow laid,
You dream of triumphs in the rural shade;
In pensive thought recall the fancied scene,
See coronations rise on every green;
Before you pass th' imaginary sights

Of lords, and earls, and dukes, and gartered knights,
While the spread fan o'ershades your closing eyes;
Then give one flirt, and all the vision flies.
Thus vanish sceptres, coronets, and balls,
And leave you in lone woods, or empty walls!⁣   40
  So when your slave, at some dear idle time,
(Not plagued with head-aches, or the want of rhyme)
Stands in the streets, abstracted from the crew,
And while he seems to study, thinks of you;
Just when his fancy points your sprightly eyes,
Or sees the blush of soft Parthenia rise,
Gay pats my shoulder, and you vanish quite,
Streets, chairs, and coxcombs rush upon my sight;
Vexed to be still in town, I knit my brow,
Look sour, and hum a tune, as you may now.⁣   50

ELOISA
TO
ABELARD

ARGUMENT

Abelard and Eloisa flourished in the twelfth century; they were two of the most distinguished persons of their age in learning and beauty, but for nothing more famous than for their unfortunate passion. After a long course of calamities, they retired each to a several convent, and consecrated the remainder of their days to religion. It was many years after this separation, that a letter of Abelard's to a friend, which contained the history of his misfortune, fell into the hands of Eloisa. This awakening all her tenderness, occasioned those celebrated letters (out of which the following is partly extracted) which give so lively a picture of the struggles of grace and nature, virtue and passion.

    In these deep solitudes and awful cells,   1
  Where heavenly-pensive contemplation dwells,
  And ever-musing melancholy reigns;
  What means this tumult in a vestal's veins?
  Why rove my thoughts beyond this last retreat?
  Why feels my heart its long-forgotten heat?

Yet, yet I love!—From Abelard it came,
And Eloïsa yet must kiss the name.
    Dear fatal name! rest ever unrevealed,
Nor pass these lips in holy silence sealed: 10
Hide it, my heart, within that close disguise,
Where, mixed with God's, his loved idea lies:
O write it not, my hand—the name appears
Already written—wash it out, my tears!
In vain lost Eloïsa weeps and prays,
Her heart still dictates, and her hand obeys.
    Relentless walls! whose darksome round contains
Repentant sighs, and voluntary pains:
Ye rugged rocks! which holy knees have worn;
Ye grots and caverns shagged with horrid thorn!   20
Shrines! where their vigils pale-eyed virgins keep,
And pitying saints, whose statues learn to weep!
Though cold like you, unmoved and silent grown,
I have not yet forgot myself to stone.
All is not heaven's while Abelard has part,
Still rebel nature holds out half my heart;
Nor prayers nor fasts its stubborn pulse restrain,
Nor tears, for ages, taught to flow in vain.
    Soon as thy letters trembling I unclose,
That well-known name awakens all my woes.   30
Oh name for ever sad! for ever dear!
Still breathed in sighs, still ushered with a tear.
I tremble too where'er my own I find,
Some dire misfortune follows close behind.
Line after line my gushing eyes o'erflow,
Led through a sad variety of woe:
Now warm in love, now withering in my bloom,
Lost in a convent's solitary gloom!
There stern religion quenched th'unwilling flame,
There died the best of passions, love and fame. 40
    Yet write, oh write me all, that I may join
Griefs to thy griefs, and echo sighs to thine.
Nor foes nor fortune take this power away;
And is my Abelard less kind than they?
Tears still are mine, and those I need not spare,
Love but demands what else were shed in prayer;
No happier task these faded eyes pursue;

To read and weep is all they now can do.
　　Then share thy pain, allow that sad relief;
Ah, more than share it! give me all thy grief.　　　　50
Heaven first taught letters for some wretch's aid,
Some banished lover, or some captive maid;
They live, they speak, they breathe what love inspires,
Warm from the soul, and faithful to its fires,
The virgin's wish without her fears impart,
Excuse the blush, and pour out all the heart,
Speed the soft intercourse from soul to soul,
And waft a sigh from Indus to the Pole.
　　Thou knowst how guiltless first I met thy flame,
When love approached me under friendship's name;　　60
My fancy formed thee of angelic kind,
Some emanation of th'all-beauteous mind.
Those smiling eyes, attempering every ray,
Shone sweetly lambent with celestial day:
Guiltless I gazed; heaven listened while you sung;
And truths divine came mended from that tongue.
From lips like those what precept failed to move?
Too soon they taught me 'twas no sin to love:
Back through the paths of pleasing sense I ran,
Nor wished an angel whom I loved a man.　　　　　　70
Dim and remote the joys of saints I see,
Nor envy them that heaven I lose for thee.
　　How oft, when pressed to marriage, have I said,
Curse on all laws but those which love has made?
Love, free as air, at sight of human ties,
Spreads his light wings, and in a moment flies.
Let wealth, let honour, wait the wedded dame,
August her deed, and sacred be her fame;
Before true passion all those views remove,
Fame, wealth, and honour! what are you to love?　　80
The jealous god, when we profane his fires,
Those restless passions in revenge inspires,
And bids them make mistaken mortals groan,
Who seek in love for aught but love alone.
Should at my feet the world's great master fall,
Himself, his throne, his world, I'd scorn 'em all:

---

66. He was her preceptor in philosophy and divinity.

Not Caesar's empress would I deign to prove;
No, make me mistress to the man I love;
If there be yet another name more free,
More fond than mistress, make me that to thee!   90
Oh happy state! when souls each other draw,
When love is liberty, and nature, law:
All then is full, possessing, and possessed,
No craving void left aching in the breast:
Ev'n thought meets thought, ere from the lips it part,
And each warm wish springs mutual from the heart.
This sure is bliss (if bliss on earth there be)
And once the lot of Abelard and me.

    Alas how changed! what sudden horrors rise!
A naked lover bound and bleeding lies!   100
Where, where was Eloïse? her voice, her hand,
Her poniard, had opposed the dire command.
Barbarian, stay! that bloody stroke restrain;
The crime was common, common be the pain.
I can no more; by shame, by rage suppressed,
Let tears, and burning blushes speak the rest.

    Canst thou forget that sad, that solemn day,
When victims at yon altar's foot we lay?
Canst thou forget what tears that moment fell,
When, warm in youth, I bade the world farewell?   110
As with cold lips I kissed the sacred veil,
The shrines all trembled, and the lamps grew pale:
Heaven scarce believed the conquest it surveyed,
And saints with wonder heard the vows I made.
Yet then, to those dread altars as I drew,
Not on the cross my eyes were fixed, but you:
Not grace, or zeal, love only was my call,
And if I lose thy love, I lose my all.
Come! with thy looks, thy words, relieve my woe,
Those still at least are left thee to bestow.   120
Still on that breast enamoured let me lie,
Still drink delicious poison from thy eye,
Pant on thy lip, and to thy heart be pressed;
Give all thou canst—and let me dream the rest.
Ah no! instruct me other joys to prize,
With other beauties charm my partial eyes,
Full in my view set all the bright abode,

And make my soul quit Abelard for God.
 Ah think at least thy flock deserve thy care,
Plants of thy hand, and children of thy prayer.   130
From the false world in early youth they fled,
By thee to mountains, wilds, and deserts led.
You raised these hallowed walls; the desert smiled,
And paradise was opened in the wild.
No weeping orphan saw his father's stores
Our shrines irradiate, or emblaze the floors;
No silver saints, by dying misers given,
Here bribed the rage of ill-requited heaven:
But such plain roofs as piety could raise,
And only vocal with the Maker's praise.   140
In these lone walls (their days eternal bound)
These moss-grown domes with spiry turrets crowned,
Where awful arches make a noon-day night,
And the dim windows shed a solemn light;
Thy eyes diffused a reconciling ray,
And gleams of glory brightened all the day.
But now no face divine contentment wears,
'Tis all blank sadness, or continual tears.
See how the force of others prayers I try,
(O pious fraud of amorous charity!)   150
But why should I on others prayers depend?
Come thou, my father, brother, husband, friend!
Ah let thy handmaid, sister, daughter move,
And all those tender names in one, thy love!
The darksome pines that o'er yon rocks reclined
Wave high, and murmur to the hollow wind,
The wandering streams that shine between the hills,
The grots that echo to the tinkling rills,
The dying gales that pant upon the trees,
The lakes that quiver to the curling breeze;   160
No more these scenes my meditation aid,
Or lull to rest the visionary maid.
But o'er the twilight groves and dusky caves,
Long-sounding isles, and intermingled graves,
Black Melancholy sits, and round her throws
A death-like silence, and a dread repose:

133. He founded the monastery.

Her gloomy presence saddens all the scene,
Shades every flower, and darkens every green,
Deepens the murmur of the falling floods,
And breathes a browner horror on the woods.   170
     Yet here for ever, ever must I stay;
Sad proof how well a lover can obey!
Death, only death, can break the lasting chain;
And here, ev'n then, shall my cold dust remain,
Here all its frailties, all its flames resign,
And wait, till 'tis no sin to mix with thine.
     Ah wretch! believed the spouse of God in vain,
Confessed within the slave of love and man.
Assist me, heaven! but whence arose that prayer?
Sprung it from piety, or from despair?   180
Ev'n here, where frozen chastity retires,
Love finds an altar for forbidden fires.
I ought to grieve, but cannot what I ought;
I mourn the lover, not lament the fault;
I view my crime, but kindle at the view,
Repent old pleasures, and solicit new;
Now turned to heaven, I weep my past offence,
Now think of thee, and curse my innocence.
Of all affliction taught a lover yet,
'Tis sure the hardest science to forget!   190
How shall I lose the sin, yet keep the sense,
And love th'offender, yet detest th'offence?
How the dear object from the crime remove,
Or how distinguish penitence from love?
Unequal task! a passion to resign,
For hearts so touched, so pierced, so lost as mine.
Ere such a soul regains its peaceful state,
How often must it love, how often hate!
How often hope, despair, resent, regret,
Conceal, disdain—do all things but forget.   200
But let heaven seize it, all at once 'tis fired;
Not touched, but rapt; not wakened, but inspired!
Oh come! oh teach me nature to subdue,
Renounce my love, my life, my self—and you.
Fill my fond heart with God alone, for he
Alone can rival, can succeed to thee.
     How happy is the blameless vestal's lot?

The world forgetting, by the world forgot:
Eternal sunshine of the spotless mind!
Each prayer accepted, and each wish resigned;   210
Labour and rest, that equal periods keep;
'Obedient slumbers that can wake and weep;'
Desires composed, affections ever even;
Tears that delight, and sighs that waft to heaven.
Grace shines around her with serenest beams,
And whispering angels prompt her golden dreams.
For her th'unfading rose of Eden blooms,
And wings of seraphs shed divine perfumes,
For her the spouse prepares the bridal ring,
For her white virgins hymeneals sing;   220
To sounds of heavenly harps she dies away,
And melts in visions of eternal day.
    Far other dreams my erring soul employ,
Far other raptures, of unholy joy:
When at the close of each sad, sorrowing day,
Fancy restores what vengeance snatched away,
Then conscience sleeps, and leaving nature free,
All my loose soul unbounded springs to thee.
O cursed, dear horrors of all-conscious night!
How glowing guilt exalts the keen delight!   230
Provoking daemons all restraint remove,
And stir within me every source of love.
I hear thee, view thee, gaze o'er all thy charms,
And round thy phantom glue my clasping arms.
I wake—no more I hear, no more I view,
The phantom flies me, as unkind as you.
I call aloud; it hears not what I say:
I stretch my empty arms; it glides away.
To dream once more I close my willing eyes;
Ye soft illusions, dear deceits, arise!   240
Alas, no more! methinks we wandering go
Through dreary wastes, and weep each other's woe,
Where round some mouldering tower pale ivy creeps,
And low-browed rocks hang nodding o'er the deeps.
Sudden you mount! you beckon from the skies;
Clouds interpose, waves roar, and winds arise.

212. Taken from Crashaw.

I shriek, start up, the same sad prospect find,
And wake to all the griefs I left behind.
　For thee the fates, severely kind, ordain
A cool suspense from pleasure and from pain;   250
Thy life a long, dead calm of fixed repose;
No pulse that riots, and no blood that glows.
Still as the sea, ere winds were taught to blow,
Or moving spirit bade the waters flow;
Soft as the slumbers of a saint forgiven,
And mild as opening gleams of promised heaven.
　Come, Abelard! for what hast thou to dread?
The torch of Venus burns not for the dead.
Nature stands checked; religion disapproves;
Ev'n thou art cold—yet Eloïsa loves.   260
Ah hopeless, lasting flames! like those that burn
To light the dead, and warm th'unfruitful urn.
　What scenes appear where'er I turn my view?
The dear ideas, where I fly, pursue,
Rise in the grove, before the altar rise,
Stain all my soul, and wanton in my eyes.
I waste the matin lamp in sighs for thee,
Thy image steals between my God and me,
Thy voice I seem in every hymn to hear,
With every bead I drop too soft a tear.   270
When from the censer clouds of fragrance roll,
And swelling organs lift the rising soul,
One thought of thee puts all the pomp to flight,
Priests, tapers, temples, swim before my sight:
In seas of flame my plunging soul is drowned,
While altars blaze, and angels tremble round.
　While prostrate here in humble grief I lie,
Kind, virtuous drops just gathering in my eye,
While praying, trembling, in the dust I roll,
And dawning grace is opening on my soul: 280
Come, if thou darest, all charming as thou art!
Oppose thyself to heaven; dispute my heart;
Come, with one glance of those deluding eyes
Blot out each bright idea of the skies;
Take back that grace, those sorrows, and those tears,
Take back my fruitless penitence and prayers,
Snatch me, just mounting, from the blest abode,

Assist the fiends, and tear me from my God!
  No, fly me, fly me, far as pole from pole;
Rise Alps between us! and whole oceans roll!   290
Ah, come not, write not, think not once of me,
Nor share one pang of all I felt for thee.
Thy oaths I quit, thy memory resign;
Forget, renounce me, hate whate'er was mine.
Fair eyes, and tempting looks (which yet I view!)
Long loved, adored ideas, all adieu!
O grace serene! oh virtue heavenly fair!
Divine oblivion of low-thoughted care!
Fresh blooming hope, gay daughter of the sky!
And faith, our early immortality!   300
Enter, each mild, each amicable guest;
Receive, and wrap me in eternal rest!
  See in her cell sad Eloïsa spread,
Propped on some tomb, a neighbour of the dead.
In each low wind methinks a spirit calls,
And more than echoes talk along the walls.
Here, as I watched the dying lamps around,
From yonder shrine I heard a hollow sound.
'Come, sister, come!', it said, or seemed to say,
'Thy place is here, sad sister, come away!   310
Once like thyself, I trembled, wept, and prayed,
Love's victim then, though now a sainted maid:
But all is calm in this eternal sleep;
Here grief forgets to groan, and love to weep,
Ev'n superstition loses every fear:
For God, not man, absolves our frailties here.'
  I come, I come! prepare your roseate bowers,
Celestial palms, and ever-blooming flowers.
Thither, where sinners may have rest, I go,
Where flames refined in breasts seraphic glow.   320
Thou, Abelard! the last sad office pay,
And smooth my passage to the realms of day;
See my lips tremble, and my eye-balls roll,
Suck my last breath, and catch my flying soul!
Ah no—in sacred vestments mayst thou stand,
The hallowed taper trembling in thy hand,
Present the cross before my lifted eye,
Teach me at once, and learn of me to die.

Ah then, thy once-loved Eloïsa see!
It will be then no crime to gaze on me.   330
See from my cheek the transient roses fly!
See the last sparkle languish in my eye!
Till every motion, pulse, and breath be o'er;
And ev'n my Abelard beloved no more.
O Death all-eloquent! you only prove
What dust we dote on, when 'tis man we love.
    Then too, when fate shall thy fair frame destroy,
(That cause of all my guilt, and all my joy)
In trance ecstatic may thy pangs be drowned,
Bright clouds descend, and angels watch thee round,   340
From opening skies may streaming glories shine,
And saints embrace thee with a love like mine.
    May one kind grave unite each hapless name,
And graft my love immortal on thy fame!
Then, ages hence, when all my woes are o'er,
When this rebellious heart shall beat no more;
If ever chance two wandering lovers brings
To Paraclete's white walls and silver springs,
O'er the pale marble shall they join their heads,
And drink the falling tears each other sheds;   350
Then sadly say, with mutual pity moved,
'Oh may we never love as these have loved!'
From the full choir when loud hosannas rise,
And swell the pomp of dreadful sacrifice,
Amid that scene, if some relenting eye
Glance on the stone where our cold relics lie,
Devotion's self shall steal a thought from heaven,
One human tear shall drop, and be forgiven.
And sure if fate some future bard shall join
In sad similitude of griefs to mine,   360
Condemned whole years in absence to deplore,
And image charms he must behold no more;
Such if there be, who loves so long, so well;
Let him our sad, our tender story tell;
The well-sung woes will soothe my pensive ghost;
He best can paint 'em, who shall feel 'em most.

343. Abelard and Eloïsa were interred in the same grave, or in monuments adjoining, in the monastery of the Paraclete: he died in the year 1142, she in 1163.

ELEGY
To the MEMORY of an
UNFORTUNATE LADY

What beckoning ghost, along the moonlight shade   1
Invites my step, and points to yonder glade?
'Tis she!—but why that bleeding bosom gored,
Why dimly gleams the visionary sword?
Oh ever beauteous, ever friendly! tell,
Is it, in heaven, a crime to love too well?
To bear too tender, or too firm a heart,
To act a lover's or a Roman's part?
Is there no bright reversion in the sky,
For those who greatly think, or bravely die?   10
  Why bade ye else, ye powers! her soul aspire
Above the vulgar flight of low desire?
Ambition first sprung from your blessed abodes;
The glorious fault of angels and of gods:
Thence to their images on earth it flows,
And in the breasts of kings and heroes glows.
Most souls, 'tis true, but peep out once an age,
Dull sullen prisoners in the body's cage:
Dim lights of life, that burn a length of years
Useless, unseen, as lamps in sepulchres;   20
Like eastern kings a lazy state they keep,
And close confined in their own palace sleep.
  From these perhaps (ere nature bade her die)
Fate snatched her early to the pitying sky.
As into air the purer spirits flow,
And separate from their kindred dregs below;
So flew the soul to its congenial place,
Nor left one virtue to redeem her race.
  But thou, false guardian of a charge too good,
Thou, mean deserter of thy brother's blood!   30
See on these ruby lips the trembling breath,
These cheeks, now fading at the blast of death;
Cold is that breast which warmed the world before,
And those love-darting eyes must roll no more.
Thus, if eternal justice rules the ball,

Thus shall your wives, and thus your children fall:
On all the line a sudden vengeance waits,
And frequent hearses shall besiege your gates.
There passengers shall stand, and pointing say,
(While the long funerals blacken all the way)   40
'Lo these were they, whose souls the Furies steeled,
And cursed with hearts unknowing how to yield.
Thus unlamented pass the proud away,
The gaze of fools, and pageant of a day!
So perish all, whose breast ne'er learned to glow
For others good, or melt at others woe.'
    What can atone (oh ever-injured shade!)
Thy fate unpitied, and thy rites unpaid?
No friend's complaint, no kind domestic tear
Pleased thy pale ghost, or graced thy mournful bier;   50
By foreign hands thy dying eyes were closed,
By foreign hands thy decent limbs composed,
By foreign hands thy humble grave adorned,
By strangers honoured, and by strangers mourned!
What though no friends in sable weeds appear,
Grieve for an hour, perhaps, then mourn a year,
And bear about the mockery of woe
To midnight dances, and the public show?
What though no weeping loves thy ashes grace,
Nor polished marble emulate thy face?   60
What though no sacred earth allow thee room,
Nor hallowed dirge be muttered o'er thy tomb?
Yet shall thy grave with rising flowers be dressed,
And the green turf lie lightly on thy breast:
There shall the morn her earliest tears bestow,
There the first roses of the year shall blow;
While angels with their silver wings o'ershade
The ground, now sacred by thy relics made.
    So peaceful rests, without a stone, a name,
What once had beauty, titles, wealth, and fame.   70
How loved, how honoured once, avails thee not,
To whom related, or by whom begot;
A heap of dust alone remains of thee;
'Tis all thou art, and all the proud shall be!
    Poets themselves must fall, like those they sung;
Deaf the praised ear, and mute the tuneful tongue.

Ev'n he, whose soul now melts in mournful lays,
Shall shortly want the generous tear he pays;
Then from his closing eyes thy form shall part,
And the last pang shall tear thee from his heart,   80
Life's idle business at one gasp be o'er,
The Muse forgot, and thou beloved no more!

EPITAPH
Intended for Sir ISAAC NEWTON
In Westminster-Abbey

Nature and Nature's Laws lay hid in Night.
GOD said, '*Let Newton be!*' and all was Light.

AN EPISTLE
TO
Richard Boyle, Earl of *Burlington*

Of the Use of RICHES

'Tis strange, the miser should his cares employ   1
To gain those riches he can ne'er enjoy.
Is it less strange, the prodigal should waste
His wealth, to purchase what he ne'er can taste?
Not for himself he sees, or hears, or eats;
Artists must choose his pictures, music, meats:
He buys for Topham, drawings and designs,
For Pembroke statues, dirty gods, and coins;
Rare monkish manuscripts for Hearne alone,
And books for Mead, and butterflies for Sloane.   10

7. *Topham*] A gentleman famous for a judicious collection of drawings.

10. *Mead—Sloane.*] Two eminent physicians; the one had an excellent library, the other the finest collection in Europe of natural curiosities; both men of great learning and humanity.

Think we all these are for himself? no more
Than his fine wife, alas! or finer whore.
 For what has Virro painted, built, and planted?
Only to show, how many tastes he wanted.
What brought Sir Visto's ill got wealth to waste?
Some demon whispered, 'Visto! have a taste.'
Heaven visits with a taste the wealthy fool,
And needs no rod but Ripley with a rule.
See! sportive fate, to punish awkward pride,
Bids Bubo build, and sends him such a guide: 20
A standing sermon, at each year's expense,
That never coxcomb reached magnificence!
 You show us, Rome was glorious, not profuse,
And pompous buildings once were things of use.
Yet shall (my Lord) your just, your noble rules
Fill half the land with imitating fools;
Who random drawings from your sheets shall take,
And of one beauty many blunders make;
Load some vain church with old theatric state,
Turn arcs of triumph to a garden-gate;   30
Reverse your ornaments, and hang them all
On some patched dog-hole eked with ends of wall,
Then clap four slices of pilaster on't,
That, laced with bits of rustic, makes a front:
Or call the winds through long arcades to roar,
Proud to catch cold at a Venetian door;
Conscious they act a true Palladian part,
And if they starve, they starve by rules of art.
 Oft have you hinted to your brother peer,
A certain truth, which many buy too dear: 40
Something there is, more needful than expense,
And something previous ev'n to taste—'tis sense:
Good sense, which only is the gift of heaven,

---

18. *Ripley*] This man was a carpenter, employed by a first minister, who raised him to an architect, without any genius in the art; and after some wretched proofs of his insufficiency in public buildings, made him Comptroller of the Board of Works.

23. The Earl of Burlington was then publishing the designs of Inigo Jones, and the Antiquities of Rome by Palladio.

36. *Venetian door*] A door or window, so called, from being much practised at Venice by Palladio and others.

And though no science, fairly worth the seven:
A light, which in yourself you must perceive;
Jones and Le Nôtre have it not to give.
   To build, to plant, whatever you intend,
To rear the column, or the arch to bend,
To swell the terrace, or to sink the grot;
In all, let nature never be forgot.   50
But treat the goddess like a modest fair,
Nor over-dress, nor leave her wholly bare;
Let not each beauty everywhere be spied,
Where half the skill is decently to hide.
He gains all points, who pleasingly confounds,
Surprises, varies, and conceals the bounds.
   Consult the genius of the place in all;
That tells the waters or to rise, or fall,
Or helps th'ambitious hill the heavens to scale,
Or scoops in circling theatres the vale;   60
Calls in the country, catches opening glades,
Joins willing woods, and varies shades from shades;
Now breaks, or now directs, th' intending lines,
Paints as you plant, and as you work, designs.
   Still follow sense, of every art the soul,
Parts answering parts shall slide into a whole,
Spontaneous beauties all around advance,
Start ev'n from difficulty, strike from chance;
Nature shall join you; time shall make it grow
A work to wonder at—perhaps a STOWE.   70
   Without it, proud Versailles! thy glory falls,
And Nero's terraces desert their walls:
The vast parterres a thousand hands shall make,
Lo! COBHAM comes, and floats them with a lake:
Or cut wide views through mountains to the plain,
You'll wish your hill or sheltered seat again.

46. Inigo Jones the celebrated architect, and M. Le Nôtre, the designer of the best gardens of France.

70. The seat and gardens of the Lord Viscount Cobham in Buckinghamshire.

75. This was done in Hertfordshire, by a wealthy citizen, at the expense of above £5000 by which means (merely to overlook a dead plain) he let in the north-wind upon his house and parterre, which were before adorned and defended by beautiful woods.

Ev'n in an ornament its place remark,
Nor in an hermitage set Dr Clarke.

Behold Villario's ten-years' toil complete;
His arbours darken, his espaliers meet;   80
The wood supports the plain, the parts unite,
And strength of shade contends with strength of light:
A waving glow the bloomy beds display,
Blushing in bright diversities of day,
With silver-quivering rills meandered o'er—
Enjoy them, you! Villario can no more;
Tired of the scene parterres and fountains yield,
He finds at last he better likes a field.

Through his young woods how pleased Sabinus strayed
Or sat delighted in the thickening shade,   90
With annual joy the reddening shoots to greet,
Or see the stretching branches long to meet.
His son's fine taste an opener vista loves,
Foe to the dryads of his father's groves,
One boundless green, or flourished carpet views,
With all the mournful family of yews;
The thriving plants ignoble broomsticks made,
Now sweep those alleys they were born to shade.

At Timon's villa let us pass a day,
Where all cry out, 'What sums are thrown away!'   100
So proud, so grand, of that stupendous air,
Soft and agreeable come never there.
Greatness, with Timon, dwells in such a draught
As brings all Brobdignag before your thought.

78. Dr S. Clarke's busto placed by the Queen in the Hermitage, while the Dr duly frequented the Court.

95. The two extremes in parterres, which are equally faulty; a *boundless green*, large and naked as a field, or a *flourished carpet*, where the greatness and nobleness of the piece is lessened by being divided into too many parts, with scrolled works and beds, of which the examples are frequent.

96. Touches upon the ill taste of those who are so fond of evergreens (particularly yews, which are the most tonsile) as to destroy the nobler forest-trees, to make way for such little ornaments as pyramids of dark-green continually repeated, not unlike a funeral procession.

99. This description is intended to comprise the principles of a false taste of magnificence, and to exemplify what was said before, that nothing but good sense can attain it.

To compass this, his building is a town,
His pond an ocean, his parterre a down:
Who but must laugh, the master when he sees?
A puny insect, shivering at a breeze.
Lo! what huge heaps of littleness around!
The whole, a laboured quarry above ground.   110
Two cupids squirt before: a lake behind
Improves the keenness of the northern wind.
His gardens next your admiration call,
On every side you look, behold the wall!
No pleasing intricacies intervene,
No artful wildness to perplex the scene;
Grove nods at grove, each alley has a brother,
And half the platform just reflects the other.
The suffering eye inverted nature sees,
Trees cut to statues, statues thick as trees,   120
With here a fountain, never to be played,
And there a summer-house, that knows no shade.
Here Amphitrite sails through myrtle bowers;
There gladiators fight, or die, in flowers;
Un-watered see the drooping sea-horse mourn,
And swallows roost in Nilus' dusty urn.

My Lord advances with majestic mien,
Smit with the mighty pleasure, to be seen:
But soft—by regular approach—not yet—
First through the length of yon hot terrace sweat,   130
And when up ten steep slopes you've dragged your
        thighs,
Just at his study-door he'll bless your eyes.

His study! with what authors is it stored?
In books, not authors, curious is my lord;
To all their dated backs he turns you round:

124. The two statues of the *Gladiator pugnans* and *Gladiator moriens*.

130. The *approaches* and *communication* of house with garden, or of one part with another, ill judged, and inconvenient.

133. The false taste in books; a satire on the vanity in collecting them, more frequent in men of fortune than the study to understand them. Many delight chiefly in the elegance of the print, or of the binding; some have carried it so far, as to cause the upper shelves to be filled with painted books of wood; others pique themselves so much upon books in a language they do not understand, as to exclude the most useful in one they do.

These Aldus printed, those Du Suëil has bound.
Lo some are vellum, and the rest as good
For all his Lordship knows, but they are wood.
For Locke or Milton 'tis in vain to look,
These shelves admit not any modern book.   140
    And now the chapel's silver bell you hear,
That summons you to all the pride of prayer:
Light quirks of music, broken and uneven,
Make the soul dance upon a jig to heaven.
On painted ceilings you devoutly stare,
Where sprawl the saints of Verrio or Laguerre,
On gilded clouds in fair expansion lie,
And bring all paradise before your eye.
To rest, the cushion and soft dean invite,
Who never mentions hell to ears polite.   150
    But hark! the chiming clocks to dinner call;
A hundred footsteps scrape the marble hall:
The rich buffet well-coloured serpents grace,
And gaping Tritons spew to wash your face.
Is this a dinner? this a genial room?
No, 'tis a temple, and a hecatomb,
A solemn sacrifice, performed in state,
You drink by measure, and to minutes eat.
So quick retires each flying course, you'd swear

143. The false taste in *music*, improper to the subjects, as of light airs in churches, often practised by the organists, &c.

145. —And in *painting* (from which even Italy is not free) of naked figures in churches, &c. which has obliged some Popes to put draperies on some of those of the best masters.

146. Verrio (Antonio) painted many ceilings, &c. at Windsor, Hampton Court, &c. and Laguerre at Blenheim Castle, and other places.

150. This is a fact; a reverend dean preaching at court, threatened the sinner with punishment in 'a place which he thought it not decent to name in so polite an assembly'.

153. Taxes the incongruity of *ornaments* (though sometimes practised by the ancients) where an open mouth ejects the water into a fountain, or where the shocking images of serpents, &c. are introduced in grottos or buffets.

155. The proud festivals of some men are here set forth to ridicule, where pride destroys the ease, and formal regularity all the pleasurable enjoyment of the entertainment.

Sancho's dread doctor and his wand were there.   160
Between each act the trembling salvers ring,
From soup to sweet-wine, and 'God bless the King'.
In plenty starving, tantalized in state,
And complaisantly helped to all I hate,
Treated, caressed, and tired, I take my leave,
Sick of his civil pride from morn to eve;
I curse such lavish cost, and little skill,
And swear no day was ever passed so ill.

   Yet hence the poor are clothed, the hungry fed;
Health to himself, and to his infants bread   170
The labourer bears: what his hard heart denies,
His charitable vanity supplies.

   Another age shall see the golden ear
Imbrown the slope, and nod on the parterre,
Deep harvests bury all his pride has planned,
And laughing Ceres reassume the land.

   Who then shall grace, or who improve the soil?
Who plants like BATHURST, or who builds like
     BOYLE.
'Tis use alone that sanctifies expense,
And splendour borrows all her rays from sense.   180

   His father's acres who enjoys in peace,
Or makes his neighbours glad, if he increase;
Whose cheerful tenants bless their yearly toil,
Yet to their Lord owe more than to the soil;
Whose ample lawns are not ashamed to feed
The milky heifer and deserving steed;
Whose rising forests, not for pride or show,
But future buildings, future navies grow:
Let his plantations stretch from down to down,
First shade a country, and then raise a town.   190

   You too proceed! make falling arts your care,
Erect new wonders, and the old repair;
Jones and Palladio to themselves restore,

---

160. See *Don Quixote*, chap. xlvii.

169. The *moral* of the whole, where PROVIDENCE is justified in giving wealth to
those who squander it in this manner. A bad taste employs more hands, and diffuses
expense more than a good one.

And be whate'er Vitruvius was before:
Till kings call forth th' ideas of your mind,
(Proud to accomplish what such hands designed,)
Bid harbours open, public ways extend,
Bid temples, worthier of the god, ascend,
Bid the broad arch the dangerous flood contain,
The mole projected break the roaring main;　　　200
Back to his bounds their subject sea command,
And roll obedient rivers through the land:
These honours, peace to happy Britain brings,
These are imperial works, and worthy kings.

AN EPISTLE
TO
Allen Lord *Bathurst*

Of the Use *of* RICHES

Who shall decide, when doctors disagree,　　　1
And soundest casuists doubt, like you and me?
You hold the word, from Jove to Momus given,
That man was made the standing jest of heaven;

195, 197, &c. The poet after having touched upon the proper objects of magnificence and expense, in the private works of great men, comes to those great and public works which become a prince. This poem was published in the year 1732, when some of the new-built churches, by the Act of Queen Anne, were ready to fall, being founded in boggy land (which is satirically alluded to in our author's imitation of Horace, *Lib.* ii. *Sat.* 2. *Shall half the new-built churches round thee fall*), others were vilely executed, through fraudulent cabals between undertakers, officers, &c. Dagenham Breach had done very great mischiefs; many of the highways throughout England were hardly passable; and most of those which were repaired by turnpikes were made jobs for private lucre, and infamously executed, even to the entrances of London itself. The proposal of building a bridge at Westminster had been petitioned against and rejected; but in two years after the publication of this poem, an Act for building a bridge passed through both houses. After many debates in the committee, the execution was left to the carpenter above-mentioned, who would have made it a wooden one, to which our author alludes in these lines,

> *Who builds a bridge that never drove a pile?*
> *Should Ripley venture, all the world would smile.*

See the notes on that place.

And gold but sent to keep the fools in play,
For some to heap, and some to throw away.
   But I, who think more highly of our kind,
(And surely, heaven and I are of a mind)
Opine, that nature, as in duty bound,
Deep hid the shining mischief under ground: 10
But when by man's audacious labour won,
Flamed forth this rival to its sire the sun,
Then careful heaven supplied two sorts of men,
To squander these, and those to hide again.
   Like doctors thus, when much dispute has passed,
We find our tenets just the same at last.
Both fairly owning, riches in effect
No grace of heaven or token of th'elect;
Given to the fool, the mad, the vain, the evil,
To Ward, to Waters, Chartres, and the devil.   20

20. JOHN WARD of Hackney Esq., Member of Parliament, being prosecuted by the Duchess of Buckingham, and convicted of forgery, was first expelled the House, and then stood in the pillory on the 17th of March 1727. He was suspected of joining in a conveyance with Sir John Blunt, to secrete fifty thousand pounds of that director's estate, forfeited to the South Sea Company by Act of Parliament. The Company recovered the fifty thousand pounds against Ward; but he set up prior conveyances of his real estate to his brother and son, and concealed all his personal, which was computed to be one hundred and fifty thousand pounds. These conveyances being also set aside by a bill in Chancery, Ward was imprisoned, and hazarded the forfeiture of his life, by not giving in his effects till the last day, which was that of his examination. During his confinement, his amusement was to give poison to dogs and cats, and see them expire by slower or quicker torments. To sum up the *worth* of this gentleman, at the several eras of his life; at his standing in the pillory he was *worth above two hundred thousand pounds*; at his commitment to prison, he was *worth one hundred and fifty thousand*; but has been since so far diminished in his reputation, as to be thought a *worse man* by *fifty or sixty thousand*.

FR. CHARTRES, a man infamous for all manner of vices. When he was an ensign in the army, he was drummed out of the regiment for a cheat; he was next banished Brussels, and drummed out of Ghent on the same account. After a hundred tricks at the gaming-tables, he took to lending of money at exorbitant interest and on great penalties, accumulating premium, interest, and capital into a new capital, and seizing to a minute when the payments became due; in a word, by a constant attention to the vices, wants, and follies of mankind, he acquired an immense fortune. His house was a perpetual bawdy house. He was twice condemned for rapes, and pardoned; but the last time not without imprisonment in Newgate, and large confiscations. He died in Scotland in 1731, aged 62. The populace at his funeral raised a great riot, almost tore the body out of the coffin, and cast dead dogs, etc. into the grave along with it ... This gentleman was *worth seven thousand pounds a year* estate in land, and about *one hundred thousand* in money.

MR WATERS, the third of these worthies, was a man no way resembling the former

What nature wants, commodious gold bestows,
'Tis thus we eat the bread another sows:
But how unequal it bestows, observe,
'Tis thus we riot, while who sow it, starve.
What nature wants (a phrase I much distrust)
Extends to luxury, extends to lust:
Useful, I grant, it serves what life requires,
But dreadful too, the dark assassin hires:
Trade it may help, society extend;
But lures the pirate, and corrupts the friend: 30
It raises armies in a nation's aid,
But bribes a senate, and the land's betrayed.
In vain may heroes fight, and patriots rave;
If secret gold saps on from knave to knave.
Once, we confess, beneath the patriot's cloak,
From the cracked bag the dropping guinea spoke,
And gingling down the backstairs, told the crew,
'Old Cato is as great a rogue as you.'
Blessed paper-credit! last and best supply!
That lends corruption lighter wings to fly!   40
Gold imped by thee, can compass hardest things,
Can pocket states, can fetch or carry kings;
A single leaf shall waft an army o'er,

in his military, but extremely so in his civil capacity; his great fortune having been raised by the like diligent attendance on the necessities of others. But this gentleman's history must be deferred till his death, when his *worth* may be known more certainly.

21. *What nature wants*, commodious *gold bestows*,] The epithet *commodious* gives us the very proper idea of a *bawd* or *pander*, and this thought produced the two following lines, which were in all the former editions, but, for their bad reasoning omitted,

> And if we count amongst the needs of life
> Another's toil, why not another's wife!

35. This is a true story, which happened in the reign of William III to an unsuspected old patriot, who coming out at the back-door from having been closeted by the king, where he had received a large bag of guineas, the bursting of the bag discovered his business there.

42. In our author's time, many princes had been sent about the world, and great changes of kings projected in Europe. The partition treaty had disposed of Spain; France had set up a king for England, who was sent to Scotland, and back again; King Stanislaus was sent to Poland, and back again; the Duke of Anjou was sent to Spain, and Don Carlos to Italy.

Or ship off senates to a distant shore;
A leaf, like sibyls, scatter to and fro
Our fates and fortunes, as the winds shall blow:
Pregnant with thousands flits the scrap unseen,
And silent sells a king, or buys a queen.

Oh! that such bulky bribes as all might see,
Still, as of old, incumbered villainy!   50
Could France or Rome divert our brave designs,
With all their brandies or with all their wines?
What could they more than knights and squires
    confound,
Or water all the quorum ten miles round?
A statesman's slumbers how this speech would spoil!
'Sir, Spain has sent a thousand jars of oil;
Huge bales of British cloth blockade the door;
A hundred oxen at your levee roar.'

Poor avarice one torment more would find;
Nor could profusion squander all, in kind.   60
Astride his cheese Sir Morgan might we meet,
And Worldly crying coals from street to street,
Whom with a wig so wild, and mien so mazed,
Pity mistakes for some poor tradesman crazed.
Had Colepepper's whole wealth been hops and hogs,
Could he himself have sent it to the dogs?
His Grace will game: to White's a bull be led,
With spurning heels and with a butting head.
To White's be carried, as to ancient games,
Fair coursers, vases, and alluring dames.   70
Shall then Uxorio, if the stakes he sweep,

44. Alludes to several ministers, counsellors, and patriots banished in our times to Siberia, and to that MORE GLORIOUS FATE of the PARLIAMENT of PARIS, banished to Pontoise in the year 1720.

62. Some misers of great wealth, proprietors of the coal mines, had entered at this time into an association to keep up coals to an extravagant price, whereby the poor were reduced almost to starve, till one of them taking the advantage of underselling the rest, defeated the design. One of these misers was *worth ten thousand*, another *seven thousand* a year.

65. Sir WILLIAM COLEPEPPER, Bart. a person of an ancient family, and ample fortune, without one other quality of a gentleman, who, after ruining himself at the gaming table, past the rest of his days in sitting there to see the ruin of others; preferring to subsist upon borrowing and begging, rather than to enter into any reputable method of life, and refusing a post in the army which was offered him.

Bear home six whores, and make his lady weep?
Or soft Adonis, so perfumed and fine,
Drive to St James's a whole herd of swine?
Oh filthy check on all industrious skill,
To spoil the nation's last great trade, quadrille!
Since then, my Lord, on such a world we fall,
What say you? 'Say? Why take it, gold and all.'
   What riches give us let us then enquire:
Meat, fire, and clothes, what more? Meat, clothes,
     and fire.   80
Is this too little? would you more than live?
Alas! 'tis more than Turner finds they give.
Alas! 'tis more than (all his visions passed)
Unhappy Wharton, waking, found at last!
What can they give? to dying Hopkins, heirs;
To Chartres, vigour; Japhet, nose and ears?
Can they, in gems bid pallid Hippia glow,
In Fulvia's buckle ease the throbs below;

82. *Turner*] One, who, being possessed of three hundred thousand pounds, laid down his coach, because interest was reduced from five to four *per cent.* and then put seventy thousand into the Charitable Corporation for better interest; which sum having lost, he took it so much to heart, that he kept his chamber ever after. It is thought he would not have outlived it, but that he was heir to another considerable estate, which he daily expected, and that by this course of life he saved both clothes and all other expenses.

84. *Unhappy Wharton.*] A nobleman of great qualities, but as unfortunate in the application of them, as if they had been vices and follies. See his character in the [*Epistle to Cobham*].

85. *Hopkins,*] A citizen, whose rapacity obtained him the name of Vulture Hopkins. He lived worthless, but died *worth three hundred thousand pounds*, which he would give to no person living, but left it so as not to be inherited till after the second generation. His counsel representing to him how many years it must be, before this could take effect, and that his money could only lie at interest all that time, he expressed great joy thereat, and said, 'They would then be as long in spending, as he had been in getting it.' But the Chancery afterwards set aside the will, and gave it to the heir at law.

86. *Japhet, nose and ears*] JAPHET CROOK, alias Sir Peter Stranger, was published with the loss of those parts, for having forged a conveyance of an estate to himself, upon which he took up several thousand pounds. He was at the same time sued in Chancery for having fraudulently obtained a will, by which he possessed another considerable estate, in wrong of the brother of the deceased. By these means he was *worth* a great sum, which (in reward for the small loss of his ears) he enjoyed in prison till his death, and quietly left to his executor.

Or heal, old Narses, thy obscener ail,
With all th'embroidery plastered at thy tail?   90
They might (were Harpax not too wise to spend)
Give Harpax self the blessing of a friend;
Or find some doctor that would save the life
Of wretched Shylock, spite of Shylock's wife:
But thousands die, without or this or that,
Die, and endow a college, or a cat:
To some, indeed, heaven grants the happier fate,
T'enrich a bastard, or a son they hate.

Perhaps you think the poor might have their part?
Bond damns the poor, and hates them from his heart: 100
The grave Sir Gilbert holds it for a rule,
That 'every man in want is knave or fool:'
'God cannot love', says Blunt, with tearless eyes,
'The wretch he starves'—and piously denies:
But the good bishop, with a meeker air,
Admits, and leaves them, Providence's care.

Yet, to be just to these poor men of pelf,
Each does but hate his neighbour as himself:
Damned to the mines, an equal fate betides
The slave that digs it, and the slave that hides.   110
Who suffer thus, mere charity should own,
Must act on motives powerful, though unknown:
Some war, some plague, or famine they foresee,
Some revelation hid from you and me.
Why Shylock wants a meal, the cause is found,
He thinks a loaf will rise to fifty pound.
What made directors cheat in South-Sea year?

---

96. *Die, and endow a college, or a cat.*] A famous Duchess of R. in her last will left considerable legacies and annuities to her cats.

100. This epistle was written in the year 1730, when a corporation was established to lend money to the poor upon pledges, by the name of the Charitable Corporation, but the whole was turned only to an iniquitous method of enriching particular people, to the ruin of such numbers, that it became a parliamentary concern to endeavour the relief of those unhappy sufferers, and three of the managers, who were members of the house, were expelled. By the report of the Committee, appointed to enquire into that iniquitous affair, it appears, that when it was objected to the intended removal of the office, that the poor, for whose use it was erected, would be hurt by it, Bond, one of the directors, replied, *Damn the poor.* That 'God hates the poor,' and, 'That every man in want is knave or fool,' &c. were the genuine apothegms of some of the persons here mentioned.

To live on venison when it sold so dear.
Ask you why Phryne the whole auction buys?
Phryne foresees a general excise.   120
Why she and Sappho raise that monstrous sum?
Alas! they fear a man will cost a plum.
  Wise Peter sees the world's respect for gold,
And therefore hopes this nation may be sold:
Glorious ambition! Peter, swell thy store,
And be what Rome's great Didius was before.
  The crown of Poland, venal twice an age,
To just three millions stinted modest Gage.
But nobler scenes Maria's dreams unfold,
Hereditary realms, and worlds of gold.   130
Congenial souls! whose life one avarice joins,
And one fate buries in th'Asturian mines.
  Much injured Blunt! why bears he Britain's hate?

118. In the extravagance and luxury of the South Sea year, the price of a haunch of venison was from three to five pounds.

120. Many people about the year 1733, had a conceit that such a thing was intended, of which it is not improbable this lady might have some intimation.

123. PETER WALTER, a person not only eminent in the wisdom of his profession, as a dexterous attorney, but allowed to be a good, if not a safe, conveyancer; extremely respected by the nobility of this land, though free from all manner of luxury and ostentation: his wealth was never seen, and his bounty never heard of, except to his own son, for whom he procured an employment of considerable profit, of which he gave him as much as was *necessary*. Therefore the taxing this gentleman with any ambition, is certainly a great wrong to him.

126. A Roman lawyer, so rich as to purchase the Empire when it was set to sale upon the death of Pertinax.

127. The two persons here mentioned were of quality, each of whom in the Mississippi despised to realise above *three hundred thousand pounds*; the gentleman with a view to the purchase of the crown of Poland, the lady on a vision of the like royal nature. They since retired into Spain, where they are still in search of gold in the mines of the Asturies.

Sir JOHN BLUNT, originally a scrivener, was one of the first projectors of the South Sea company, and afterwards one of the directors and chief managers of the famous scheme in 1720. He was also one of those who suffered most severely by the bill of pains and penalties on the said directors. He was a dissenter of a most religious deportment, and professed to be a great believer. Whether he did really credit the prophecy here mentioned is not certain, but it was constantly in this very style he declaimed against the corruption and luxury of the age, the partiality of Parliaments, and the misery of party-spirit. He was particularly eloquent against *avarice* in great and noble persons, of which he had indeed lived to see many miserable examples. He died in the year 1732.

A wizard told him in these words our fate:
'At length corruption, like a general flood,
(So long by watchful ministers withstood)
Shall deluge all; and avarice creeping on,
Spread like a low-born mist, and blot the sun;
Statesman and patriot ply alike the stocks,
Peeress and butler share alike the box,   140
And judges job, and bishops bite the town,
And mighty dukes pack cards for half a crown.
See Britain sunk in lucre's sordid charms,
And France revenged of ANNE's and EDWARD's
        arms!'
'Twas no court-badge, great scrivener! fired thy
        brain,
Nor lordly luxury, nor city gain:
No, 'twas thy righteous end, (ashamed to see
Senates degenerate, patriots disagree,
And nobly wishing party-rage to cease)
To buy both sides, and give thy country peace.   150
    'All this is madness,' cries a sober sage:
But who, my friend, has reason in his rage?
'The ruling passion, be it what it will,
The ruling passion conquers reason still.'
Less mad the wildest whimsy we can frame,
That ev'n that passion, if it has no aim;
For though such motives folly you may call,
The folly's greater to have none at all.
    Hear then the truth: ' 'Tis heaven each passion
        sends,
And different men directs to different ends.   160
Extremes in nature equal good produce,
Extremes in man concur to general use.'
Ask we what makes one keep, and one bestow?
That POWER who bids the ocean ebb and flow;
Bids seed-time, harvest, equal course maintain,
Through reconciled extremes of drought and rain;
Builds life on death, on change duration founds,
And gives th'eternal wheels to know their rounds.
    Riches, like insects, when concealed they lie,
Wait but for wings, and in their season fly.   170
Who sees pale Mammon pine amidst his store,

Sees but a backward steward for the poor;
This year a reservoir, to keep and spare;
The next, a fountain, spouting through his heir,
In lavish streams to quench a country's thirst,
And men and dogs shall drink him till they burst.

   Old Cotta shamed his fortune and his birth,
Yet was not Cotta void of wit or worth:
What though (the use of barbarous spits forgot)
His kitchen vied in coolness with his grot?   180
His court with nettles, moats with cresses stored,
With soups unbought and salads blessed his board?
If Cotta lived on pulse, it was no more
Than Brahmins, saints, and sages did before;
To cram the rich was prodigal expense,
And who would take the poor from Providence?
Like some lone Chartreux stands the good old hall,
Silence without, and fasts within the wall;
No raftered roofs with dance and tabor sound,
No noontide-bell invites the country round: 190
Tenants with sighs the smokeless towers survey,
And turn th'unwilling steeds another way:
Benighted wanderers, the forest o'er,
Curse the saved candle, and unopening door;
While the gaunt mastiff growling at the gate,
Affrights the beggar whom he longs to eat.

   Not so his son, he marked this oversight,
And then mistook reverse of wrong for right.
(For what to shun will no great knowledge need,
But what to follow, is a task indeed.)   200
Yet sure, of qualities deserving praise,
More go to ruin fortunes, than to raise.
Whole slaughtered hecatombs, and floods of wine,
Fill the capacious squire, and deep divine!
Yet no mean motive this profusion draws,
His oxen perish in his country's cause;
'Tis GEORGE and LIBERTY that crowns the cup,
And zeal for that great house which eats him up.
The woods recede around the naked seat,
The sylvans groan—no matter—for the fleet: 210
Next goes his wool—to clothe our valiant bands,
Last, for his country's love, he sells his lands.

To town he comes, completes the nation's hope,
And heads the bold train-bands, and burns a Pope.
And shall not Britain now reward his toils,
Britain, that pays her patriots with her spoils?
In vain at court the bankrupt pleads his cause,
His thankless country leaves him to her laws.

 The sense to value riches, with the art
T'enjoy them, and the virtue to impart,   220
Not meanly, nor ambitiously pursued,
Not sunk by sloth, not raised by servitude;
To balance fortune by a just expense,
Join with economy, magnificence;
With splendour, charity; with plenty, health;
Oh teach us, BATHURST! yet unspoiled by wealth!
That secret rare, between th' extremes to move
Of mad good nature, and of mean self-love.

 To worth or want well-weighed, be bounty given,
And ease, or emulate, the care of heaven;   230
(Whose measure full o'erflows on human race)
Mend fortune's fault, and justify her grace.
Wealth in the gross is death, but life diffused;
As poison heals, in just proportion used:
In heaps, like ambergris, a stink it lies,
But well-dispersed, is incense to the skies.

 Who starves by nobles, or with nobles eats?
The wretch that trusts them, and the rogue that
  cheats.
Is there a lord, who knows a cheerful noon
Without a fiddler, flatterer, or buffoon?   240
Whose table, wit, or modest merit share,
Un-elbowed by a gamester, pimp, or player?
Who copies yours, or OXFORD's better part,
To ease th'oppressed, and raise the sinking heart?
Where'er he shines, oh fortune, gild the scene,
And angels guard him in the golden mean!
There, English bounty yet awhile may stand,

243. Edward Harley, Earl of Oxford. The son of Robert, created Earl of Oxford
and Earl Mortimer by Queen Anne. This nobleman died regretted by all men of
letters, great numbers of whom had experienced his benefits. He left behind him
one of the most noble libraries in Europe.

And honour linger e'er it leaves the land.
   But all our praises why should lords engross?
Rise, honest Muse! and sing the MAN of ROSS: 250
Pleased Vaga echoes through her winding bounds,
And rapid Severn hoarse applause resounds.
Who hung with woods yon mountain's sultry brow?
From the dry rock who bade the waters flow?
Not to the skies in useless columns tossed,
Or in proud falls magnificently lost,
But clear and artless, pouring through the plain
Health to the sick, and solace to the swain.
Whose causeway parts the vale with shady rows?
Whose seats the weary traveller repose?   260
Who taught that heaven-directed spire to rise?
'The MAN of ROSS,' each lisping babe replies.
Behold the market-place with poor o'erspread!
The MAN of ROSS divides the weekly bread:
He feeds yon alms-house, neat, but void of state,
Where age and want sit smiling at the gate:
Him portioned maids, apprenticed orphans blessed,
The young who labour, and the old who rest.
Is any sick? the MAN of ROSS relieves,
Prescribes, attends, the medicine makes, and gives.   270
Is there a variance? enter but his door,
Balked are the courts, and contest is no more.
Despairing quacks with curses fled the place,
And vile attorneys, now an useless race.
   'Thrice happy man! enabled to pursue
What all so wish, but want the power to do!
Oh say, what sums that generous hand supply?
What mines, to swell that boundless charity?'
Of debts, and taxes, wife and children clear,
This man possessed—five hundred pounds a year.   280
Blush, grandeur, blush! proud courts, withdraw your
    blaze!
Ye little stars! hide your diminished rays.

---

250. The person here celebrated, who with a small estate actually performed all these good works, and whose true name was almost lost (partly by the title of the Man of Ross given him by way of eminence, and partly by being buried without so much as an inscription) was called Mr John Kyrle. He died in the year 1724, aged 90, and lies interred in the chancel of the church of Ross in Herefordshire.

'And what? no monument, inscription, stone?
His race, his form, his name almost unknown?'
    Who builds a church to God, and not to fame,
Will never mark the marble with his name:
Go search it there, where to be born and die,
Of rich and poor makes all the history;
Enough, that virtue filled the space between;
Proved, by the ends of being, to have been.   290
When Hopkins dies, a thousand lights attend
The wretch, who living saved a candle's end:
Shouldering God's altar a vile image stands,
Belies his features, nay extends his hands;
That live-long wig which Gorgon's self might own,
Eternal buckle takes in Parian stone.
Behold what blessings wealth to life can lend!
And see, what comfort it affords our end.
    In the worst inn's worst room, with mat half-hung,
The floors of plaster, and the walls of dung,   300
On once a flock-bed, but repaired with straw,
With tape-tied curtains, never meant to draw,
The George and garter dangling from that bed
Where tawdry yellow strove with dirty red,
Great Villers lies—alas! how changed from him,
That life of pleasure, and that soul of whim!
Gallant and gay, in Cliveden's proud alcove,
The bower of wanton Shrewsbury and love;
Or just as gay, at council, in a ring
Of mimicked statesmen, and their merry king.   310
No wit to flatter, left of all his store!

287. The parish registers.

296. The poet ridicules the wretched taste of carving large periwigs on bustos, of which there are several vile examples in the tombs at Westminster and elsewhere.

305. This lord, yet more famous for his vices than his misfortunes, after having been possessed of about £50,000 a year, and passed through many of the highest posts in the kingdom, died in the year 1687, in a remote inn in Yorkshire, reduced to the utmost misery.

307. *Cliveden*] A delightful palace, on the banks of the Thames, built by the Duke of Buckingham.

308. *Shrewsbury*] The Countess of Shrewsbury, a woman abandoned to gallantries. The Earl her husband was killed by the Duke of Buckingham in a duel; and it has been said, that during the combat she held the Duke's horses in the habit of a page.

No fool to laugh at, which he valued more.
There, victor of his health, of fortune, friends,
And fame, this lord of useless thousands ends.
   His Grace's fate sage Cutler could foresee,
And well (he thought) advised him, 'Live like me.'
As well his Grace replied, 'Like you, Sir John?
That I can do, when all I have is gone.'
Resolve me, reason, which of these is worse,
Want with a full, or with an empty purse?   320
Thy life more wretched, Cutler, was confessed,
Arise, and tell me, was thy death more blessed?
Cutler saw tenants break, and houses fall,
For very want; he could not build a wall.
His only daughter in a stranger's power,
For very want; he could not pay a dower.
A few grey hairs his reverend temples crowned,
'Twas very want that sold them for two pound.
What ev'n denied a cordial at his end,
Banished the doctor, and expelled the friend?   330
What but a want, which you perhaps think mad,
Yet numbers feel, the want of what he had!
Cutler and Brutus, dying both exclaim,
'Virtue! and wealth! what are ye but a name!'
   Say, for such worth are other worlds prepared?
Or are they both, in this, their own reward?
A knotty point! to which we now proceed.
But you are tired—I'll tell a tale——'Agreed.'
   Where London's column, pointing at the skies,
Like a tall bully, lifts the head, and lies;   340
There dwelt a citizen of sober fame,
A plain good man, and Balaam was his name;
Religious, punctual, frugal, and so forth;
His word would pass for more than he was worth.
One solid dish his weekday meal affords,
An added pudding solemnized the Lord's:
Constant at church, and Change; his gains were sure,
His givings rare, save farthings to the poor.
   The devil was piqued such saintship to behold,

---

339. The Monument, built in memory of the fire of London, with an inscription,
importing that city to have been burnt by the Papists.

And longed to tempt him like good Job of old: 350
But Satan now is wiser than of yore,
And tempts by making rich, not making poor.

Roused by the prince of air, the whirlwinds sweep
The surge, and plunge his father in the deep;
Then full against his Cornish lands they roar,
And two rich shipwrecks bless the lucky shore.

Sir Balaam now, he lives like other folks,
He takes his chirping pint, and cracks his jokes:
'Live like yourself,' was soon my Lady's word;
And lo! two puddings smoked upon the board. 360

Asleep and naked as an Indian lay,
An honest factor stole a gem away:
He pledged it to the knight; the knight had wit,
So kept the diamond, and the rogue was bit.
Some scruple rose, but thus he eased his thought,
'I'll now give sixpence where I gave a groat;
Where once I went to church, I'll now go twice—
And am so clear too of all other vice.'

The tempter saw his time; the work he plied;
Stocks and subscriptions pour on every side, 370
Till all the demon makes his full descent
In one abundant shower of cent per cent,
Sinks deep within him, and possesses whole,
Then dubs director, and secures his soul.

Behold Sir Balaam, now a man of spirit,
Ascribes his gettings to his parts and merit;
What late he called a blessing, now was wit,
And God's good Providence, a lucky hit.
Things change their titles, as our manners turn:
His counting house employed the Sunday morn; 380
Seldom at church ('twas such a busy life)
But duly sent his family and wife.
There (so the devil ordained) one Christmas-tide
My good old Lady catched a cold, and died.

355. The author has placed the scene of these shipwrecks in Cornwall, not only from their frequency on that coast, but from the inhumanity of the inhabitants to those to whom that misfortune arrives. When a ship happens to be stranded there, they have been known to bore holes in it, to prevent its getting off; to plunder, and sometimes even to massacre the people. Nor has the Parliament of England been yet able wholly to suppress these barbarities.

A nymph of quality admires our knight;
He marries, bows at court, and grows polite:
Leaves the dull cits, and joins (to please the fair)
The well-bred cuckolds in St James's air:
First, for his son a gay commission buys,
Who drinks, whores, fights, and in a duel dies: 390
His daughter flaunts a viscount's tawdry wife;
She bears a coronet and p—x for life.
In Britain's senate he a seat obtains,
And one more pensioner St Stephen gains.
My Lady falls to play; so bad her chance,
He must repair it; takes a bribe from France;
The House impeach him; Coningsby harangues;
The court forsake him, and Sir Balaam hangs:
Wife, son, and daughter, Satan! are thy own,
His wealth, yet dearer, forfeit to the crown: 400
The devil and the king divide the prize,
And sad Sir Balaam curses God and dies.

THE
FIRST SATIRE
OF THE
SECOND BOOK
OF
HORACE IMITATED

To Mr FORTESCUE

P. There are (I scarce can think it, but am told)   1
There are, to whom my satire seems too bold:
Scarce to wise Peter complaisant enough,
And something said of Chartres much too rough.
The lines are weak, another's pleased to say,
Lord Fanny spins a thousand such a day.
Timorous by nature, of the rich in awe,
I come to counsel learned in the law:
You'll give me, like a friend both sage and free,

Advice; and (as you use) without a fee.   10
   F. I'd write no more.
                P. Not write? but then I think,
And for my soul I cannot sleep a wink.
I nod in company, I wake at night,
Fools rush into my head, and so I write.
   F. You could not do a worse thing for your life.
Why, if the nights seem tedious—take a wife:
Or rather truly, if your point be rest,
Lettuce and cowslip-wine; *probatum est*.
But talk with Celsus, Celsus will advise
Hartshorn, or something that shall close your eyes.   20
Or, if you needs must write, write CAESAR's praise,
You'll gain at least a *knighthood*, or the *bays*.
   P. What? like Sir Richard, rumbling, rough, and
     fierce,
With ARMS, and GEORGE, and BRUNSWICK crowd the
     verse,
Rend with tremendous sound your ears asunder,
With gun, drum, trumpet, blunderbuss, and thunder?
Or nobly wild, with Budgell's fire and force,
Paint angels trembling round his falling horse?
   F. Then all your muse's softer art display,
Let CAROLINA smooth the tuneful lay,   30
Lull with AMELIA's liquid name the nine,
And sweetly flow through all the royal line.
   P. Alas! few verses touch their nicer ear;
They scarce can bear their *Laureate* twice a year;
And justly CAESAR scorns the poet's lays,
It is to *history* he trusts for praise.
   F. Better be Cibber, I'll maintain it still,
Than ridicule all taste, blaspheme quadrille,
Abuse the city's best good men in metre,
And laugh at peers that put their trust in Peter.   40
Ev'n those you touch not, hate you.
                P. What should ail them?
   F. A hundred smart in Timon and in Balaam:
The fewer still you name, you wound the more;
Bond is but one, but Harpax is a score.
   P. Each mortal has his pleasure: none deny
Scarsdale his bottle, Darty his ham-pie;

Ridotta sips and dances, till she see
The doubling lustres dance as fast as she;
Fox loves the senate, Hockley Hole his brother,
Like in all else, as one egg to another.   50
I love to pour out all myself, as plain
As downright SHIPPEN, or as old Montaigne:
In them, as certain to be loved as seen,
The soul stood forth, nor kept a thought within;
In me what spots (for spots I have) appear,
Will prove at least the medium must be clear.
In this impartial glass, my muse intends
Fair to expose myself, my foes, my friends;
Publish the present age; but where my text
Is vice too high, reserve it for the next: 60
My foes shall wish my life a longer date,
And every friend the less lament my fate.
My head and heart thus flowing through my quill,
Verse-man or prose-man, term me which you will,
Papist or Protestant, or both between,
Like good Erasmus in an honest mean,
In moderation placing all my glory,
While Tories call me Whig, and Whigs a Tory.
    Satire's my weapon, but I'm too discreet
To run amuck, and tilt at all I meet;   70
I only wear it in a land of Hectors,
Thieves, supercargoes, sharpers, and directors.
Save but our *army!* and let Jove incrust
Swords, pikes, and guns, with everlasting rust!
Peace is my dear delight—not FLEURY's more:
But touch me, and no minister so sore.
Whoe'er offends, at some unlucky time
Slides into verse, and hitches in a rhyme,
Sacred to ridicule his whole life long,
And the sad burden of some merry song.   80
    Slander or poison, dread from Delia's rage,
Hard words or hanging, if your judge be Page.
From furious Sappho scarce a milder fate,
P-xed by her love, or libelled by her hate.
Its proper power to hurt, each creature feels;
Bulls aim their horns, and asses lift their heels;
'Tis a bear's talent not to kick, but hug;

And no man wonders he's not stung by Pug.
So drink with Walter, or with Chartres eat,
They'll never poison you, they'll only cheat.   90
    Then, learned Sir! (to cut the matter short)
Whate'er my fate, or well or ill at court,
Whether old age, with faint but cheerful ray,
Attends to gild the evening of my day,
Or death's black wing already be displayed,
To wrap me in the universal shade;
Whether the darkened room to muse invite,
Or whitened wall provoke the skewer to write:
In durance, exile, Bedlam, or the Mint,
Like Lee or Budgell, I will rhyme and print.   100
    F. Alas young man! your days can ne'er be long,
In flower of age you perish for a song!
Plums and directors, Shylock and his wife,
Will club their testers, now, to take your life!
    P. What, armed for virtue when I point the pen,
Brand the bold front of shameless, guilty men;
Dash the proud gamester in his gilded car;
Bare the mean heart that lurks beneath a *star*;
Can there be wanting, to defend her cause,
Lights of the church, or guardians of the laws?   110
Could pensioned Boileau lash in honest strain
Flatterers and bigots ev'n in Louis' reign?
Could Laureate Dryden pimp and friar engage,
Yet neither Charles nor James be in a rage?
And I not strip the gilding off a knave,
Unplaced, unpensioned, no man's heir, or slave?
I will, or perish in the generous cause:
Hear this, and tremble! you, who 'scape the laws.
Yes, while I live, no rich or noble knave
Shall walk the world, in credit, to his grave.   120
To VIRTUE ONLY and HER FRIENDS, A FRIEND,
The world beside may murmur, or commend.
Know, all the distant din that world can keep,
Rolls o'er my grotto, and but soothes my sleep.
There, my retreat the best companions grace,
Chiefs out of war, and statesmen out of place.
There ST JOHN mingles with my friendly bowl
The feast of reason and the flow of soul:

And HE, whose lightning pierced th' Iberian lines,
Now forms my quincunx, and now ranks my vines,   130
Or tames the genius of the stubborn plain,
Almost as quickly as he conquered Spain.

Envy must own, I live among the great,
No pimp of pleasure, and no spy of state,
With eyes that pry not, tongue that ne'er repeats,
Fond to spread friendships, but to cover heats;
To help who want, to forward who excel;
This, all who know me, know; who love me, tell;
And who unknown defame me, let them be
Scribblers or peers, alike are *mob* to me.   140
This is my plea, on this I rest my cause—
What saith my counsel learned in the laws?

   F. Your plea is good; but still I say, beware!
Laws are explained by men—so have a care.
It stands on record, that in Richard's times
A man was hanged for very honest rhymes.
Consult the statute: *quart.* I think, it is,
Edwardi sext. or *prim. et quint. Eliz.*
See *Libels, Satires*—here you have it—read.

   P. Libels and *Satires!* lawless things indeed!   150
But grave *Epistles*, bringing vice to light,
Such as a king might read, a bishop write,
Such as Sir ROBERT would approve—
                                          F. Indeed?
The case is altered—you may then proceed;
In such a cause the plaintiff will be hissed,
My lords the judges laugh, and you're dismissed.

---

129. Charles Mordaunt, Earl of Peterborough, who in the year 1705 took Barcelona, and in the winter following with only 280 horse and 900 foot enterprised and accomplished the conquest of Valentia.

EPISTLE to Dr ARBUTHNOT

Neque sermonibus *Vulgi* dederis te, nec in *Praemiis* humanis
spem posueris rerum tuarum: suis te oportet illecebris *ipsa
Virtus* trahat ad verum decus. Quid de te alii loquantur, ipsi
videant, sed loquentur tamen.

TULLY [*De Re Publica*, vi. 23].

Advertisement

This paper is a sort of bill of complaint, begun many years since, and
drawn up by snatches, as the several occasions offered. I had no thoughts
of publishing it, till it pleased some persons of rank and fortune [the authors
of *Verses to the Imitator of Horace*, and of an *Epistle to a Doctor of Divinity
from a Nobleman at Hampton Court*] to attack in a very extraordinary manner,
not only my writings (of which being public the public judge) but my *person*,
morals, and *family*, whereof to those who know me not, a true information
may be requisite. Being divided between the necessity to say something of
myself, and my own laziness to undertake so awkward a task, I thought it
the shortest way to put the last hand to this epistle. If it have any thing
pleasing, it will be that by which I am most desirous to please, the *truth*
and the *sentiment*; and if any thing offensive, it will be only to those I am
least sorry to offend, the *vicious* or *the ungenerous*.

Many will know their own pictures in it, there being not a circumstance
but what is true; but I have, for the most part spared their *names*, and they
may escape being laughed at, if they please.

I would have some of them know, it was owing to the request of the
learned and candid friend to whom it is inscribed, that I make not as free
use of theirs as they have done of mine. However I shall have this advantage,
and honour, on my side, that whereas by their proceeding, any abuse may
be directed at any man, no injury can possibly be done by mine, since a
nameless character can never be found out, but by its *truth* and *likeness*.

'Shut, shut the door, good John!', fatigued I said,   1
'Tie up the knocker, say I'm sick, I'm dead.'
The dog-star rages! nay 'tis past a doubt,
All Bedlam, or Parnassus, is let out:
Fire in each eye, and papers in each hand,
They rave, recite, and madden round the land.

What walls can guard me, or what shades can hide?
They pierce my thickets, through my grot they glide,

By land, by water, they renew the charge,
They stop the chariot, and they board the barge.   10
No place is sacred, not the church is free,
Ev'n Sunday shines no sabbath day to me:
Then from the Mint walks forth the man of rhyme,
Happy! to catch me, just at dinner time.

   Is there a parson, much bemused in beer,
A maudlin poetess, a rhyming peer,
A clerk, foredoomed his father's soul to cross,
Who pens a stanza, when he should *engross*?
Is there, who, locked from ink and paper, scrawls
With desperate charcoal round his darkened walls?   20
All fly to TWIT'NAM, and in humble strain
Apply to me, to keep them mad or vain.
Arthur, whose giddy son neglects the laws,
Imputes to me and my damned works the cause:
Poor Cornus sees his frantic wife elope,
And curses wit, and poetry, and Pope.

   Friend to my life! (which did not you prolong,
The world had wanted many an idle song)
What *drop* or *nostrum* can this plague remove?
Or which must end me, a fool's wrath or love?   30
A dire dilemma! either way I'm sped,
If foes, they write, if friends, they read me dead.
Seized and tied down to judge, how wretched I!
Who can't be silent, and who will not lie:
To laugh, were want of goodness and of grace,
And to be grave, exceeds all power of face.
I sit with sad civility, I read
With honest anguish, and an aching head;
And drop at last, but in unwilling ears,
This saving counsel, 'Keep your piece nine years.'   40

   'Nine years!', cries he, who high in Drury Lane
Lulled by soft zephyrs through the broken pane,
Rhymes ere he wakes, and prints before *term* ends,
Obliged by hunger, and request of friends:
'The piece, you think, is incorrect? why take it,
I'm all submission, what you'd have it, make it.'

   Three things another's modest wishes bound,
My friendship, and a prologue, and ten pound.

    Pitholeon sends to me: 'You know his Grace,
I want a patron; ask him for a place.'   50
Pitholeon libelled me—'but here's a letter
Informs you, sir, 'twas when he knew no better.
Dare you refuse him? Curll invites to dine,
He'll write a *Journal*, or he'll turn divine.'
    Bless me! a packet—' 'Tis a stranger sues,
A virgin tragedy, an orphan muse.'
If I dislike it, 'Furies, death and rage!'
If I approve, 'Commend it to the stage.'
There (thank my stars) my whole commission ends,
The players and I are, luckily, no friends.   60
Fired that the house reject him, ' 'Sdeath I'll print it,
And shame the fools—your interest, sir, with Lintot.'
Lintot, dull rogue! will think your price too much:
'Not, sir, if you revise it, and retouch.'
All my demurs but double his attacks;
At last he whispers, 'Do, and we go snacks.'
Glad of a quarrel, straight I clap the door,
Sir, let me see your works and you no more.
    'Tis sung, when Midas' ears began to spring,
(Midas, a sacred person and a king)   70
His very minister who spied them first,
(Some say his queen) was forced to speak, or burst.
And is not mine, my friend, a sorer case,
When every coxcomb perks them in my face?
    'Good friend forbear! you deal in dangerous things.
I'd never name queens, ministers, or kings;
Keep close to ears, and those let asses prick,
'Tis nothing'—Nothing? if they bite and kick?
Out with it, *Dunciad*! let the secret pass,
That secret to each fool, that he's an ass: 80
The truth once told (and wherefore should we lie?)
The queen of Midas slept, and so may I.
    You think this cruel? take it for a rule,
No creature smarts so little as a fool.

    49. *Pitholeon*] The name taken from a foolish poet of Rhodes, who pretended much to Greek.

    72. The story is told, by some, of his barber, but by Chaucer of his queen. See 'Wife of Bath's Tale' in Dryden's *Fables*.

Let peals of laughter, Codrus! round thee break,
Thou unconcerned canst hear the mighty crack:
Pit, box, and gallery in convulsions hurled,
Thou standst unshook amidst a bursting world.
Who shames a scribbler? break one cobweb through,
He spins the slight, self-pleasing thread anew: 90
Destroy his fib or sophistry; in vain,
The creature's at his dirty work again,
Throned in the centre of his thin designs,
Proud of a vast extent of flimsy lines!
Whom have I hurt? has poet yet, or peer,
Lost the arched eyebrow, or Parnassian sneer?
And has not Colley still his lord, and whore?
His butchers Henley, his freemasons Moore?
Does not one table Bavius still admit?
Still to one bishop Philips seem a wit?   100
Still Sappho—'Hold! for God sake—you'll offend,
No names—be calm—learn prudence of a friend:
I too could write, and I am twice as tall;
But foes like these'—One flatterer's worse than all;
Of all mad creatures, if the learned are right,
It is the slaver kills, and not the bite.
A fool quite angry is quite innocent:
Alas! 'tis ten times worse when they *repent*.

    One dedicates in high heroic prose,
And ridicules beyond a hundred foes: 110
One from all Grub Street will my fame defend,
And more abusive, calls himself my friend.
This prints my *Letters*, that expects a bribe,
And others roar aloud, 'Subscribe, subscribe.'

    There are, who to my person pay their court:
I cough like Horace, and, though lean, am short,
Ammon's great son one shoulder had too high,
Such Ovid's nose, and 'Sir! you have an eye—'
Go on, obliging creatures, make me see
All that disgraced my betters, met in me.   120
Say for my comfort, languishing in bed,
'Just so immortal Maro held his head:'
And when I die, be sure you let me know
Great Homer died three thousand years ago.

    Why did I write? what sin to me unknown

Dipped me in ink, my parents', or my own?
As yet a child, nor yet a fool to fame,
I lisped in numbers, for the numbers came.
I left no calling for this idle trade,
No duty broke, no father disobeyed.   130
The Muse but served to ease some friend, not wife,
To help me through this long disease, my life,
To second, ARBUTHNOT! thy art and care,
And teach, the being you preserved, to bear.
   But why then publish? Granville the polite,
And knowing Walsh, would tell me I could write;
Well-natured Garth inflamed with early praise,
And Congreve loved, and Swift endured my lays;
The courtly Talbot, Somers, Sheffield read,
Ev'n mitred Rochester would nod the head,   140
And St John's self (great Dryden's friends before)
With open arms received one poet more.
Happy my studies, when by these approved!
Happier their author, when by these beloved!
From these the world will judge of men and books,
Not from the Burnets, Oldmixons, and Cookes.
   Soft were my numbers; who could take offence
While pure description held the place of sense?
Like gentle Fanny's was my flowery theme,
A painted mistress, or a purling stream.   150
Yet then did Gildon draw his venal quill;
I wished the man a dinner, and sate still:
Yet then did Dennis rave in furious fret;
I never answered, I was not in debt:
If want provoked, or madness made them print,

139. All these were patrons and admirers of Mr Dryden; though a scandalous libel against him, entitled, *Dryden's Satire to his Muse*, has been printed in the name of the Lord Somers, of which he was wholly ignorant.
   These are the persons to whose account the author charges the publication of his first pieces: persons with whom he was conversant (and he adds beloved) at 16 or 17 years of age; an early period for such acquaintance. The catalogue might be made yet more illustrious, had he not confined it to that time when he writ the *Pastorals* and *Windsor Forest*, on which he passes a sort of censure in the lines following, *While pure description held the place of sense? &c.*

146. Authors of secret and scandalous history.

150. *A painted meadow, or a purling stream* is a verse of Mr Addison.

I waged no war with Bedlam or the Mint.
　　Did some more sober critic come abroad?
If wrong, I smiled; if right, I kissed the rod.
Pains, reading, study, are their just pretence,
And all they want is spirit, taste, and sense.　　　　160
Commas and points they set exactly right,
And 'twere a sin to rob them of their mite.
Yet ne'er one sprig of laurel graced these ribalds,
From slashing Bentley down to piddling Tibbalds:
Each wight who reads not, and but scans and spells,
Each word-catcher that lives on syllables,
Ev'n such small critics some regard may claim,
Preserved in Milton's or in Shakespeare's name.
Pretty! in amber to observe the forms
Of hairs, or straws, or dirt, or grubs, or worms!　　170
The things, we know, are neither rich nor rare,
But wonder how the devil they got there?
　　Were others angry? I excused them too;
Well might they rage, I gave them but their due.
A man's true merit 'tis not hard to find,
But each man's secret standard in his mind,
That casting-weight pride adds to emptiness,
This, who can gratify? for who can *guess*?
The bard whom pilfered pastorals renown,
Who turns a Persian tale for half a crown,　　　　180
Just writes to make his barrenness appear,
And strains from hard-bound brains, eight lines a year;
He, who still wanting, though he lives on theft,
Steals much, spends little, yet has nothing left:
And he, who now to sense, now nonsense leaning,
Means not, but blunders round about a meaning:
And he, whose fustian's so sublimely bad,
It is not poetry, but prose run mad:
All these, my modest satire bad *translate*,
And owned that nine such poets made a Tate.　　　190
How did they fume, and stamp, and roar, and chafe!
And swear, not ADDISON himself was safe.
　　Peace to all such! but were there one whose fires
True genius kindles, and fair fame inspires;

180. Amb. Philips translated a book called the *Persian Tales*.

Blessed with each talent and each art to please,
And born to write, converse, and live with ease:
Should such a man, too fond to rule alone,
Bear, like the Turk, no brother near the throne,
View him with scornful, yet with jealous eyes,
And hate for arts that caused himself to rise;   200
Damn with faint praise, assent with civil leer,
And without sneering, teach the rest to sneer;
Willing to wound, and yet afraid to strike,
Just hint a fault, and hesitate dislike;
Alike reserved to blame, or to commend,
A timorous foe, and a suspicious friend;
Dreading ev'n fools, by flatterers besieged,
And so obliging, that he ne'er obliged;
Like Cato, give his little senate laws,
And sit attentive to his own applause;   210
While wits and templars every sentence raise,
And wonder with a foolish face of praise—
Who but must laugh, if such a man there be?
Who would not weep, if ATTICUS were he!
    What though my name stood rubric on the walls,
Or plastered posts, with claps, in capitals?
Or smoking forth, a hundred hawkers load,
On wings of winds came flying all abroad?
I sought no homage from the race that write;
I kept, like Asian monarchs, from their sight: 220
Poems I heeded (now berhymed so long)
No more than thou, great GEORGE! a birthday song.
I ne'er with wits or witlings passed my days,
To spread about the itch of verse and praise;
Nor like a puppy daggled through the town,
To fetch and carry singsong up and down;
Nor at rehearsals sweat, and mouthed, and cried,
With handkerchief and orange at my side;
But sick of fops, and poetry, and prate,
To Bufo left the whole Castalian state.   230

214. ATTICUS] It was a great falsehood, which some of the libels reported, that
this character was written after the gentleman's death; which see refuted in the
testimonies prefixed to the *Dunciad*. But the occasion of writing it was such as he
would not make public out of regard to his memory: and all that could further be
done was to omit the name, in the editions of his Works.

Proud as Apollo on his forked hill,
Sate full-blown Bufo, puffed by every quill;
Fed with soft dedication all day long,
Horace and he went hand in hand in song.
His library (where busts of poets dead
And a true Pindar stood without a head)
Received of wits an undistinguished race,
Who first his judgment asked, and then a place:
Much they extolled his pictures, much his seat,
And flattered every day, and some days eat: 240
Till grown more frugal in his riper days,
He paid some bards with port, and some with praise.
To some a dry rehearsal was assigned,
And others (harder still) he paid in kind.
Dryden alone (what wonder?) came not nigh,
Dryden alone escaped this judging eye:
But still the great have kindness in reserve,
He helped to bury whom he helped to starve.
    May some choice patron bless each gray goose quill!
May every Bavius have his Bufo still!   250
So when a statesman wants a day's defence,
Or envy holds a whole week's war with sense,
Or simple pride for flattery makes demands,
May dunce by dunce be whistled off my hands!
Blessed be the great! for those they take away,
And those they left me; for they left me GAY;
Left me to see neglected genius bloom,
Neglected die, and tell it on his tomb:
Of all thy blameless life the sole return
My verse, and QUEENSBERRY weeping o'er thy urn!   260
    Oh let me live my own, and die so too!
(To live and die is all I have to do:)
Maintain a poet's dignity and ease,
And see what friends, and read what books I please:
Above a patron, though I condescend
Sometimes to call a minister my friend:

236. Ridicules the affectation of antiquaries, who frequently exhibit the headless *trunks* and *terms* of statues, for Plato, Homer, Pindar, &c.

248. Mr Dryden, after having lived in exigencies, had a magnificent funeral bestowed upon him by the contribution of several persons of quality.

I was not born for courts or great affairs;
I pay my debts, believe, and say my prayers;
Can sleep without a poem in my head,
Nor know, if Dennis be alive or dead.   270
    Why am I asked what next shall see the light?
Heavens! was I born for nothing but to write?
Has life no joys for me? or (to be grave)
Have I no friend to serve, no soul to save?
'I found him close with Swift'—'Indeed? no doubt',
Cries prating Balbus, 'something will come out.'
'Tis all in vain, deny it as I will.
'No, such a genius never can lie still;'
And then for mine obligingly mistakes
The first lampoon Sir Will or Bubo makes.   280
Poor guiltless I! and can I choose but smile,
When every coxcomb knows me by my *style*?
    Cursed be the verse, how well soe'er it flow,
That tends to make one worthy man my foe,
Give virtue scandal, innocence a fear,
Or from the soft-eyed virgin steal a tear!
But he who hurts a harmless neighbour's peace,
Insults fallen worth, or beauty in distress,
Who loves a lie, lame slander helps about,
Who writes a libel, or who copies out: 290
That fop, whose pride affects a patron's name,
Yet absent, wounds an author's honest fame:
Who can *your* merit *selfishly* approve,
And show the *sense* of it without the *love*;
Who has the vanity to call you friend,
Yet wants the honour, injured, to defend;
Who tells whate'er you think, whate'er you say,
And, if he lie not, must at least betray:
Who to the dean and *silver bell* can swear,
And sees at Cannons what was never there;   300
Who reads, but with a lust to misapply,
Make satire a lampoon, and fiction lie.
A lash like mine no honest man shall dread,
But all such babbling blockheads in his stead.
    Let Sporus tremble—'What? that thing of silk,

---

299. *Dean.*] See the *Epistle to the Earl of Burlington.*

Sporus, that mere white curd of ass's milk?
Satire or sense, alas! can Sporus feel?
Who breaks a butterfly upon a wheel?'
   Yet let me flap this bug with gilded wings,
This painted child of dirt, that stinks and stings;   310
Whose buzz the witty and the fair annoys,
Yet wit ne'er tastes, and beauty ne'er enjoys:
So well-bred spaniels civilly delight
In mumbling of the game they dare not bite.
Eternal smiles his emptiness betray,
As shallow streams run dimpling all the way.
Whether in florid impotence he speaks,
And, as the prompter breathes, the puppet squeaks;
Or at the ear of Eve, familiar toad,
Half froth, half venom, spits himself abroad,   320
In puns, or politics, or tales, or lies,
Or spite, or smut, or rhymes, or blasphemies.
His wit all seesaw, between *that* and *this*,
Now high, now low, now master up, now miss,
And he himself one vile antithesis.
Amphibious thing! that acting either part,
The trifling head, or the corrupted heart,
Fop at the toilet, flatterer at the board,
Now trips a lady, and now struts a lord.
Eve's tempter thus the rabbins have expressed,   330
A cherub's face, a reptile all the rest,
Beauty that shocks you, parts that none will trust,
Wit that can creep, and pride that licks the dust.
   Not fortune's worshipper, nor fashion's fool,
Not lucre's madman, nor ambition's tool,
Not proud, nor servile; be one poet's praise,
That, if he pleased, he pleased by manly ways:
That flattery, ev'n to kings, he held a shame,
And thought a lie in verse or prose the same:
That not in fancy's maze he wandered long,   340
But stooped to truth, and moralized his song:
That not for fame, but virtue's better end,
He stood the furious foe, the timid friend,
The damning critic, half approving wit,

319. See Milton, [*Paradise Lost*], Book iv.

The coxcomb hit, or fearing to be hit;
Laughed at the loss of friends he never had,
The dull, the proud, the wicked, and the mad;
The distant threats of vengeance on his head,
The blow unfelt, the tear he never shed;
The tale revived, the lie so oft o'erthrown;   350
Th' imputed trash, and dulness not his own;
The morals blackened when the writings 'scape,
The libelled person, and the pictured shape;
Abuse, on all he loved, or loved him, spread,
A friend in exile, or a father, dead;
The whisper, that to greatness still too near,
Perhaps, yet vibrates on his SOVEREIGN's ear—
Welcome for thee, fair virtue! all the past:
For thee, fair virtue! welcome ev'n the *last!*
　　'But why insult the poor, affront the great?'   360
A knave's a knave, to me, in every state:
Alike my scorn, if he succeed or fail,
Sporus at court, or Japhet in a jail,
A hireling scribbler, or a hireling peer,
Knight of the post corrupt, or of the shire;
If on a pillory, or near a throne,
He gain his prince's ear, or lose his own.
　　Yet soft by nature, more a dupe than wit,
Sappho can tell you how this man was bit:
This dreaded satirist Dennis will confess   370
Foe to his pride, but friend to his distress:
So humble, he has knocked at Tibbald's door,
Has drunk with Cibber, nay has rhymed for Moore.
Full ten years slandered, did he once reply?

350. *the lie so oft o'erthrown*] As that he received subscriptions for Shakespeare, that he set his name to Mr Broome's verses, &c. which, though publicly disproved, were nevertheless shamelessly repeated in the libels, and even in that called the *Nobleman's Epistle.*

351. *Th' imputed trash*] Such as profane *Psalms, Court Poems,* and other scandalous things, printed in his name by Curll and others.

354. Namely on the Duke of Buckingham, the Earl of Burlington, Lord Bathurst, Lord Bolingbroke, Bishop Atterbury, Dr Swift, Dr Arbuthnot, Mr Gay, his friends, his parents, and his very nurse, aspersed in printed papers, by James Moore, G. Ducket, I. Welsted, Tho. Bentley, and other obscure persons.

374. *ten years*] It was so long after many libels before the author of the *Dunciad* published that poem, till when, he never writ a word in answer to the many scurrilities and falsehoods concerning him.

Three thousand suns went down on Welsted's lie.
To please a mistress, one aspersed his life;
He lashed him not, but let her be his wife:
Let Budgell charge low Grub Street on his quill,
And write whate'er he pleased, except his will;
Let the two Curlls of town and court, abuse   380
His father, mother, body, soul, and muse.
Yet why? that father held it for a rule,
It was a sin to call our neighbour fool:
That harmless mother thought no wife a whore:
Hear this, and spare his family, James Moore!
Unspotted names, and memorable long!
If there be force in virtue, or in song.

Of gentle blood (part shed in honour's cause,
While yet in Britain honour had applause)
Each parent sprung—'What fortune, pray?'—
    Their own,   390
And better got, than Bestia's from the throne.
Born to no pride, inheriting no strife,

---

375. *Welsted's lie.*] This man had the impudence to tell in print, that Mr P. had occasioned a *lady's death*, and to name a person he never heard of. He also published that he libelled the Duke of Chandos; with whom (it was added) that he had lived in familiarity, and received from him a present of *five hundred pounds*: the falsehood of both which is known to his Grace. Mr P. never received any present, farther than the subscription for Homer, from him, or from *Any great Man* whatsoever.

378. Budgell, in a weekly pamphlet called the *Bee*, bestowed much abuse on him, in the imagination that he writ some things about the *Last Will* of Dr Tindal, in the *Grub Street Journal*; a paper wherein he never had the least hand, direction, or supervisal, nor the least knowledge of its author.

381. In some of Curll's and other pamphlets, Mr Pope's father was said to be a mechanic, a hatter, a farmer, nay a bankrupt. But, what is stranger, a nobleman (if such a reflection could be thought to come from a nobleman) had dropped an allusion to that pitiful untruth, in a paper called an *Epistle to a Doctor of Divinity*: and the following line,

Hard as thy heart, and as thy birth obscure,

had fallen from a like *courtly* pen, in certain *Verses to the Imitator of Horace*. Mr Pope's father was of a gentleman's family in Oxfordshire, the head of which was the Earl of Downe, whose sole heiress married the Earl of Lindsey—His mother was the daughter of William Turner, Esq. of York. She had three brothers, one of whom was killed, another died in the service of King Charles; the eldest following his fortunes, and becoming a general officer in Spain, left her what estate remained after the sequestrations and forfeitures of her family—Mr Pope died in 1717, aged 75; she in 1733, aged 93, a very few weeks after this poem was finished.

Nor marrying discord in a noble wife,
Stranger to civil and religious rage,
The good man walked innoxious through his age.
No courts he saw, no suits would ever try,
Nor dared an oath, nor hazarded a lie:
Unlearned, he knew no schoolman's subtle art,
No language, but the language of the heart.
By nature honest, by experience wise, 400
Healthy by temperance, and by exercise;
His life, though long, to sickness past unknown,
His death was instant, and without a groan.
O grant me, thus to live, and thus to die!
Who sprung from kings shall know less joy than I.
  O friend! may each domestic bliss be thine!
Be no unpleasing melancholy mine:
Me, let the tender office long engage
To rock the cradle of reposing age,
With lenient arts extend a mother's breath, 410
Make languor smile, and smooth the bed of death,
Explore the thought, explain the asking eye,
And keep a while one parent from the sky!
On cares like these if length of days attend,
May heaven, to bless those days, preserve my friend,
Preserve him social, cheerful, and serene,
And just as rich as when he served a QUEEN.
Whether that blessing be denied or given,
Thus far was right, the rest belongs to heaven.

AN EPISTLE
TO
A LADY

Of the Characters *of* WOMEN

Nothing so true as what you once let fall,   1
'Most women have no characters at all.'
Matter too soft a lasting mark to bear,
And best distinguished by black, brown, or fair.
  How many pictures of one nymph we view,
All how unlike each other, all how true!
Arcadia's Countess, here, in ermined pride,
Is there, Pastora by a fountain side.
Here Fannia, leering on her own good man,
And there, a naked Leda with a swan.   10
Let then the fair one beautifully cry,
In Magdalen's loose hair and lifted eye,
Or dressed in smiles of sweet Cecilia shine,
With simpering angels, palms, and harps divine;
Whether the charmer sinner it, or saint it,
If folly grow romantic, I must paint it!
  Come then, the colours and the ground prepare!
Dip in the rainbow, trick her off in air;
Choose a firm cloud before it fall, and in it
Catch, e'er she change, the Cynthia of this minute.   20
  Rufa, whose eye quick-glancing o'er the park,

---

1. Of the CHARACTERS of WOMEN, *treating of this sex only as contradistinguished from the other.*
  That their particular characters are not so strongly marked as those of men, seldom so fixed, and still more inconsistent with themselves.

7, 8, 10, &c. *Arcadia's Countess,—Pastora by a fountain—Leda with a swan.— Magdalen—Cecilia—*] Attitudes in which several ladies affected to be drawn, and sometimes one lady in them all—The poet's politeness and compliance to the sex is observable in this instance, amongst others, that, whereas in the *Characters of Men* [*Epistle to Cobham*] he has sometimes made use of real names, in the *Characters of Women* always fictitious.

21. Instances of contrarieties, given even from such characters as are most strongly marked, and seemingly, therefore most consistent: as, I. In the *Affected*, v. 21, &c.

Attracts each light gay meteor of a spark,
Agrees as ill with Rufa studying Locke,
As Sappho's diamonds with her dirty smock;
Or Sappho at her toilet's greasy task,
With Sappho fragrant at an evening mask:
So morning insects that in muck begun,
Shine, buzz, and fly-blow in the setting-sun.

How soft is Silia! fearful to offend,
The frail one's advocate, the weak one's friend: 30
To her, Calista proved her conduct nice,
And good Simplicius asks of her advice.
Sudden, she storms! she raves! You tip the wink,
But spare your censure; Silia does not drink.
All eyes may see from what the change arose,
All eyes may see—a pimple on her nose.

Papillia, wedded to her amorous spark,
Sighs for the shades—'How charming is a park!'
A park is purchased; but the fair he sees
All bathed in tears—'Oh odious, odious trees!'   40

Ladies like variegated tulips show;
'Tis to their changes half their charms we owe;
Their happy spots the nice admirer take,
Fine by defect, and delicately weak.
'Twas thus Calypso once each heart alarmed,
Awed without virtue, without beauty charmed;
Her tongue bewitched as oddly as her eyes,
Less wit than mimic, more a wit than wise;
Strange graces still, and stranger flights she had,
Was just not ugly, and was just not mad;   50
Yet ne'er so sure our passion to create,
As when she touched the brink of all we hate.

Narcissa's nature, tolerably mild,
To make a wash, would hardly stew a child;
Has ev'n been proved to grant a lover's prayer,
And paid a tradesman once to make him stare;
Gave alms at Easter, in a Christian trim,
And made a widow happy, for a whim.

29-40. II. Contrarieties in the *soft-natured*.

45. III. Contrarieties in the *cunning* and *artful*.

53. IV. In the *whimsical*.

Why then declare good nature is her scorn,
When 'tis by that alone she can be born?   60
Why pique all mortals, yet affect a name?
A fool to pleasure, yet a slave to fame:
Now deep in Taylor and the Book of Martyrs,
Now drinking citron with his Grace and Chartres:
Now conscience chills her, and now passion burns;
And atheism and religion take their turns;
A very heathen in the carnal part,
Yet still a sad, good Christian at her heart.
    See sin in state, majestically drunk;
Proud as a peeress, prouder as a punk;   70
Chaste to her husband, frank to all beside,
A teeming mistress, but a barren bride.
What then? let blood and body bear the fault,
Her head's untouched, that noble seat of thought:
Such this day's doctrine—in another fit
She sins with poets through pure love of wit.
What has not fired her bosom or her brain?
Caesar and Tallboy, Charles and Charlemagne.
As Helluo, late dictator of the feast,
The nose of hautgout, and the tip of taste,   80
Critiqued your wine, and analyzed your meat,
Yet on plain pudding deigned at home to eat;
So Philomedé, lecturing all mankind
On the soft passion, and the taste refined,
Th'address, the delicacy—stoops at once,
And makes her hearty meal upon a dunce.
    Flavia's a wit, has too much sense to pray;
To toast our wants and wishes, is her way;
Nor asks of God, but of her stars, to give
The mighty blessing, 'while we live, to live.'   90
Then all for death, that opiate of the soul!
Lucretia's dagger, Rosamonda's bowl.
Say, what can cause such impotence of mind?
A spark too fickle, or a spouse too kind.
Wise wretch! with pleasures too refined to please,
With too much spirit to be e'er at ease,

69. V. In the *lewd* and *vicious*.
87. VI. Contrarieties in the *witty* and *refined*.

With too much quickness ever to be taught,
With too much thinking to have common thought:
You purchase pain with all that joy can give,
And die of nothing but a rage to live.   100
  Turn then from wits; and look on Simo's mate,
No ass so meek, no ass so obstinate:
Or her, that owns her faults, but never mends,
Because she's honest, and the best of friends:
Or her, whose life the church and scandal share,
For ever in a passion, or a prayer:
Or her, who laughs at hell, but (like her Grace)
Cries, 'Ah! how charming if there's no such place!'
Or who in sweet vicissitude appears
Of mirth and opium, ratafee and tears,   110
The daily anodyne, and nightly draught,
To kill those foes to fair ones, time and thought.
Woman and fool are two hard things to hit;
For true no-meaning puzzles more than wit.
  But what are these to great Atossa's mind?
Scarce once herself, by turns all womankind!
Who, with herself, or others, from her birth
Finds all her life one warfare upon earth:
Shines, in exposing knaves, and painting fools,
Yet is, whate'er she hates and ridicules.   120
No thought advances, but her eddy brain
Whisks it about, and down it goes again.
Full sixty years the world has been her trade,
The wisest fool much time has ever made.
From loveless youth to unrespected age,
No passion gratified except her rage.
So much the fury still outran the wit,
The pleasure missed her, and the scandal hit.
Who breaks with her, provokes revenge from hell,
But he's a bolder man who dares be well.   130
Her every turn with violence pursued,
Nor more a storm her hate than gratitude:
To that each passion turns, or soon or late;
Love, if it makes her yield, must make her hate:
Superiors? death! and equals? what a curse!
But an inferior not dependant? worse.
Offend her, and she knows not to forgive;

Oblige her, and she'll hate you while you live:
But die, and she'll adore you—Then the bust
And temple rise—then fall again to dust.   140
Last night, her lord was all that's good and great;
A knave this morning, and his will a cheat.
Strange! by the means defeated of the ends,
By spirit robbed of power, by warmth of friends,
By wealth of followers! without one distress
Sick of herself through very selfishness!
Atossa, cursed with every granted prayer,
Childless with all her children, wants an heir.
To heirs unknown descends th'unguarded store
Or wanders, heaven-directed, to the poor.   150
   Pictures like these, dear Madam, to design,
Asks no firm hand, and no unerring line;
Some wandering touches, some reflected light,
Some flying stroke alone can hit 'em right:
For how should equal colours do the knack?
Chameleons who can paint in white and black?
   'Yet Cloe sure was formed without a spot'—
Nature in her then erred not, but forgot.
'With every pleasing, every prudent part,
Say, what can Cloe want?'—She wants a heart.   160
She speaks, behaves, and acts just as she ought;
But never, never, reached one generous thought.
Virtue she finds too painful an endeavour,
Content to dwell in decencies for ever.
So very reasonable, so unmoved,
As never yet to love, or to be loved.
She, while her lover pants upon her breast,
Can mark the figures on an Indian chest;
And when she sees her friend in deep despair,
Observes how much a chintz exceeds mohair.   170
Forbid it heaven, a favour or a debt
She e'er should cancel—but she may forget.
Safe is your secret still in Cloe's ear;
But none of Cloe's shall you ever hear.
Of all her dears she never slandered one,
But cares not if a thousand are undone.
Would Cloe know if you're alive or dead?
She bids her footman put it in her head.

Cloe is prudent—Would you too be wise?
Then never break your heart when Cloe dies.   180
   One certain portrait may (I grant) be seen,
Which heaven has varnished out, and made a Queen:
THE SAME FOR EVER! and described by all
With truth and goodness, as with crown and ball.
Poets heap virtues, painters gems at will,
And show their zeal, and hide their want of skill,
'Tis well—but, artists! who can paint or write,
To draw the naked is your true delight.
That robe of quality so struts and swells,
None see what parts or nature it conceals: 190
Th'exactest traits of body or of mind,
We owe to models of an humble kind.
If QUEENSBERRY to strip there's no compelling,
'Tis from a handmaid we must take a Helen.
From peer or bishop 'tis no easy thing
To draw the man who loves his God, or king:
Alas! I copy (or my draught would fail)
From honest Mah'met, or plain Parson Hale.
   But grant, in public men sometimes are shown,
A woman's seen in private life alone: 200
Our bolder talents in full light displayed;
Your virtues open fairest in the shade.
Bred to disguise, in public 'tis you hide;
There, none distinguish 'twixt your shame or pride,
Weakness or delicacy; all so nice,
That each may seem a virtue, or a vice.
   In men, we various ruling passions find;
In women, two almost divide the kind;
Those, only fixed, they first or last obey,
The love of pleasure, and the love of sway.   210
   That, nature gives; and where the lesson taught .

198. *Mah'met*, servant to the late king, said to be the son of a Turkish Bassa, whom he took at the Siege of Buda, and constantly kept about his person.

207. The former part having shown, that the *particular characters* of women are more various than those of men, it is nevertheless observed, that the *general* characteristic of the sex, as to the *ruling passion*, is more uniform.

211. This is occasioned partly by their *nature*, partly their *education*, and in some degree by *necessity*.

Is but to please, can pleasure seem a fault?
Experience, this; by man's oppression cursed,
They seek the second not to lose the first.
　　Men, some to business, some to pleasure take;
But every woman is at heart a rake:
Men, some to quiet, some to public strife;
But every lady would be queen for life.
　　Yet mark the fate of a whole sex of queens!
Power all their end, but beauty all the means: 220
In youth they conquer with so wild a rage,
As leaves them scarce a subject in their age:
For foreign glory, foreign joy, they roam;
No thought of peace or happiness at home.
But wisdom's triumph is well-timed retreat,
As hard a science to the fair as great!
Beauties, like tyrants, old and friendless grown,
Yet hate repose, and dread to be alone,
Worn out in public, weary every eye,
Nor leave one sigh behind them when they die.   230
　　Pleasures the sex, as children birds, pursue,
Still out of reach, yet never out of view;
Sure, if they catch, to spoil the toy at most,
To covet flying, and regret when lost:
At last, to follies youth could scarce defend,
It grows their age's prudence to pretend;
Ashamed to own they gave delight before,
Reduced to feign it, when they give no more:
As hags hold sabbaths, less for joy than spite,
So these their merry, miserable night;   240
Still round and round the ghosts of beauty glide,
And haunt the places where their honour died.
　　See how the world its veterans rewards!
A youth of frolics, an old age of cards;
Fair to no purpose, artful to no end,
Young without lovers, old without a friend;
A fop their passion, but their prize a sot,
Alive, ridiculous, and dead, forgot!
　　Ah! friend! to dazzle let the vain design;

219. What are the *aims* and the *fate* of this sex?—I. As to *power*.
231. II. As to *pleasure*.

To raise the thought, and touch the heart be thine!   250
That charm shall grow, while what fatigues the ring
Flaunts and goes down, an unregarded thing:
So when the sun's broad beam has tired the sight,
All mild ascends the moon's more sober light,
Serene in virgin modesty she shines,
And unobserved the glaring orb declines.

Oh! blessed with temper, whose unclouded ray
Can make tomorrow cheerful as today;
She, who can love a sister's charms, or hear
Sighs for a daughter with unwounded ear;   260
She, who ne'er answers till a husband cools,
Or, if she rules him, never shows she rules;
Charms by accepting, by submitting sways,
Yet has her humour most, when she obeys;
Let fops or fortune fly which way they will;
Disdains all loss of tickets, or codille;
Spleen, vapours, or smallpox, above them all,
And mistress of herself, though China fall.

And yet, believe me, good as well as ill,
Woman's at best a contradiction still.   270
Heaven, when it strives to polish all it can
Its last best work, but forms a softer man;
Picks from each sex, to make the favourite blessed,
Your love of pleasure, our desire of rest:
Blends, in exception to all general rules,
Your taste of follies, with our scorn of fools,
Reserve with frankness, art with truth allied,
Courage with softness, modesty with pride,
Fixed principles, with fancy ever new;
Shakes all together, and produces—You.   280
Be this a woman's fame: with this unblessed,
Toasts live a scorn, and queens may die a jest.
This Phoebus promised (I forget the year)
When those blue eyes first opened on the sphere;
Ascendant Phoebus watched that hour with care,
Averted half your parents' simple prayer,
And gave you beauty, but denied the pelf

249. Advice for their true interest.

269. The picture of an estimable woman, with the best kind of contrarieties.

That buys your sex a tyrant o'er itself.
The generous God, who wit and gold refines,
And ripens spirits as he ripens mines,   290
Kept dross for duchesses, the world shall know it,
To you gave sense, good humour, and a poet.

EPILOGUE
TO THE
SATIRES

Written in MDCCXXXVIII

DIALOGUE I

Fr. Not twice a twelve-month you appear in print,   1
And when it comes, the court see nothing in't.
You grow *correct*, that once with rapture writ,
And are, besides, too *moral* for a wit.
Decay of parts, alas! we all must feel—
Why now, this moment, don't I see you steal?
'Tis all from Horace; Horace long before ye
Said, 'Tories called him Whig, and Whigs a Tory,'
And taught his Romans, in much better metre,
'To laugh at fools who put their trust in Peter.'   10
    But Horace, sir, was delicate, was nice;
Bubo observes, he lashed no sort of *vice:*
Horace would say, Sir Billy *served the crown,*
Blunt could *do business,* Huggins *knew the town,*
In Sappho touch the *failings of the sex,*
In reverend bishops note some *small neglects,*
And own, the Spaniard did a *waggish thing,*

1, 2. These two lines are from Horace; and the only lines that are so in the whole poem; being meant to give a handle to that which follows in the character of an impertinent censurer,

            'Tis all from Horace; etc.

14. *Huggins*] Formerly gaoler of the Fleet prison, enriched himself by many exactions, for which he was tried and expelled.

Who cropped our ears, and sent them to the King.
His sly, polite, insinuating style
Could please at Court, and make AUGUSTUS smile: 20
An artful manager, that crept between
His friend and shame, and was a kind of *screen*.
But 'faith your very friends will soon be sore;
Patriots there are, who wish you'd jest no more—
And where's the glory? 'twill be only thought
The great man never offered you a groat.
Go see Sir ROBERT—

                P. See Sir ROBERT!—hum—
And never laugh—for all my life to come?
Seen him I have, but in his happier hour
Of social pleasure, ill-exchanged for power;   30
Seen him, uncumbered with the venal tribe,
Smile without art, and win without a bribe.
Would he oblige me? let me only find,
He does not think me what he thinks mankind.
Come, come, at all I laugh he laughs, no doubt;
The only difference is, I dare laugh out.

    F. Why yes: with *scripture* still you may be free;
A horse-laugh, if you please, at *honesty*;
A joke on JEKYLL, or some odd *Old Whig*
Who never changed his principle, or wig: 40
A patriot is a fool in every age,
Whom all Lord Chamberlains allow the stage:
These nothing hurts; they keep their fashion still,

---

18. *Who cropped our ears*] Said to be executed by the captain of a Spanish ship on one Jenkins, a captain of an English one. He cut off his ears, and bid him carry them to the King, his master.

Screen.] A metaphor peculiarly appropriated to a certain person in power.

24. *Patriots*] This appellation was generally given to those in opposition to the court. Though some of them (which our author hints at) had views too mean and interested to deserve that name.

26. *The great man*] A phrase, by common use, appropriated to the first minister.

31–32. These two verses were originally in the poem, though omitted in all the first editions.

39. Sir Joseph Jekyll, Master of the Rolls, a true Whig in his principles, and a man of the utmost probity. He sometimes voted against the court, which drew upon him the laugh here described of ONE, who bestowed it equally upon religion and honesty. He died a few months after the publication of this poem.

And wear their strange old virtue as they will.
   If any ask you, 'Who's the man, so near
His prince, that writes in verse, and has his ear?'
Why, answer LYTTELTON, and I'll engage
The worthy youth shall ne'er be in a rage:
But were his verses vile, his whisper base,
You'd quickly find him in Lord Fanny's case.   50
Sejanus, Wolsey, hurt not honest FLEURY,
But well may put some statesmen in a fury.
   Laugh then at any, but at fools or foes;
These you but anger, and you mend not those.
Laugh at your friends, and, if your friends are sore,
So much the better, you may laugh the more.
To vice and folly to confine the jest,
Sets half the world, God knows, against the rest;
Did not the sneer of more impartial men
At sense and virtue, balance all again.   60
Judicious wits spread wide the ridicule,
And charitably comfort knave and fool.
   P. Dear sir, forgive the prejudice of youth:
Adieu distinction, satire, warmth, and truth!
Come, harmless characters that no one hit;
Come, Henley's oratory, Osborne's wit!
The honey dropping from Favonio's tongue,
The flowers of Bubo, and the flow of Young!
The gracious dew of pulpit eloquence,
And all the well-whipped cream of courtly sense,   70
That first was Hervey's, Fox's next, and then

47. George Lyttelton, Secretary to the Prince of Wales, distinguished both for his writings and speeches in the spirit of liberty.

51. *Sejanus, Wolsey*] The one the wicked minister of Tiberius; the other, of Henry VIII. The writers against the court usually bestowed these and other odious names on the minister, without distinction, and in the most injurious manner. See Dial. II. 137.

   Fleury] Cardinal: and Minister to Louis XV. It was a patriot fashion, at that time, to cry up his wisdom and honesty.

66. *Henley—Osborne*] See them in their places in the *Dunciad*.

69. Alludes to some court sermons, and florid panegyrical speeches; particularly one very full of puerilities and flatteries; which afterwards got into an address in the same pretty style; and was lastly served up in an epitaph, between Latin and English, published by its author.

The senate's, and then Hervey's once again.
O come, that easy Ciceronian style,
So Latin, yet so English all the while,
As, though the pride of Middleton and Bland,
All boys may read, and girls may understand!
Then might I sing, without the least offence,
And all I sung should be the *nation's sense*;
Or teach the melancholy muse to mourn,
Hang the sad verse on CAROLINA's urn,   80
And hail her passage to the realms of rest,
All parts performed, and *all* her children blessed!
So—satire is no more—I feel it die—
No *gazetteer* more innocent than I—
And let, a-God's name, every fool and knave
Be graced through life, and flattered in his grave.
   F. Why so? if satire knows its time and place,
You still may lash the greatest—in disgrace:
For merit will by turns forsake them all;
Would you know when? exactly when they fall.   90
But let all satire in all changes spare
Immortal Selkirk, and grave De la Ware!
Silent and soft, as saints remove to heaven,
All ties dissolved, and every sin forgiven,
These may some gentle, ministerial wing
Receive, and place for ever near a king!
There, where no passion, pride, or shame transport,
Lulled with the sweet nepenthe of a court;
There, where no father's, brother's, friend's disgrace
Once break their rest, or stir them from their place: 100
But past the sense of human miseries,
All tears are wiped for ever from all eyes;
No cheek is known to blush, no heart to throb,
Save when they lose a question, or a job.

80. *Carolina*] Queen consort to King George II. She died in 1737. Her death gave occasion, as is observed above, to many indiscreet and mean performances unworthy of her memory, whose last moments manifested the utmost courage and resolution.

   92. *Immortal Selkirk, and grave De la Ware!*] A title given *that* Lord by King James II. He was of the Bedchamber to King William; he was so to King George I, he was so to King George II. *This* Lord was very skilful in all the forms of the House, in which he discharged himself with great gravity.

P. Good heaven forbid, that I should blast their glory,
Who know how like Whig ministers to Tory,
And when three sovereigns died, could scarce be vexed,
Considering what a *gracious Prince* was next.
Have I, in silent wonder, seen such things
As pride in slaves, and avarice in kings;   110
And at a peer, or peeress, shall I fret,
Who starves a sister, or forswears a debt?
Virtue, I grant you, is an empty boast;
But shall the dignity of *Vice* be lost?
Ye Gods! shall Cibber's son, without rebuke,
Swear like a lord, or Rich out-whore a duke?
A favourite's porter with his master vie,
Be bribed as often, and as often lie?
Shall Ward draw contracts with a statesman's skill?
Or Japhet pocket, like his Grace, a will?   120
Is it for Bond, or Peter (paltry things)
To pay their debts, or keep their faith, like kings?
If Blount dispatched himself, he played the man,
And so mayst thou, illustrious Passeran!
But shall a printer, weary of his life,
Learn, from their books, to hang himself and wife?
This, this, my friend, I cannot, must not bear;
Vice thus abused, demands a nation's care:
This calls the church to deprecate our sin.
And hurls the thunder of the laws on *gin*.   130
    Let modest FOSTER, if he will, excel
Ten metropolitans in preaching well;
A simple Quaker, or a Quaker's wife,
Outdo Llandaff in doctrine,—yea in life:

115, 116. *Cibber's Son,—Rich*] Two players: look for them in the *Dunciad*.

123. *Blount*] Author of a book entitled *The Oracles of Reason*, who being in love with a near kinswoman of his, and rejected, gave himself a stab in the arm, as pretending to kill himself, of the consequence of which he really died.

124. *Passeran!*] Author of another, called *A philosophical discourse on death*.

125. A fact that happened in London a few years past. The unhappy man left behind him a paper justifying his action by the reasonings of some of these authors.

130. *Gin*] A spirituous liquor, the exorbitant use of which had almost destroyed the lowest rank of the people till it was restrained by an act of Parliament in 1736.

134. *Llandaff*] A poor bishopric in Wales, as poorly supplied.

Let humble ALLEN, with an awkward shame,
Do good by stealth, and blush to find it fame.
Virtue may choose the high or low degree,
'Tis just alike to Virtue, and to me;
Dwell in a monk, or light upon a king,
She's still the same, beloved, contented thing.   140
Vice is undone, if she forgets her birth,
And stoops from angels to the dregs of earth:
But 'tis the *fall* degrades her to a whore;
Let *Greatness* own her, and she's mean no more:
Her birth, her beauty, crowds and courts confess,
Chaste matrons praise her, and grave bishops bless;
In golden chains the willing world she draws,
And hers the gospel is, and hers the laws,
Mounts the tribunal, lifts her scarlet head,
And sees pale Virtue carted in her stead.   150
Lo! at the wheels of her triumphal car,
Old England's genius, rough with many a scar,
Dragged in the dust! his arms hang idly round,
His flag inverted trails along the ground!
Our youth, all liveried o'er with foreign gold,
Before her dance: behind her, crawl the old!
See thronging millions to the pagod run,
And offer country, parent, wife, or son!
Hear her black trumpet through the land proclaim,
That 'not to be corrupted is the shame.'   160
In soldier, churchman, patriot, man in power,
'Tis avarice all, ambition is no more!
See, all our nobles begging to be slaves!
See, all our fools aspiring to be knaves!
The wit of cheats, the courage of a whore,
Are what ten thousand envy and adore:
All, all look up, with reverential awe,
At crimes that 'scape, or triumph o'er the law:
While truth, worth, wisdom, daily they decry—
'Nothing is sacred now but villainy.'   170
   Yet may this verse (if such a verse remain)
Show, there was one who held it in disdain.

EPILOGUE
TO THE
SATIRES

DIALOGUE II

Fr. 'Tis all a libel—Paxton, sir, will say.   1
P. Not yet, my friend! tomorrow 'faith it may;
And for that very cause I print today.
How should I fret, to mangle every line,
In reverence to the sins of Thirty-nine!
Vice with such giant strides comes on amain,
Invention strives to be before in vain;
Feign what I will, and paint it e'er so strong,
Some rising genius sins up to my song.

F. Yet none but you by name the guilty lash;   10
Ev'n Guthrie saves half Newgate by a dash.
Spare then the person, and expose the vice.

P. How, sir! not damn the sharper, but the dice?
Come on then, satire! general, unconfined,
Spread thy broad wing, and souze on all the kind.
Ye statesmen, priests, of one religion all!
Ye tradesmen vile, in army, court, or hall!
Ye reverend atheists. *F.* Scandal! name them, who?

P. Why that's the thing you bid me not to do.
'Who starved a sister, who forswore a debt,'   20
I never named; the town's enquiring yet.
The poisoning dame—*F.* You mean—*P.* I don't. *F.* You do.

P. See, now I keep the secret, and not you!
The bribing statesman—*F.* Hold, too high you go.

P. The bribed elector—*F.* There you stoop too low.

P. I fain would please you, if I knew with what;
Tell me, which knave is lawful game, which not?
Must great offenders, once escaped the crown,
Like royal harts, be never more run down?

11. *Guthrie*] The Ordinary of Newgate, who publishes the memoirs of the malefactors.

Admit your law to spare the knight requires,   30
As beasts of nature may we hunt the squires?
Suppose I censure—you know what I mean—
To save a bishop, may I name a dean?

    F. A dean, Sir? no: his fortune is not made,
You hurt a man that's rising in the trade.

    P. If not the tradesman who set up today,
Much less the prentice who tomorrow may.
Down, down, proud satire! though a realm be spoiled,
Arraign no mightier thief than wretched Wild;
Or, if a court or country's made a job,   40
Go drench a pickpocket, and join the mob.

    But, sir, I beg you (for the love of vice!)
The matter's weighty, pray consider twice:
Have you less pity for the needy cheat,
The poor and friendless villain, than the great?
Alas! the small discredit of a bribe
Scarce hurts the lawyer, but undoes the scribe.
Then better sure it charity becomes
To tax directors, who (thank God) have plums;
Still better, ministers; or, if the thing   50
May pinch ev'n there—why lay it on a king.

    F. Stop! stop!

             P. Must satire, then, nor rise nor fall?
Speak out, and bid me blame no rogues at all.

    F. Yes, strike that Wild, I'll justify the blow.

    P. Strike? why the man was hanged ten years ago:
Who now that obsolete example fears?
Ev'n Peter trembles only for his ears.

    F. What always Peter? Peter thinks you mad,
You make men desperate if they once are bad:
Else might he take to virtue some years hence—   60

    P. As Selkirk, if he lives, will love the PRINCE.

    F. Strange spleen to Selkirk!

             P. Do I wrong the man?
God knows, I praise a courtier where I can.

---

39. Jonathan Wild, a famous thief, and thief-impeacher, who was at last caught in his own train and hanged.

57. Peter had, the year before this, narrowly escaped the pillory for forgery: and got off with a severe rebuke only from the bench.

When I confess, there is who feels for fame,
And melts to goodness, need I SCARBOROUGH name?
Pleased let me own, in Esher's peaceful grove
(Where Kent and nature vie for PELHAM's love)
The scene, the master, opening to my view,
I sit and dream I see my CRAGGS anew!
    Ev'n in a bishop I can spy desert;   70
Secker is decent, Rundle has a heart,
Manners with candour are to *Benson* given,
To Berkeley, every virtue under heaven.
    But does the court a worthy man remove?
That instant, I declare, he has my love:
I shun his zenith, court his mild decline;
Thus SOMERS once, and HALIFAX were mine.
Oft, in the clear, still mirror of retreat,
I studied SHREWSBURY, the wise and great:
CARLETON's calm sense, and STANHOPE's noble flame,   80
Compared, and knew their generous end the same:
How pleasing ATTERBURY's softer hour!
How shined the soul, unconquered in the Tower!

65. *Scarborough*] Earl of; and Knight of the Garter, whose personal attachments to the king appeared from his steady adherence to the royal interest, after his resignation of his great employment of Master of the Horse; and whose known honour and virtue made him esteemed by all parties.

66. The house and gardens of Esher in Surrey, belonging to the Honourable Mr Pelham, brother of the Duke of Newcastle. The author could not have given a more amiable idea of his character than in comparing him to Mr Craggs.

77. *Somers*] John Lord Somers died in 1716. He had been Lord Keeper in the reign of William III, who took from him the seals in 1700. The author had the honour of knowing him in 1706. A faithful, able, and incorrupt minister; who, to the qualities of a consummate statesman, added those of a man of learning and politeness.

Halifax] A peer, no less distinguished by his love of letters than his abilities in Parliament. He was disgraced in 1710, on the change of Queen Anne's ministry.

79. *Shrewsbury*] Charles Talbot, Duke of Shrewsbury, had been Secretary of State, Ambassador in France, Lord Lieutenant of Ireland, Lord Chamberlain, and Lord Treasurer. He several times quitted his employments, and was often recalled. He died in 1718.

80. *Carleton*] Henry Boyle, Lord Carleton (nephew of the famous Robert Boyle) who was Secretary of State under William III, and President of the Council under Queen Anne.

Stanhope] James Earl Stanhope. A nobleman of equal courage, spirit, and learning. General in Spain, and Secretary of State.

How can I PULTENEY, CHESTERFIELD forget,
While Roman spirit charms, and Attic wit:
ARGYLL, the state's whole thunder born to wield,
And shake alike the senate and the field:
Or WYNDHAM, just to freedom and the throne,
The master of our passions, and his own.
Names, which I long have loved, nor loved in vain,   90
Ranked with their friends, not numbered with their
    train:
And if yet higher the proud list should end,
Still let me say, 'No follower, but a friend.'
    Yet think not, friendship only prompts my lays;
I follow *virtue*; where she shines, I praise:
Point she to priest or elder, Whig or Tory,
Or round a Quaker's beaver cast a glory.
I never (to my sorrow I declare)
Dined with the MAN of ROSS, or my LORD MAYOR.
Some, in their choice of friends (nay, look not grave)   100
Have still a secret bias to a knave:
To find an honest man I beat about,
And love him, court him, praise him, in or out.
    F. Then why so few commended?
                            P. Not so fierce;
Find you the virtue, and I'll find the verse.
But random praise—the task can ne'er be done;
Each mother asks it for her booby son,
Each widow asks it for *the best of men*,
For him she weeps, and him she weds again.
Praise cannot stoop, like satire, to the ground;   110
The number may be hanged, but not be crowned.
Enough for half the greatest of these days,
To 'scape my censure, not expect my praise.
Are they not rich? what more can they pretend?
Dare they to hope a poet for their friend?
What RICHELIEU wanted, LOUIS scarce could gain,
And what young AMMON wished, but wished in vain.

88. *Wyndham*] Sir William Wyndham, Chancellor of the Exchequer under Queen
Anne, made early a considerable figure; but since a much greater both by his ability
and eloquence, joined with the utmost judgment and temper.

99. *my Lord Mayor.*] Sir John Barnard.

No power the muse's friendship can command;
No power, when virtue claims it, can withstand:
To Cato, Virgil paid one honest line;   120
O let my country's friends illumine mine!
—What are you thinking? *F.* Faith the thought's no sin,
I think your friends are out, and would be in.
    P. If merely to come in, sir, they go out,
The way they take is strangely round about.
    F. They too may be corrupted, you'll allow?
    P. I only call those knaves who are so now.
    Is that too little? Come then, I'll comply—
Spirit of *Arnall!* aid me while I lie.
COBHAM's a coward, POLWARTH is a slave,   130
And LYTTELTON a dark, designing knave,
ST JOHN has ever been a wealthy fool—
But let me add, Sir ROBERT's mighty dull,
Has never made a friend in private life,
And was, besides, a tyrant to his wife.
    But pray, when others praise him, do I blame?
Call Verres, Wolsey, any odious name?
Why rail they then, if but a wreath of mine,
Oh all-accomplished ST JOHN! deck thy shrine?
    What? shall each spur-galled hackney of the day,   140
When Paxton gives him double pots and pay,
Or each new-pensioned sycophant, pretend
To break my windows, if I treat a friend?
Then wisely plead, to me they meant no hurt,
But 'twas my guest at whom they threw the dirt?
Sure, if I spare the minister, no rules
Of honour bind me, not to maul his tools;
Sure, if they cannot cut, it may be said
His saws are toothless, and his hatchets lead.
    It angered TURENNE, once upon a day,   150
To see a footman kicked that took his pay:
But when he heard th' affront the fellow gave,
Knew one a man of honour, one a knave;
The prudent general turned it to a jest,

---

130. *Polwarth*] The Hon. Hugh Hume, son of Alexander Earl of Marchmont, grandson of Patric Earl of Marchmont, and distinguished, like them, in the cause of liberty.

And begged, he'd take the pains to kick the rest:
Which not at present having time to do—
    F. Hold sir! for God's sake where's th' affront to
    you?
Against your worship when had Selkirk writ?
Or Page poured forth the torrent of his wit?
Or grant the bard whose distich all commend   160
'*In power a servant, out of power a friend*'
To Walpole guilty of some venial sin;
What's that to you who ne'er was out nor in?
    The priest whose flattery bedropped the crown,
How hurt he you? he only stained the gown.
And how did, pray, the florid youth offend,
Whose speech you took, and gave it to a friend?
    P. Faith, it imports not much from whom it came,
Whoever borrowed, could not be to blame,
Since the whole House did afterwards the same.   170
Let courtly wits to wits afford supply,
As hog to hog in huts of Westphaly;
If one, through nature's bounty or his lord's,
Has what the frugal, dirty soil affords,
From him the next receives it, thick or thin,
As pure a mess almost as it came in;
The blessed benefit, not there confined,
Drops to the third, who nuzzles close behind;
From tail to mouth, they feed and they carouse:
The last full fairly gives it to the House.   180
    F. This filthy simile, this beastly line
Quite turns my stomach—
                     P. So does flattery mine;
And all your courtly civet-cats can vent,
Perfume to you, to me is excrement.
But hear me further—Japhet, 'tis agreed,
Writ not, and Chartres scarce could write or read,
In all the courts of Pindus guiltless quite;
But pens can forge, my friend, that cannot write;

160. A verse taken out of a poem to Sir R. W.

164. Spoken not of any particular priest, but of many priests.

166. This seems to allude to a complaint made v. 71. of the preceding Dialogue.

185–6. *Japhet—Chartres*] See the *Epistle to Lord Bathurst.*

And must no egg in Japhet's face be thrown,
Because the deed he forged was not my own? 190
Must never patriot then declaim at gin,
Unless, good man! he has been fairly in?
No zealous pastor blame a failing spouse,
Without a staring reason on his brows?
And each blasphemer quite escape the rod,
Because the insult's not on man, but God?
   Ask you what provocation I have had?
The strong antipathy of good to bad.
When truth or virtue an affront endures,
Th'affront is mine, my friend, and should be yours. 200
Mine, as a foe professed to false pretence,
Who think a coxcomb's honour like his sense;
Mine, as a friend to every worthy mind;
And mine as man, who feel for all mankind.
   F. You're strangely proud.
                P. So proud, I am no slave:
So impudent, I own myself no knave:
So odd, my country's ruin makes me grave.
Yes, I am proud; I must be proud to see
Men not afraid of God, afraid of me:
Safe from the bar, the pulpit, and the throne, 210
Yet touched and shamed by ridicule alone.
   O sacred weapon! left for truth's defence,
Sole dread of folly, vice, and insolence!
To all but heaven-directed hands denied,
The muse may give thee, but the God must guide:
Reverent I touch thee! but with honest zeal;
To rouse the watchmen of the public weal,
To virtue's work provoke the tardy Hall,
And goad the prelate slumbering in his stall.
Ye tinsel insects! whom a court maintains, 220
That counts your beauties only by your stains,
Spin all your cobwebs o'er the eye of day!
The muse's wing shall brush you all away:
All his Grace preaches, all his Lordship sings,

204. From Terence: 'Homo sum; humani nihil a me alienum puto.'

222. *Cobwebs*] Weak and slight sophistry against virtue and honour. Thin colours over vice, as unable to hide the light of truth, as cobwebs to shade the sun.

All that makes saints of queens, and gods of kings,
All, all but truth, drops dead-born from the press,
Like the last Gazette, or the last address.
   When black ambition stains a public cause,
A monarch's sword when mad vainglory draws,
Not Waller's wreath can hide the nation's scar,   230
Nor Boileau turn the feather to a star.
   Not so, when diademed with rays divine,
Touched with the flame that breaks from virtue's
    shrine,
Her priestess muse forbids the good to die,
And opes the temple of eternity.
There, other trophies deck the truly brave,
Than such as Anstis casts into the grave;
Far other stars than * and ** wear,
And may descend to Mordington from STAIR:
(Such as on HOUGH's unsullied mitre shine,   240
Or beam, good DIGBY, from a heart like thine)
Let envy howl, while heaven's whole chorus sings,
And bark at honour not conferred by kings;
Let flattery sickening see the incense rise,
Sweet to the world, and grateful to the skies:
Truth guards the poet, sanctifies the line,
And makes immortal, verse as mean as mine.
   Yes, the last pen for freedom let me draw,
When truth stands trembling on the edge of law;
Here, last of Britons! let your names be read;   250
Are none, none living? let me praise the dead,

---

228. The case of Cromwell in the Civil War of England; and (229) of Louis XIV in his conquest of the Low Countries.

231. *Nor Boileau turn the feather to a Star.*] See his *Ode on Namur*, where (to use his own words) 'il a fait un Astre de la Plume blanche que le Roy porte ordinairement à son Chapeau, et qui est en effet une espece de Comete, fatale à nos ennemis.'

237. *Anstis*] The chief Herald at Arms. It is the custom, at the funeral of great peers, to cast into the grave the broken staves and ensigns of honour.

239. *Stair*] John Dalrymple, Earl of Stair, Knight of the Thistle; served in all the wars under the Duke of Marlborough; and afterwards as Ambassador in France.

240, 241. *Hough and Digby*] Dr John Hough, Bishop of Worcester, and the Lord Digby. The one an assertor of the Church of England in opposition to the false measures of King James II. The other as firmly attached to the cause of that king. Both acting out of principle, and equally men of honour and virtue.

And for that cause which made your fathers shine,
Fall by the votes of their degenerate line.
   F. Alas! alas! pray end what you began,
And write next winter more *Essays on Man*.

EPIGRAM

*Engraved on the Collar of a Dog which
I gave to his Royal Highness*

I am his Highness' dog at Kew;
Pray tell me, sir, whose dog are you?

255. This was the last poem of the kind printed by our author, with a resolution
to publish no more; but to enter thus, in the most plain and solemn manner he
could, a sort of PROTEST against that insuperable corruption and depravity of
manners, which he had been so unhappy as to live to see. Could he have hoped to
have amended any, he had continued those attacks; but bad men were grown so
shameless and so powerful, that ridicule was become as unsafe as it was ineffectual.
The poem raised him, as he knew it would, some enemies; but he had reason
to be satisfied with the approbation of good men, and the testimony of his own
conscience.

THE
DUNCIAD
IN
FOUR BOOKS
Printed according to the complete Copy
found in the Year 1742

Tandem *Phoebus* adest, morsusque inferre parantem
Congelat, et patulos, ut erant, indurat hiatus.

OVID.

THE
DUNCIAD
TO
Dr JONATHAN SWIFT

BOOK the FIRST

The Mighty Mother, and her son who brings   1
The Smithfield muses to the ear of kings,
I sing. Say you, her instruments the great!
Called to this work by Dulness, Jove, and Fate;
You by whose care, in vain decried and cursed,
Still Dunce the second reigns like Dunce the first;
Say how the Goddess bade Britannia sleep,
And poured her spirit o'er the land and deep.
    In eldest time, e'er mortals writ or read,
E'er Pallas issued from the Thunderer's head,   10
Dulness o'er all possessed her ancient right,
Daughter of Chaos and eternal Night:
Fate in their dotage this fair idiot gave,
Gross as her sire, and as her mother grave,
Laborious, heavy, busy, bold, and blind,
She ruled, in native anarchy, the mind.
    Still her old empire to restore she tries,

For, born a goddess, Dulness never dies.
  O thou! whatever title please thine ear,
Dean, Drapier, Bickerstaff, or Gulliver!   20
Whether thou choose Cervantes' serious air,
Or laugh and shake in Rabelais' easy chair,
Or praise the court, or magnify mankind,
Or thy grieved country's copper chains unbind;
From thy Boeotia though her power retires,
Mourn not, my SWIFT, at ought our realm acquires,
Here pleased behold her mighty wings out-spread
To hatch a new Saturnian age of lead.
  Close to those walls where Folly holds her throne,
And laughs to think Monroe would take her down,   30
Where o'er the gates, by his famed father's hand
Great Cibber's brazen, brainless brothers stand;
One cell there is, concealed from vulgar eye,
The cave of poverty and poetry.
Keen, hollow winds howl through the bleak recess,
Emblem of music caused by emptiness.
Hence bards, like Proteus long in vain tied down,
Escape in monsters, and amaze the town.
Hence miscellanies spring, the weekly boast
Of Curll's chaste press, and Lintot's rubric post: 40
Hence hymning Tyburn's elegiac lines,
Hence *Journals*, *Medleys*, *Merc'ries*, *Magazines*:
Sepulchral lies, our holy walls to grace,
And New Year odes, and all the Grub Street race.
  In clouded majesty here Dulness shone;
Four guardian virtues, round, support her throne:
Fierce champion Fortitude, that knows no fears
Of hisses, blows, or want, or loss of ears:
Calm Temperance, whose blessings those partake
Who hunger, and who thirst for scribbling sake: 50
Prudence, whose glass presents th' approaching gaol.
Poetic justice, with her lifted scale,
Where, in nice balance, truth with gold she weighs,
And solid pudding against empty praise.
  Here she beholds the chaos dark and deep,
Where nameless somethings in their causes sleep,
Till genial Jacob, or a warm third day,
Call forth each mass, a poem, or a play:

How hints, like spawn, scarce quick in embryo lie,
How new-born nonsense first is taught to cry,   60
Maggots half-formed in rhyme exactly meet,
And learn to crawl upon poetic feet.
Here one poor word an hundred clenches makes,
And ductile dulness new meanders takes;
There motley images her fancy strike,
Figures ill paired, and similes unlike.
She sees a mob of metaphors advance,
Pleased with the madness of the mazy dance:
How tragedy and comedy embrace;
How farce and epic get a jumbled race;   70
How time himself stands still at her command,
Realms shift their place, and ocean turns to land.
Here gay description Egypt glads with showers,
Or gives to Zembla fruits, to Barca flowers;
Glittering with ice here hoary hills are seen,
There painted valleys of eternal green,
In cold December fragrant chaplets blow,
And heavy harvests nod beneath the snow.
     All these, and more, the cloud-compelling Queen
Beholds through fogs, that magnify the scene.   80
She, tinselled o'er in robes of varying hues,
With self-applause her wild creation views;
Sees momentary monsters rise and fall,
And with her own fools-colours gilds them all.
     'Twas on the day, when * * rich and grave,
Like Cimon, triumphed both on land and wave:
(Pomps without guilt, of bloodless swords and maces,
Glad chains, warm furs, broad banners, and broad faces)
Now night descending, the proud scene was o'er,
But lived, in Settle's numbers, one day more.   90
Now mayors and shrieves all hushed and satiate lay,
Yet eat, in dreams, the custard of the day;
While pensive poets painful vigils keep,
Sleepless themselves, to give their readers sleep.
Much to the mindful Queen the feast recalls
What city swans once sung within the walls;
Much she revolves their arts, their ancient praise,
And sure succession down from Heywood's days.
She saw, with joy, the line immortal run,

Each sire impressed and glaring in his son: 100
So watchful Bruin forms, with plastic care,
Each growing lump, and brings it to a bear.
She saw old Prynne in restless Daniel shine,
And Eusden eke out Blackmore's endless line;
She saw slow Philips creep like Tate's poor page,
And all the mighty mad in Dennis rage.
  In each she marks her image full expressed,
But chief in BAYS's monster-breeding breast;
Bays, formed by nature stage and town to bless,
And act, and be, a coxcomb with success.   110
Dulness with transport eyes the lively dunce,
Remembering she herself was pertness once.
Now (shame to fortune!) an ill run at play
Blanked his bold visage, and a thin third day:
Swearing and supperless the hero sate,
Blasphemed his gods, the dice, and damned his fate.
Then gnawed his pen, then dashed it on the ground,
Sinking from thought to thought, a vast profound!
Plunged for his sense, but found no bottom there,
Yet wrote and floundered on, in mere despair.   120
Round him much embryo, much abortion lay,
Much future ode, and abdicated play;
Nonsense precipitate, like running lead,
That slipped through cracks and zigzags of the head;
All that on folly frenzy could beget,
Fruits of dull heat, and sooterkins of wit.
Next, o'er his books his eyes began to roll,
In pleasing memory of all he stole,
How here he sipped, how there he plundered snug
And sucked all o'er, like an industrious bug.   130
Here lay poor Fletcher's half-eat scenes, and here
The frippery of crucified Molière;
There hapless Shakespeare, yet of Tibbald sore,
Wished he had blotted for himself before.
The rest on outside merit but presume,
Or serve (like other fools) to fill a room;
Such with their shelves as due proportion hold,
Or their fond parents dressed in red and gold;
Or where the pictures for the page atone,
And Quarles is saved by beauties not his own.   140

Here swells the shelf with Ogilby the great;
There, stamped with arms, Newcastle shines complete:
Here all his suffering brotherhood retire,
And 'scape the martyrdom of jakes and fire:
A Gothic library! of Greece and Rome
Well purged, and worthy Settle, Banks, and Broome.
  But, high above, more solid learning shone,
The classics of an age that heard of none;
There Caxton slept, with Wynkyn at his side,
One clasped in wood, and one in strong cow-hide;   150
There, saved by spice, like mummies, many a year,
Dry bodies of divinity appear:
De Lyra there a dreadful front extends,
And here the groaning shelves Philemon bends.
  Of these twelve volumes, twelve of amplest size,
Redeemed from tapers and defrauded pies,
Inspired he seizes: these an altar raise:
An hecatomb of pure, unsullied lays
That altar crowns: a folio commonplace
Founds the whole pile, of all his works the base: 160
Quartos, octavos, shape the lessening pyre;
A twisted birthday ode completes the spire.
  Then he: 'Great tamer of all human art!
First in my care, and ever at my heart;
Dulness! whose good old cause I yet defend,
With whom my muse began, with whom shall end;
E'er since Sir Fopling's periwig was praise,
To the last honours of the butt and bays:
O thou! of business the directing soul!
To this our head like bias to the bowl,   170
Which, as more ponderous, made its aim more true,
Obliquely waddling to the mark in view:
O! ever gracious to perplexed mankind,
Still spread a healing mist before the mind;
And lest we err by wit's wild dancing light,
Secure us kindly in our native night.
Or, if to wit a coxcomb make pretence,
Guard the sure barrier between that and sense;
Or quite unravel all the reasoning thread,
And hang some curious cobweb in its stead!   180
As, forced from wind-guns, lead itself can fly,

And ponderous slugs cut swiftly through the sky;
As clocks to weight their nimble motion owe,
The wheels above urged by the load below:
Me emptiness, and dulness could inspire,
And were my elasticity, and fire.
Some daemon stole my pen (forgive th'offence)
And once betrayed me into common sense:
Else all my prose and verse were much the same;
This, prose on stilts, that, poetry fallen lame.   190
Did on the stage my fops appear confined?
My life gave ampler lessons to mankind.
Did the dead letter unsuccessful prove?
The brisk example never failed to move.
Yet sure had heaven decreed to save the state,
Heaven had decreed these works a longer date.
Could Troy be saved by any single hand,
This grey-goose weapon must have made her stand.
What can I now? my Fletcher cast aside,
Take up the Bible, once my better guide?   200
Or tread the path by venturous heroes trod,
This box my thunder, this right hand my god?
Or chaired at White's amidst the doctors sit,
Teach oaths to gamesters, and to nobles wit?
Or bidst thou rather party to embrace?
(A friend to party thou, and all her race;
'Tis the same rope at different ends they twist;
To Dulness Ridpath is as dear as Mist.)
Shall I, like Curtius, desperate in my zeal,
O'er head and ears plunge for the commonweal?   210
Or rob Rome's ancient geese of all their glories,
And cackling save the monarchy of Tories?
Hold—to the minister I more incline;
To serve his cause, O Queen! is serving thine.
And see! thy very gazetteers give o'er,
Ev'n Ralph repents, and Henley writes no more.
What then remains? Ourself. Still, still remain
Cibberian forehead, and Cibberian brain.
This brazen brightness, to the 'squire so dear;
This polished hardness, that reflects the peer;   220
This arch absurd, that wit and fool delights;
This mess, tossed up of Hockley Hole and White's;

Where dukes and butchers join to wreathe my crown,
At once the bear and fiddle of the town.
  O born in sin, and forth in folly brought!
Works damned, or to be damned! (your father's fault)
Go, purified by flames ascend the sky,
My better and more Christian progeny!
Unstained, untouched, and yet in maiden sheets;
While all your smutty sisters walk the streets.   230
Ye shall not beg, like gratis-given Bland,
Sent with a pass, and vagrant through the land;
Not sail, with Ward, to ape-and-monkey climes,
Where vile mundungus trucks for viler rhymes;
Not sulphur-tipped, emblaze an alehouse fire;
Not wrap up oranges, to pelt your sire!
O! pass more innocent, in infant state,
To the mild limbo of our father Tate:
Or peaceably forgot, at once be blessed
In Shadwell's bosom with eternal rest!   240
Soon to that mass of nonsense to return,
Where things destroyed are swept to things unborn.'
    With that, a tear (portentous sign of grace!)
Stole from the master of the sevenfold face:
And thrice he lifted high the birthday brand,
And thrice he dropped it from his quivering hand;
Then lights the structure, with averted eyes:
The rolling smokes involve the sacrifice.
The opening clouds disclose each work by turns,
Now flames the *Cid*, and now *Perolla* burns;   250
Great *Caesar* roars, and hisses in the fires;
King John in silence modestly expires:
No merit now the dear *Nonjuror* claims,
Molière's old stubble in a moment flames.
Tears gushed again, as from pale Priam's eyes
When the last blaze sent Ilion to the skies.
    Roused by the light, old Dulness heaved the head;
Then snatched a sheet of Thulè from her bed,
Sudden she flies, and whelms it o'er the pyre;
Down sink the flames, and with a hiss expire.   260
    Her ample presence fills up all the place;
A veil of fogs dilates her awful face:
Great in her charms! as when on shrieves and mayors

She looks, and breathes herself into their airs.
She bids him wait her to her sacred dome:
Well pleased he entered, and confessed his home.
So spirits ending their terrestrial race,
Ascend, and recognize their native place.
This the Great Mother dearer held than all
The clubs of quidnuncs, or her own Guildhall: 270
Here stood her opium, here she nursed her owls,
And here she planned th' imperial seat of Fools.

Here to her chosen all her works she shows;
Prose swelled to verse, verse loitering into prose:
How random thoughts now meaning chance to find,
Now leave all memory of sense behind:
How prologues into prefaces decay,
And these to notes are frittered quite away:
How index-learning turns no student pale,
Yet holds the eel of science by the tail: 280
How, with less reading than makes felons 'scape,
Less human genius than God gives an ape,
Small thanks to France, and none to Rome or Greece,
A past, vamped, future, old, revived, new piece,
'Twixt Plautus, Fletcher, Shakespeare, and Corneille,
Can make a Cibber, Tibbald, or Ozell.

The Goddess then, o'er his anointed head,
With mystic words, the sacred opium shed.
And lo! her bird, (a monster of a fowl,
Something betwixt a Heidegger and owl,)   290
Perched on his crown: 'All hail! and hail again,
My son! the promised land expects thy reign.
Know, Eusden thirsts no more for sack or praise;
He sleeps among the dull of ancient days;
Safe, where no critics damn, no duns molest,
Where wretched Withers, Ward, and Gildon rest,
And high-born Howard, more majestic sire,
With fool of quality completes the quire.
Thou Cibber! thou, his laurel shalt support,
Folly, my son, has still a friend at court.   300
Lift up your gates, ye princes, see him come!
Sound, sound ye viols, be the catcall dumb!
Bring, bring the madding bay, the drunken vine;
The creeping, dirty, courtly ivy join.

And thou! his aide de camp, lead on my sons,
Light-armed with points, antitheses, and puns.
Let bawdry, Billingsgate, my daughters dear,
Support his front, and oaths bring up the rear:
And under his, and under Archer's wing,
Gaming and Grub Street skulk behind the king.   310
  O! when shall rise a monarch all our own,
And I, a nursing-mother, rock the throne,
'Twixt prince and people close the curtain draw,
Shade him from light, and cover him from law;
Fatten the courtier, starve the learned band,
And suckle armies, and dry-nurse the land:
Till senates nod to lullabies divine,
And all be asleep, as at an ode of thine.'

  She ceased. Then swells the Chapel Royal throat:
'God save King Cibber!' mounts in every note.   320
Familiar White's, 'God save King Colley!' cries;
'God save King Colley!' Drury Lane replies:
To Needham's quick the voice triumphal rode,
But pious Needham dropped the name of God;
Back to the Devil the last echoes roll,
And 'Coll!' each butcher roars at Hockley Hole.
  So when Jove's block descended from on high
(As sings thy great forefather Ogilby)
Loud thunder to its bottom shook the bog,
And the hoarse nation croaked, 'God save King Log!'   330

The End of the FIRST BOOK.

THE

DUNCIAD

BOOK the SECOND

High on a gorgeous seat, that far outshone   1
Henley's gilt tub, or Flecknoe's Irish throne,
Or that where on her Curlls the public pours,
All-bounteous, fragrant grains and golden showers,

Great Cibber sate: the proud Parnassian sneer,
The conscious simper, and the jealous leer,
Mix on his look: all eyes direct their rays
On him, and crowds turn coxcombs as they gaze.
His peers shine round him with reflected grace,
New edge their dulness, and new bronze their face.   10
So from the sun's broad beam, in shallow urns
Heaven's twinkling sparks draw light, and point their
       horns.
   Not with more glee, by hands pontific crowned,
With scarlet hats wide-waving circled round,
Rome in her Capitol saw Querno sit,
Throned on seven hills, the Antichrist of wit.
   And now the Queen, to glad her sons, proclaims
By herald hawkers, high heroic games.
They summon all her race: an endless band
Pours forth, and leaves unpeopled half the land.   20
A motley mixture! in long wigs, in bags,
In silks, in crapes, in garters, and in rags,
From drawing rooms, from colleges, from garrets,
On horse, on foot, in hacks, and gilded chariots:
All who true dunces in her cause appeared,
And all who knew those dunces to reward.
   Amid that area wide they took their stand,
Where the tall maypole once o'erlooked the Strand;
But now (so ANNE and piety ordain)
A church collects the saints of Drury Lane.   30
   With authors, stationers obeyed the call,
(The field of glory is a field for all).
Glory, and gain, th'industrious tribe provoke;
And gentle Dulness ever loves a joke.
A poet's form she placed before their eyes,
And bade the nimblest racer seize the prize;
No meagre, muse-rid mope, adust and thin,
In a dun nightgown of his own loose skin;
But such a bulk as no twelve bards could raise,
Twelve starveling bards of these degenerate days.   40
All as a partridge plump, full-fed, and fair,
She formed this image of well-bodied air;
With pert flat eyes she windowed well its head;
A brain of feathers, and a heart of lead;

And empty words she gave, and sounding strain,
But senseless, lifeless! idol void and vain!
Never was dashed out, at one lucky hit,
A fool, so just a copy of a wit;
So like, that critics said, and courtiers swore,
A wit it was, and called the phantom More.   50
    All gaze with ardour: some a poet's name,
Others a sword-knot and laced suit inflame.
But lofty Lintot in the circle rose:
'This prize is mine; who tempt it are my foes;
With me began this genius, and shall end.'
He spoke: and who with Lintot shall contend?
    Fear held them mute. Alone, untaught to fear,
Stood dauntless Curll; 'Behold that rival here!
The race by vigour, not by vaunts is won;
So take the hindmost, Hell.'—He said, and run.   60
Swift as a bard the bailiff leaves behind,
He left huge Lintot, and out-stripped the wind.
As when a dabchick waddles through the copse
On feet and wings, and flies, and wades, and hops;
So labouring on, with shoulders, hands, and head,
Wide as a windmill all his figure spread,
With arms expanded Bernard rows his state,
And left-legged Jacob seems to emulate:
Full in the middle way there stood a lake,
Which Curll's Corinna chanced that morn to make: 70
(Such was her wont, at early dawn to drop
Her evening cates before his neighbour's shop,)
Here fortuned Curll to slide; loud shout the band,
And 'Bernard! Bernard!' rings through all the Strand.
Obscene with filth the miscreant lies bewrayed,
Fallen in the plash his wickedness had laid:
Then first (if poets aught of truth declare)
The caitiff vaticide conceived a prayer.
    'Hear Jove! whose name my bards and I adore,
As much at least as any god's, or more;   80
And him and his, if more devotion warms,
Down with the Bible, up with the Pope's Arms.'
    A place there is, betwixt earth, air, and seas,
Where, from Ambrosia, Jove retires for ease.
There in his seat two spacious vents appear,

On this he sits, to that he leans his ear.
And hears the various vows of fond mankind;
Some beg an eastern, some a western wind:
All vain petitions, mounting to the sky,
With reams abundant this abode supply;   90
Amused he reads, and then returns the bills
Signed with that Ichor which from gods distils.
  In office here fair Cloacina stands,
And ministers to Jove with purest hands.
Forth from the heap she picked her votary's prayer,
And placed it next him, a distinction rare!
Oft had the Goddess heard her servant's call,
From her black grottos near the Temple wall,
Listening delighted to the jest unclean
Of link-boys vile, and watermen obscene;   100
Where as he fished her nether realms for wit,
She oft had favoured him, and favours yet.
Renewed by ordure's sympathetic force,
As oiled with magic juices for the course,
Vigorous he rises; from th' effluvia strong
Imbibes new life, and scours and stinks along;
Repasses Lintot, vindicates the race,
Nor heeds the brown dishonours of his face.
  And now the victor stretched his eager hand
Where the tall nothing stood, or seemed to stand;   110
A shapeless shade, it melted from his sight,
Like forms in clouds, or visions of the night.
To seize his papers, Curll, was next thy care;
His papers light, fly diverse, tossed in air;
Songs, sonnets, epigrams the winds uplift,
And whisk 'em back to Evans, Young, and Swift.
Th'embroidered suit at least he deemed his prey;
That suit an unpaid tailor snatched away.
No rag, no scrap, of all the beau, or wit,
That once so fluttered, and that once so writ.   120
  Heaven rings with laughter: of the laughter vain,
Dulness, good Queen, repeats the jest again.
Three wicked imps, of her own Grub Street choir,
She decked like Congreve, Addison, and Prior;
Mears, Warner, Wilkins run: delusive thought!
Breval, Bond, Besaleel, the varlets caught.

Curll stretches after Gay, but Gay is gone,
He grasps an empty Joseph for a John:
So Proteus, hunted in a nobler shape,
Became, when seized, a puppy, or an ape.   130
   To him the Goddess: 'Son! thy grief lay down,
And turn this whole illusion on the town:
As the sage dame, experienced in her trade,
By names of toasts retails each battered jade;
(Whence hapless Monsieur much complains at Paris
Of wrongs from Duchesses and Lady Maries);
Be thine, my stationer! this magic gift;
Cooke shall be Prior, and Concanen, Swift:
So shall each hostile name become our own,
And we too boast our Garth and Addison.'   140
   With that she gave him (piteous of his case,
Yet smiling at his rueful length of face)
A shaggy tapestry, worthy to be spread
On Codrus' old, or Dunton's modern bed;
Instructive work! whose wry-mouthed portraiture
Displayed the fates her confessors endure.
Earless on high, stood unabashed Defoe,
And Tutchin flagrant from the scourge below.
There Ridpath, Roper, cudgelled might ye view,
The very worsted still looked black and blue.   150
Himself among the storied chiefs he spies,
As from the blanket high in air he flies,
'And oh!', he cried, 'what street, what lane but knows,
Our purgings, pumpings, blankettings, and blows?
In every loom our labours shall be seen,
And the fresh vomit run for ever green!'
   See in the circle next, Eliza placed,
Two babes of love close clinging to her waist;
Fair as before her works she stands confessed,
In flowers and pearls by bounteous Kirkall dressed.   160
The Goddess then: 'Who best can send on high
The salient spout, far-streaming to the sky;
His be yon Juno of majestic size,
With cow-like udders, and with ox-like eyes.
This China jordan let the chief o'ercome
Replenish, not ingloriously, at home.'
Osborne and Curll accept the glorious strife,

(Though this his son dissuades, and that his wife.)
One on his manly confidence relies,
One on his vigour and superior size.   170
First Osborne leaned against his lettered post;
It rose, and laboured to a curve at most.
So Jove's bright bow displays its watery round,
(Sure sign, that no spectator shall be drowned).
A second effort brought but new disgrace,
The wild meander washed the artist's face:
Thus the small jet, which hasty hands unlock,
Spurts in the gardener's eyes who turns the cock.
Not so from shameless Curll; impetuous spread
The stream, and smoking flourished o'er his head.   180
So (famed like thee for turbulence and horns)
Eridanus his humble fountain scorns;
Through half the heavens he pours th'exalted urn;
His rapid waters in their passage burn.
    Swift as it mounts, all follow with their eyes:
Still happy impudence obtains the prize.
Thou triumph'st, victor of the high-wrought day,
And the pleased dame, soft-smiling, leadst away.
Osborne, through perfect modesty o'ercome,
Crowned with the jordan, walks contented home.   190
    But now for authors nobler palms remain;
Room for my Lord! three jockeys in his train;
Six huntsmen with a shout precede his chair:
He grins, and looks broad nonsense with a stare.
His honour's meaning Dulness thus expressed,
'He wins this patron, who can tickle best.'
    He chinks his purse, and takes his seat of state:
With ready quills the dedicators wait;
Now at his head the dexterous task commence,
And, instant, fancy feels th' imputed sense;   200
Now gentle touches wanton o'er his face,
He struts Adonis, and affects grimace:
Rolli the feather to his ear conveys,
Then his nice taste directs our operas:
Bentley his mouth with classic flattery opes,
And the puffed orator bursts out in tropes.
But Welsted most the poet's healing balm
Strives to extract from his soft, giving palm;

Unlucky Welsted! thy unfeeling master,
The more thou ticklest, gripes his fist the faster.   210
  While thus each hand promotes the pleasing pain,
And quick sensations skip from vein to vein;
A youth unknown to Phoebus, in despair,
Puts his last refuge all in heaven and prayer.
What force have pious vows! The Queen of Love
His sister sends, her votress, from above.
As taught by Venus, Paris learnt the art
To touch Achilles' only tender part;
Secure, through her, the noble prize to carry,
He marches off, his Grace's secretary.   220
  'Now turn to different sports,' the Goddess cries,
'And learn, my sons, the wondrous power of noise.
To move, to raise, to ravish every heart,
With Shakespeare's nature, or with Jonson's art,
Let others aim: 'tis yours to shake the soul
With thunder rumbling from the mustard bowl,
With horns and trumpets now to madness swell,
Now sink in sorrows with a tolling bell;
Such happy arts attention can command,
When fancy flags, and sense is at a stand.   230
Improve we these. Three catcalls be the bribe
Of him, whose chattering shames the monkey tribe:
And his this drum, whose hoarse heroic bass
Drowns the loud clarion of the braying ass.'
  Now thousand tongues are heard in one loud din:
The monkey-mimics rush discordant in;
'Twas chattering, grinning, mouthing, jabbering all,
And noise and Norton, brangling and Breval,
Dennis and dissonance, and captious art,
And snipsnap short, and interruption smart,   240
And demonstration thin, and theses thick,
And major, minor, and conclusion quick.
'Hold', cried the Queen, 'a catcall each shall win;
Equal your merits! equal is your din!
But that this well-disputed game may end,
Sound forth my brayers, and the welkin rend.'
  As when the long-eared milky mothers wait
At some sick miser's triple-bolted gate,
For their defrauded, absent foals they make

A moan so loud, that all the guild awake;   250
Sore sighs Sir Gilbert, starting at the bray,
From dreams of millions, and three groats to pay.
So swells each wind-pipe; ass intones to ass,
Harmonic twang! of leather, horn, and brass;
Such as from labouring lungs th' enthusiast blows,
High sound, attempered to the vocal nose;
Or such as bellow from the deep divine;
There Webster! pealed thy voice, and Whitfield! thine.
But far o'er all, sonorous Blackmore's strain;
Walls, steeples, skies, bray back to him again.   260
In Tottenham fields, the brethren, with amaze,
Prick all their ears up, and forget to graze;
Long Chancery Lane retentive rolls the sound,
And courts to courts return it round and round;
Thames wafts it thence to Rufus' roaring hall,
And Hungerford re-echoes bawl for bawl.
All hail him victor in both gifts of song,
Who sings so loudly, and who sings so long.
    This labour past, by Bridewell all descend,
(As morning prayer, and flagellation end)   270
To where Fleet Ditch with disemboguing streams
Rolls the large tribute of dead dogs to Thames,
The King of dykes! than whom no sluice of mud
With deeper sable blots the silver flood.
'Here strip, my children! here at once leap in,
Here prove who best can dash through thick and thin,
And who the most in love of dirt excel,
Or dark dexterity of groping well.
Who flings most filth, and wide pollutes around
The stream, be his the *Weekly Journals* bound,   280
A pig of lead to him who dives the best;
A peck of coals apiece shall glad the rest.'
    In naked majesty Oldmixon stands,
And Milo-like surveys his arms and hands;
Then sighing, thus, 'And am I now three score?
Ah why, ye gods! should two and two make four?'
He said, and climbed a stranded lighter's height,
Shot to the black abyss, and plunged downright.
The senior's judgment all the crowd admire,
Who but to sink the deeper, rose the higher.   290

Next Smedley dived; slow circles dimpled o'er
The quaking mud, that closed, and oped no more.
All look, all sigh, and call on Smedley lost;
'Smedley' in vain resounds through all the coast.

   Then * essayed; scarce vanished out of sight,
He buoys up instant, and returns to light:
He bears no token of the sabler streams,
And mounts far off among the swans of Thames.

   True to the bottom, see Concanen creep,
A cold, long-winded, native of the deep: 300
If perseverance gain the diver's prize,
Not everlasting Blackmore this denies:
No noise, no stir, no motion canst thou make,
Th' unconscious stream sleeps o'er thee like a lake.

   Next plunged a feeble, but a desperate pack,
With each a sickly brother at his back:
Sons of a day! just buoyant on the flood,
Then numbered with the puppies in the mud.
Ask ye their names? I could as soon disclose
The names of these blind puppies as of those.   310
Fast by, like Niobe (her children gone)
Sits Mother Osborne, stupefied to stone!
And monumental brass this record bears,
'These are,—ah no! these were, the *Gazetteers*!'

   Not so bold Arnall; with a weight of skull,
Furious he dives, precipitately dull.
Whirlpools and storms his circling arm invest,
With all the might of gravitation blessed:
No crab more active in the dirty dance,
Downward to climb, and backward to advance.   320
He brings up half the bottom on his head,
And loudly claims the journals and the lead.

   The plunging prelate, and his ponderous Grace,
With holy envy gave one layman place.
When lo! a burst of thunder shook the flood.
Slow rose a form, in majesty of mud;
Shaking the horrors of his sable brows,
And each ferocious feature grim with ooze.
Greater he looks, and more than mortal stares:
Then thus the wonders of the deep declares.   330

   First he relates, how sinking to the chin,

Smit with his mien, the mud-nymphs sucked him in:
How young Lutetia, softer than the down,
Nigrina black, and Merdamante brown,
Vied for his love in jetty bowers below,
As Hylas fair was ravished long ago.
Then sung, how shown him by the nut-brown maids
A branch of Styx here rises from the shades,
That tinctured as it runs with Lethe's streams,
And wafting vapours from the land of dreams,   340
(As under seas Alpheus' secret sluice
Bears Pisa's offerings to his Arethuse)
Pours into Thames: and hence the mingled wave
Intoxicates the pert, and lulls the grave:
Here brisker vapours o'er the Temple creep,
There, all from Paul's to Aldgate drink and sleep.
    Thence to the banks where reverend bards repose,
They led him soft; each reverend bard arose;
And Milbourne chief, deputed by the rest,
Gave him the cassock, surcingle, and vest.   350
'Receive', he said, 'these robes which once were
        mine,
Dulness is sacred in a sound divine.'
    He ceased, and spread the robe; the crowd confess,
The reverend flamen in his lengthened dress.
Around him wide a sable army stand,
A low-born, cell-bred, selfish, servile band,
Prompt or to guard or stab, to saint or damn,
Heaven's Swiss, who fight for any god, or man.
    Through Lud's famed gates, along the well-known
        Fleet
Rolls the black troop, and overshades the street,   360
Till showers of sermons, characters, essays,
In circling fleeces whiten all the ways:
So clouds replenished from some bog below,
Mount in dark volumes, and descend in snow.
Here stopped the Goddess; and in pomp proclaims
A gentler exercise to close the games.
    'Ye critics! in whose heads, as equal scales,
I weigh what author's heaviness prevails;
Which most conduce to soothe the soul in slumbers,
My Henley's periods, or my Blackmore's numbers;   370

Attend the trial we propose to make:
If there be man, who o'er such works can wake,
Sleep's all-subduing charms who dares defy,
And boasts Ulysses' ear with Argus' eye;
To him we grant our amplest powers to sit
Judge of all present, past, and future wit;
To cavil, censure, dictate, right or wrong,
Full and eternal privilege of tongue.'
  Three college sophs, and three pert templars came,
The same their talents, and their tastes the same;   380
Each prompt to query, answer, and debate,
And smit with love of poesy and prate.
The ponderous books two gentle readers bring;
The heroes sit, the vulgar form a ring.
The clamorous crowd is hushed with mugs of mum,
Till all tuned equal, send a general hum.
Then mount the clerks, and in one lazy tone
Through the long, heavy, painful page drawl on;
Soft creeping, words on words, the sense compose,
At every line they stretch, they yawn, they doze.   390
As to soft gales top-heavy pines bow low
Their heads, and lift them as they cease to blow:
Thus oft they rear, and oft the head decline,
As breathe, or pause, by fits, the airs divine.
And now to this side, now to that they nod,
As verse, or prose, infuse the drowsy god.
Thrice Budgell aimed to speak, but thrice suppressed
By potent Arthur, knocked his chin and breast.
Toland and Tindal, prompt at priests to jeer,
Yet silent bowed to Christ's no kingdom here.   400
Who sate the nearest, by the words o'ercome,
Slept first; the distant nodded to the hum.
Then down are rolled the books; stretched o'er
    'em lies
Each gentle clerk, and muttering seals his eyes.
As what a Dutchman plumps into the lakes,
One circle first, and then a second makes;
What Dulness dropped among her sons impressed
Like motion from one circle to the rest;
So from the midmost the nutation spreads
Round and more round, o'er all the sea of heads.   410

At last Centlivre felt her voice to fail,
Motteux himself unfinished left his tale,
Boyer the state, and Law the stage gave o'er,
Morgan and Mandeville could prate no more;
Norton, from Daniel and Ostroea sprung,
Blessed with his father's front, and mother's tongue,
Hung silent down his never-blushing head;
And all was hushed, as folly's self lay dead.

Thus the soft gifts of sleep conclude the day,
And stretched on bulks, as usual, poets lay.   420
Why should I sing what bards the nightly muse
Did slumbering visit, and convey to stews;
Who prouder marched, with magistrates in state,
To some famed round-house, ever open gate!
How Henley lay inspired beside a sink,
And to mere mortals seemed a priest in drink:
While others, timely, to the neighbouring Fleet
(Haunt of the muses) made their safe retreat.

The End of the SECOND BOOK

THE
DUNCIAD

BOOK the THIRD

But in her temple's last recess enclosed,   1
On Dulness' lap th' anointed head reposed.
Him close she curtains round with vapours blue,
And soft besprinkles with Cimmerian dew.
Then raptures high the seat of sense o'erflow,
Which only heads refined from reason know.
Hence, from the straw where Bedlam's prophet nods,
He hears loud oracles, and talks with gods:
Hence the fool's paradise, the statesman's scheme,
The air-built castle, and the golden dream,   10
The maid's romantic wish, the chemist's flame,
And poet's vision of eternal fame.

And now, on fancy's easy wing conveyed,

The King descending, views th' Elysian shade.
A slipshod sibyl led his steps along,
In lofty madness meditating song;
Her tresses staring from poetic dreams,
And never washed, but in Castalia's streams.
Taylor, their better Charon, lends an oar,
(Once swan of Thames, though now he sings no
      more.)   20
Benlowes, propitious still to blockheads, bows;
And Shadwell nods the poppy on his brows.
Here, in a dusky vale where Lethe rolls,
Old Bavius sits, to dip poetic souls,
And blunt the sense, and fit it for a skull
Of solid proof, impenetrably dull:
Instant, when dipped, away they wing their flight,
Where Brown and Mears unbar the gates of Light,
Demand new bodies, and in calf's array,
Rush to the world, impatient for the day.   30
Millions and millions on these banks he views,
Thick as the stars of night, or morning dews,
As thick as bees o'er vernal blossoms fly,
As thick as eggs at Ward in pillory.
  Wondering he gazed: when lo! a sage appears,
By his broad shoulders known, and length of ears,
Known by the band and suit which Settle wore
(His only suit) for twice three years before:
All as the vest, appeared the wearer's frame,
Old in new state, another yet the same.   40
Bland and familiar as in life, begun
Thus the great father to the greater son.
  'Oh, born to see what none can see awake!
Behold the wonders of th' oblivious lake.
Thou, yet unborn, hast touched this sacred shore;
The hand of Bavius drenched thee o'er and o'er.
But blind to former as to future fate,
What mortal knows his pre-existent state?
Who knows how long thy transmigrating soul
Might from Boeotian to Boeotian roll?   50
How many Dutchmen she vouchsafed to thrid?
How many stages through old monks she rid?
And all who since, in mild benighted days,

Mixed the owl's ivy with the poet's bays.
As man's meanders to the vital spring
Roll all their tides, then back their circles bring;
Or whirligigs, twirled round by skilful swain,
Suck the thread in, then yield it out again:
All nonsense thus, of old or modern date,
Shall in thee centre, from thee circulate.   60
For this our Queen unfolds to vision true
Thy mental eye, for thou hast much to view:
Old scenes of glory, times long cast behind
Shall, first recalled, rush forward to thy mind:
Then stretch thy sight o'er all her rising reign,
And let the past and future fire thy brain.

Ascend this hill, whose cloudy point commands
Her boundless empire over seas and lands.
See, round the poles where keener spangles shine,
Where spices smoke beneath the burning line,   70
(Earth's wide extremes) her sable flag displayed,
And all the nations covered in her shade!

Far eastward cast thine eye, from whence the sun
And orient science their bright course begun:
One godlike monarch all that pride confounds,
He, whose long wall the wandering Tartar bounds;
Heavens! what a pile! whole ages perish there,
And one bright blaze turns learning into air.

Thence to the south extend thy gladdened eyes;
There rival flames with equal glory rise,   80
From shelves to shelves see greedy Vulcan roll,
And lick up all their physic of the soul.

How little, mark! that portion of the ball,
Where, faint at best, the beams of science fall:
Soon as they dawn, from Hyperborean skies
Embodied dark, what clouds of Vandals rise!
Lo! where Maeotis sleeps, and hardly flows
The freezing Tanais through a waste of snows,
The North by myriads pours her mighty sons,
Great nurse of Goths, of Alans and of Huns!   90
See Alaric's stern port! the martial frame
Of Genseric! and Attila's dread name!
See the bold Ostrogoths on Latium fall;
See the fierce Visigoths on Spain and Gaul!

See, where the morning gilds the palmy shore
(The soil that arts and infant letters bore)
His conquering tribes th' Arabian prophet draws,
And saving ignorance enthrones by laws.
See Christians, Jews, one heavy sabbath keep,
And all the western world believe and sleep. 100
    Lo! Rome herself, proud mistress now no more
Of arts, but thundering against heathen lore;
Her grey-haired synods damning books unread,
And Bacon trembling for his brazen head.
Padua, with sighs, beholds her Livy burn,
And ev'n th' Antipodes Virgilius mourn.
See, the cirque falls, th' unpillared temple nods,
Streets paved with heroes, Tiber choked with gods;
Till Peter's keys some christened Jove adorn,
And Pan to Moses lends his pagan horn; 110
See graceless Venus to a Virgin turned,
Or Phidias broken, and Apelles burned.
    Behold yon isle, by palmers, pilgrims trod,
Men bearded, bald, cowled, uncowled, shod, unshod,
Peeled, patched and piebald, linsey-wolsey brothers,
Grave mummers! sleeveless some, and shirtless others.
That once was Britain—Happy! had she seen
No fiercer sons, had Easter never been.
In peace, great Goddess, ever be adored;
How keen the war, if Dulness draw the sword! 120
Thus visit not thy own! on this blessed age
Oh spread thy influence, but restrain thy rage.
    And see, my son! the hour is on its way,
That lifts our Goddess to imperial sway;
This favourite isle, long severed from her reign,
Dovelike, she gathers to her wings again.
Now look through fate! behold the scene she draws!
What aids, what armies to assert her cause!
See all her progeny, illustrious sight!
Behold, and count them, as they rise to light. 130
As Berecynthia, while her offspring vie
In homage to the mother of the sky,
Surveys around her, in the blessed abode,
An hundred sons, and every son a god:
Not with less glory mighty Dulness crowned,

Shall take through Grub Street her triumphant round;
And her Parnassus glancing o'er at once,
Behold an hundred sons, and each a Dunce.

Mark first that youth who takes the foremost place,
And thrusts his person full into your face.   140
With all thy Father's virtues blessed, be born!
And a new Cibber shall the stage adorn.

A second see, by meeker manners known,
And modest as the maid that sips alone;
From the strong fate of drams if thou get free,
Another Durfey, Ward! shall sing in thee.
Thee shall each alehouse, thee each gillhouse mourn,
And answering gin-shops sourer sighs return.

Jacob, the scourge of grammar, mark with awe,
Nor less revere him, blunderbuss of Law.   150
Lo Popple's brow, tremendous to the town,
Horneck's fierce eye, and Roome's funereal frown.
Lo sneering Goode, half malice and half whim,
A fiend in glee, ridiculously grim.
Each cygnet sweet of Bath and Tunbridge race,
Whose tuneful whistling makes the waters pass:
Each songster, riddler, every nameless name,
All crowd, who foremost shall be damned to fame.
Some strain in rhyme; the muses, on their racks,
Scream like the winding of ten thousand jacks: 160
Some free from rhyme or reason, rule or check,
Break Priscian's head, and Pegasus's neck;
Down, down they larum, with impetuous whirl,
The Pindars, and the Miltons of a Curll.

Silence, ye wolves! while Ralph to Cynthia howls,
And makes night hideous—Answer him, ye owls!

Sense, speech, and measure, living tongues and
    dead,
Let all give way—and Morris may be read.

Flow Welsted, flow! like thine inspirer, beer,
Though stale, not ripe; though thin, yet never clear;   170
So sweetly mawkish, and so smoothly dull;
Heady, not strong; o'erflowing, though not full.

Ah Dennis! Gildon ah! what ill-starred rage
Divides a friendship long confirmed by age?
Blockheads with reason wicked wits abhor,

But fool with fool is barbarous civil war.
Embrace, embrace my sons! be foes no more!
Nor glad vile poets with true critics' gore.

Behold yon pair, in strict embraces joined;
How like in manners, and how like in mind! 180
Equal in wit, and equally polite,
Shall this a *Pasquin*, that a *Grumbler* write;
Like are their merits, like rewards they share,
That shines a consul, this commissioner.

'But who is he, in closet close y-pent,
Of sober face, with learned dust besprent?'
Right well mine eyes arede the myster wight,
On parchment scraps y-fed, and Wormius hight.
To future ages may thy dulness last,
As thou preserv'st the dulness of the past! 190

There, dim in clouds, the poring scholiasts mark,
Wits, who like owls, see only in the dark,
A lumberhouse of books in every head,
For ever reading, never to be read!

But, where each science lifts its modern type,
History her pot, divinity her pipe,
While proud philosophy repines to show,
Dishonest sight! his breeches rent below;
Imbrowned with native bronze, lo! Henley stands,
Tuning his voice, and balancing his hands. 200
How fluent nonsense trickles from his tongue!
How sweet the periods, neither said, nor sung!
Still break the benches, Henley! with thy strain,
While Sherlock, Hare, and Gibson preach in vain.
Oh great restorer of the good old stage,
Preacher at once, and zany of thy age!
Oh worthy thou of Egypt's wise abodes,
A decent priest, where monkeys were the gods!
But fate with butchers placed thy priestly stall,
Meek modern faith to murder, hack, and maul; 210
And bade thee live, to crown Britannia's praise,
In Toland's, Tindal's, and in Woolston's days.

Yet oh, my sons! a father's words attend:
(So may the fates preserve the ears you lend)
'Tis yours, a Bacon or a Locke to blame,
A Newton's genius, or a Milton's flame:

But oh! with one, immortal one dispense,
The source of Newton's light, of Bacon's sense!
Content, each emanation of his fires
That beams on earth, each virtue he inspires,   220
Each art he prompts, each charm he can create,
Whate'er he gives, are given for you to hate.
Persist, by all divine in man unawed,
But, "Learn, ye DUNCES! not to scorn your GOD".'
   Thus he, for then a ray of reason stole
Half through the solid darkness of his soul;
But soon the cloud returned—and thus the sire:
'See now, what Dulness and her sons admire!
See what the charms, that smite the simple heart
Not touched by nature, and not reached by art.'   230
   His never-blushing head he turned aside,
(Not half so pleased when Goodman prophesied)
And looked, and saw a sable sorcerer rise,
Swift to whose hand a winged volume flies:
All sudden, gorgons hiss, and dragons glare,
And ten-horned fiends and giants rush to war.
Hell rises, Heaven descends, and dance on earth:
Gods, imps, and monsters, music, rage, and mirth,
A fire, a jig, a battle, and a ball,
Till one wide conflagration swallows all.   240
   Thence a new world to nature's laws unknown,
Breaks out refulgent, with a heaven its own:
Another Cynthia her new journey runs,
And other planets circle other suns.
The forests dance, the rivers upward rise,
Whales sport in woods, and dolphins in the skies;
And last, to give the whole creation grace,
Lo! one vast egg produces human race.
   Joy fills his soul, joy innocent of thought;
'What power,' he cries, 'what power these wonders
      wrought?   250
Son; what thou seekst is in thee! Look, and find
Each monster meets his likeness in thy mind.
Yet wouldst thou more? In yonder cloud behold,
Whose sarsenet skirts are edged with flamey gold,
A matchless youth! his nod these worlds controls,
Wings the red lightning, and the thunder rolls.

Angel of Dulness, sent to scatter round
Her magic charms o'er all unclassic ground:
Yon stars, yon suns, he rears at pleasure higher,
Illumes their light, and sets their flames on fire.   260
Immortal Rich! how calm he sits at ease
'Mid snows of paper, and fierce hail of pease;
And proud his mistress' orders to perform,
Rides in the whirlwind, and directs the storm.
　　But lo! to dark encounter in mid air
New wizards rise; I see my Cibber there!
Booth in his cloudy tabernacle shrined,
On grinning dragons thou shalt mount the wind.
Dire is the conflict, dismal is the din,
Here shouts all Drury, there all Lincoln's Inn;   270
Contending theatres our empire raise,
Alike their labours, and alike their praise.
　　And are these wonders, son, to thee unknown?
Unknown to thee? These wonders are thy own.
These fate reserved to grace thy reign divine,
Foreseen by me, but ah! withheld from mine.
In Lud's old walls though long I ruled, renowned
Far as loud Bow's stupendous bells resound;
Though my own aldermen conferred the bays,
To me committing their eternal praise,   280
Their full-fed heroes, their pacific mayors,
Their annual trophies, and their monthly wars:
Though long my party built on me their hopes,
For writing pamphlets, and for roasting popes;
Yet lo! in me what authors have to brag on!
Reduced at last to hiss in my own dragon.
Avert it heaven! that thou, my Cibber, e'er
Shouldst wag a serpent-tail in Smithfield Fair!
Like the vile straw that's blown about the streets,
The needy poet sticks to all he meets,   290
Coached, carted, trod upon, now loose, now fast,
And carried off in some dog's tail at last.
Happier thy fortunes! like a rolling stone,
Thy giddy dulness still shall lumber on,
Safe in its heaviness, shall never stray,
But lick up every blockhead in the way.
Thee shall the patriot, thee the courtier taste,

And every year be duller than the last.
Till raised from booths, to theatre, to court,
Her seat imperial Dulness shall transport.   300
Already opera prepares the way,
The sure forerunner of her gentle sway:
Let her thy heart, next drabs and dice, engage,
The third mad passion of thy doting age.
Teach thou the warbling Polypheme to roar,
And scream thyself as none e'er screamed before!
To aid our cause, if heaven thou canst not bend,
Hell thou shalt move; for Faustus is our friend:
Pluto with Cato thou for this shalt join,
And link the *Mourning Bride* to *Proserpine*.   310
Grub Street! thy fall should men and gods
        conspire.
Thy stage shall stand, ensure it but from fire.
Another Aeschylus appears! prepare
For new abortions, all ye pregnant fair!
In flames, like Semele's, be brought to bed,
While opening hell spouts wildfire at your head.
   Now Bavius take the poppy from thy brow,
And place it here! here all ye heroes bow!
This, this is he, foretold by ancient rhymes:
Th' Augustus born to bring Saturnian times.   320
Signs following signs lead on the mighty year!
See! the dull stars roll round and reappear.
See, see, our own true Phoebus wears the bays!
Our Midas sits Lord Chancellor of Plays!
On poets' tombs see Benson's titles writ!
Lo! Ambrose Philips is preferred for wit!
See under Ripley rise a new Whitehall,
While Jones' and Boyle's united labours fall:
While Wren with sorrow to the grave descends,
Gay dies unpensioned with a hundred friends.   330
Hibernian politics, O Swift! thy fate;
And Pope's, ten years to comment and translate.
   Proceed, great days! till Learning fly the shore,
Till Birch shall blush with noble blood no more,
Till Thames see Eton's sons for ever play,
Till Westminster's whole year be holiday,
Till Isis' elders reel, their pupils sport,

And alma mater lie dissolved in port!'
  'Enough! enough!' the raptured monarch cries;
And through the ivory gate the vision flies.   340

The End of the THIRD BOOK

THE
DUNCIAD

BOOK the FOURTH

Yet, yet a moment, one dim ray of light   1
Indulge, dread Chaos, and eternal Night!
Of darkness visible so much be lent,
As half to show, half veil the deep intent.
Ye powers! whose mysteries restored I sing,
To whom time bears me on his rapid wing,
Suspend a while your force inertly strong,
Then take at once the poet and the song.
  Now flamed the dog-star's unpropitious ray,
Smote every brain, and withered every bay;   10
Sick was the sun, the owl forsook his bower,
The moonstruck prophet felt the madding hour:
Then rose the seed of Chaos, and of Night,
To blot out order, and extinguish light,
Of dull and venal a new world to mould,
And bring Saturnian days of lead and gold.
  She mounts the throne: her head a cloud
      concealed,
In broad effulgence all below revealed,
('Tis thus aspiring Dulness ever shines)
Soft on her lap her laureate son reclines.   20
  Beneath her footstool, Science groans in chains,
And Wit dreads exile, penalties and pains.
There foamed rebellious Logic, gagged and bound,
There, stripped, fair Rhetoric languished on the
      ground;
His blunted arms by Sophistry are borne,
And shameless Billingsgate her robes adorn.

Morality, by her false guardians drawn,
Chicane in furs, and Casuistry in lawn,
Gasps, as they straiten at each end the cord,
And dies, when Dulness gives her Page the word.   30
Mad Mathesis alone was unconfined,
Too mad for mere material chains to bind,
Now to pure space lifts her ecstatic stare,
Now running round the circle, finds it square.
But held in tenfold bonds the muses lie,
Watched both by envy's and by flattery's eye:
There to her heart sad Tragedy addressed
The dagger wont to pierce the tyrant's breast;
But sober History restrained her rage,
And promised vengeance on a barbarous age.   40
There sunk Thalia, nerveless, cold, and dead,
Had not her sister Satire held her head:
Nor couldst thou, CHESTERFIELD! a tear refuse,
Thou wept'st, and with thee wept each gentle muse.
    When lo! a harlot form soft sliding by,
With mincing step, small voice, and languid eye;
Foreign her air, her robe's discordant pride
In patchwork fluttering, and her head aside:
By singing peers upheld on either hand,
She tripped and laughed, too pretty much to stand;   50
Cast on the prostrate nine a scornful look,
Then thus in quaint recitativo spoke.
    'O *Cara! Cara!* silence all that train:
Joy to great Chaos! let division reign:
Chromatic tortures soon shall drive them hence,
Break all their nerves, and fritter all their sense:
One trill shall harmonize joy, grief, and rage,
Wake the dull church, and lull the ranting stage;
To the same notes thy sons shall hum, or snore,
And all thy yawning daughters cry, *encore*.   60
Another Phoebus, thy own Phoebus, reigns,
Joys in my jigs, and dances in my chains.
But soon, ah soon rebellion will commence,
If music meanly borrows aid from sense:
Strong in new arms, lo! giant Handel stands,
Like bold Briareus, with a hundred hands;
To stir, to rouse, to shake the soul he comes,

And Jove's own thunders follow Mars's drums.
Arrest him, Empress; or you sleep no more'—
She heard, and drove him to th' Hibernian shore. 70
    And now had Fame's posterior trumpet blown,
And all the nations summoned to the throne.
The young, the old, who feel her inward sway,
One instinct seizes, and transports away.
None need a guide, by sure attraction led,
And strong impulsive gravity of head:
None want a place, for all their centre found,
Hung to the Goddess, and cohered around.
Not closer, orb in orb, conglobed are seen
The buzzing bees about their dusky queen. 80
    The gathering number, as it moves along,
Involves a vast involuntary throng,
Who gently drawn, and struggling less and less,
Roll in her vortex, and her power confess.
Not those alone who passive own her laws,
But who, weak rebels, more advance her cause.
Whate'er of dunce in college or in town
Sneers at another, in toupee or gown;
Whate'er of mongrel no one class admits,
A wit with dunces, and a dunce with wits. 90
    Nor absent they, no members of her state,
Who pay her homage in her sons, the great;
Who false to Phoebus, bow the knee to Baal;
Or impious, preach his word without a call.
Patrons, who sneak from living worth to dead,
Withhold the pension, and set up the head;
Or vest dull flattery in the sacred gown;
Or give from fool to fool the laurel crown.
And (last and worst) with all the cant of wit,
Without the soul, the muse's hypocrite. 100
    There marched the bard and blockhead, side by
        side,
Who rhymed for hire, and patronized for pride.
Narcissus, praised with all a parson's power,
Looked a white lily sunk beneath a shower.
There moved Montalto with superior air;
His stretched-out arm displayed a volume fair;
Courtiers and patriots in two ranks divide,

Through both he passed, and bowed from side to
    side:
But as in graceful act, with awful eye
Composed he stood, bold Benson thrust him by: 110
On two unequal crutches propped he came,
Milton's on this, on that one Johnston's name.
The decent knight retired with sober rage,
Withdrew his hand, and closed the pompous page.

    *   *   *   *   *   *
    *   *   *   *   *   *
    *   *   *   *   *   *
    *   *   *   *   *   *

    When Dulness, smiling—'Thus revive the wits!
But murder first, and mince them all to bits;   120
As erst Medea (cruel, so to save!)
A new edition of old Aeson gave,
Let standard-authors, thus, like trophies born,
Appear more glorious as more hacked and torn,
And you, my critics! in the chequered shade,
Admire new light through holes yourselves have made.
    Leave not a foot of verse, a foot of stone,
A page, a grave, that they can call their own;
But spread, my sons, your glory thin or thick,
On passive paper, or on solid brick.   130
So by each bard an alderman shall sit,
A heavy lord shall hang at every wit,
And while on Fame's triumphal car they ride,
Some slave of mine be pinioned to their side.'
    Now crowds on crowds around the Goddess press,
Each eager to present the first address.
Dunce scorning dunce beholds the next advance,
But fop shows fop superior complaisance.
When lo! a spectre rose, whose index-hand
Held forth the virtue of the dreadful wand;   140
His beavered brow a birchen garland wears,
Dropping with infant's blood, and mother's tears.
O'er every vein a shuddering horror runs;
Eton and Winton shake through all their sons.
All flesh is humbled, Westminster's bold race

Shrink, and confess the genius of the place:
The pale boy-senator yet tingling stands,
And holds his breeches close with both his hands.
    Then thus: 'Since man from beast by words is
        known,
Words are man's province, words we teach alone.   150
When reason doubtful, like the Samian letter,
Points him two ways, the narrower is the better.
Placed at the door of learning, youth to guide,
We never suffer it to stand too wide.
To ask, to guess, to know, as they commence,
As fancy opens the quick springs of sense,
We ply the memory, we load the brain,
Bind rebel wit, and double chain on chain,
Confine the thought, to exercise the breath;
And keep them in the pale of words till death.   160
Whate'er the talents, or howe'er designed,
We hang one jingling padlock on the mind:
A poet the first day, he dips his quill;
And what the last? a very poet still.
Pity! the charm works only in our wall,
Lost, lost too soon in yonder house or hall.
There truant WYNDHAM every muse gave o'er,
There TALBOT sunk, and was a wit no more!
How sweet an Ovid, MURRAY was our boast!
How many Martials were in PULTENEY lost!   170
Else sure some bard, to our eternal praise,
In twice ten thousand rhyming nights and days,
Had reached the work, the all that mortal can;
And south beheld that masterpiece of man.'
    'Oh,' cried the Goddess, 'for some pedant
        reign!
Some gentle JAMES, to bless the land again;
To stick the doctor's chair into the throne,
Give law to words, or war with words alone,
Senates and courts with Greek and Latin rule,
And turn the council to a grammar school!   180
For sure, if Dulness sees a grateful day,
'Tis in the shade of arbitrary sway.
O! if my sons may learn one earthly thing,
Teach but that one, sufficient for a king;

That which my priests, and mine alone, maintain,
Which as it dies, or lives, we fall, or reign:
May you, may Cam, and Isis preach it long!
The RIGHT DIVINE of kings to govern wrong.'
   Prompt at the call, around the Goddess roll
Broad hats, and hoods, and caps, a sable shoal: 190
Thick and more thick the black blockade extends,
A hundred head of Aristotle's friends.
Nor wert thou, Isis! wanting to the day,
[Though Christ Church long kept prudishly away.]
Each staunch polemic, stubborn as a rock,
Each fierce logician, still expelling Locke,
Came whip and spur, and dashed through thin and
    thick
On German Crousaz, and Dutch Burgersdyck.
As many quit the streams that murmuring fall
To lull the sons of Margaret and Clare Hall,   200
Where Bentley late tempestuous wont to sport
In troubled waters, but now sleeps in port.
Before them marched that awful aristarch;
Ploughed was his front with many a deep remark:
His hat, which never vailed to human pride,
Walker with reverence took, and laid aside.
Low bowed the rest: he, kingly, did but nod;
So upright Quakers please both man and God.
'Mistress! dismiss that rabble from your throne:
Avaunt——is Aristarchus yet unknown?   210
Thy mighty scholiast, whose unwearied pains
Made Horace dull, and humbled Milton's strains.
Turn what they will to verse, their toil is vain,
Critics like me shall make it prose again.
Roman and Greek grammarians! know your better:
Author of something yet more great than letter;
While towering o'er your alphabet, like Saul,
Stands our digamma, and o'ertops them all.
'Tis true, on words is still our whole debate,
Disputes of *me* or *te*, of *aut* or *at*,   220
To sound or sink in *cano*, O or A,
Or give up Cicero to C or K.
Let Freind affect to speak as Terence spoke,
And Alsop never but like Horace joke:

For me, what Virgil, Pliny may deny,
Manilius or Solinus shall supply:
For Attic phrase in Plato let them seek,
I poach in Suidas for unlicensed Greek.
In ancient sense if any needs will deal,
Be sure I give them fragments, not a meal;   230
What Gellius or Stobaeus hashed before,
Or chewed by blind old scholiasts o'er and o'er.
The critic eye, that microscope of wit,
Sees hairs and pores, examines bit by bit:
How parts relate to parts, or they to whole,
The body's harmony, the beaming soul,
Are things which Kuster, Burman, Wasse shall see,
When man's whole frame is obvious to a *flea*.
    Ah, think not, mistress! more true Dulness lies
In folly's cap, than wisdom's grave disguise.   240
Like buoys, that never sink into the flood,
On learning's surface we but lie and nod.
Thine is the genuine head of many a house,
And much divinity without a *Νοῦς*.
Nor could a BARROW work on every block,
Nor has one ATTERBURY spoiled the flock.
See! still thy own, the heavy canon roll,
And metaphysic smokes involve the pole.
For thee we dim the eyes, and stuff the head
With all such reading as was never read: 250
For thee explain a thing till all men doubt it,
And write about it, Goddess, and about it:
So spins the silk-worm small its slender store,
And labours till it clouds itself all o'er.
    What though we let some better sort of fool
Thrid every science, run through every school?
Never by tumbler through the hoops was shown
Such skill in passing all, and touching none.
He may indeed (if sober all this time)
Plague with dispute, or persecute with rhyme.   260
We only furnish what he cannot use,
Or wed to what he must divorce, a muse:
Full in the midst of Euclid dip at once,
And petrify a genius to a dunce:
Or set on metaphysic ground to prance,

Show all his paces, not a step advance.
With the same cement, ever sure to bind,
We bring to one dead level every mind.
Then take him to develop, if you can,
And hew the block off, and get out the man.   270
But wherefore waste I words? I see advance
Whore, pupil, and laced governor from France.
Walker! our hat'——nor more he deigned to say,
But, stern as Ajax' spectre, strode away.
      In flowed at once a gay embroidered race,
And tittering pushed the pedants off the place:
Some would have spoken, but the voice was drowned
By the French horn, or by the opening hound.
The first came forwards, with as easy mien,
As if he saw St James's and the Queen.   280
When thus th'attendant orator begun:
'Receive, great Empress! thy accomplished son:
Thine from the birth, and sacred from the rod,
A dauntless infant! never scared with God.
The sire saw, one by one, his virtues wake:
The mother begged the blessing of a rake.
Thou gavest that ripeness, which so soon began,
And ceased so soon, he ne'er was boy, nor man.
Through school and college, thy kind cloud o'ercast,
Safe and unseen the young Aeneas passed: 290
Thence bursting glorious, all at once let down,
Stunned with his giddy larum half the town.
Intrepid then, o'er seas and lands he flew:
Europe he saw, and Europe saw him too.
There all thy gifts and graces we display,
Thou, only thou, directing all our way!
To where the Seine, obsequious as she runs,
Pours at great Bourbon's feet her silken sons;
Or Tiber, now no longer Roman, rolls,
Vain of Italian arts, Italian souls: 300
To happy convents, bosomed deep in vines,
Where slumber abbots, purple as their wines:
To isles of fragrance, lily-silvered vales,
Diffusing languor in the panting gales:
To lands of singing, or of dancing slaves,
Love-whispering woods, and lute-resounding waves.

But chief her shrine where naked Venus keeps,
And Cupids ride the lion of the deeps;
Where, eased of fleets, the Adriatic main
Wafts the smooth eunuch and enamoured swain.   310
Led by my hand, he sauntered Europe round,
And gathered every vice on Christian ground;
Saw every court, heard every king declare
His royal sense, of operas or the fair;
The stews and palace equally explored,
Intrigued with glory, and with spirit whored;
Tried all *hors d'oeuvres*, all *liqueurs* defined,
Judicious drank, and greatly daring dined;
Dropped the dull lumber of the Latin store,
Spoiled his own language, and acquired no more;   320
All classic learning lost on classic ground;
And last turned *air*, the echo of a sound!
See now, half-cured, and perfectly well-bred,
With nothing but a solo in his head;
As much estate, and principle, and wit,
As Jansen, Fleetwood, Cibber shall think fit;
Stolen from a duel, followed by a nun,
And, if a borough choose him, not undone;
See, to my country happy I restore
This glorious youth, and add one Venus more.   330
Her too receive (for her my soul adores)
So may the sons of sons of sons of whores,
Prop thine, O Empress! like each neighbour throne,
And make a long posterity thy own.'
    Pleased, she accepts the hero, and the dame,
Wraps in her veil, and frees from sense of shame.
    Then looked, and saw a lazy, lolling sort,
Unseen at church, at senate, or at court,
Of ever-listless loiterers, that attend
No cause, no trust, no duty, and no friend.   340
Thee too, my Paridel! she marked thee there,
Stretched on the rack of a too easy chair,
And heard thy everlasting yawn confess
The pains and penalties of idleness.
She pitied! but her pity only shed
Benigner influence on thy nodding head.
    But Annius, crafty seer, with ebon wand,

And well dissembled emerald on his hand,
False as his gems, and cankered as his coins,
Came, crammed with capon, from where Pollio
    dines.   350
Soft, as the wily fox is seen to creep,
Where bask on sunny banks the simple sheep,
Walk round and round, now prying here, now there;
So he; but pious, whispered first his prayer.
  'Grant, gracious Goddess! grant me still to cheat,
O may thy cloud still cover the deceit!
Thy choicer mists on this assembly shed,
But pour them thickest on the noble head.
So shall each youth, assisted by our eyes,
See other Caesars, other Homers rise;   360
Through twilight ages hunt th' Athenian fowl,
Which Chalcis gods, and mortals call an owl,
Now see an Attys, now a Cecrops clear,
Nay, Mahomet! the pigeon at thine ear;
Be rich in ancient brass, though not in gold,
And keep his Lares, though his house be sold;
To headless Phoebe his fair bride postpone,
Honour a Syrian prince above his own;
Lord of an Otho, if I vouch it true;
Blessed in one Niger, till he knows of two.'   370
  Mummius o'erheard him; Mummius, fool-
    renowned,
Who like his Cheops stinks above the ground,
Fierce as a startled adder, swelled, and said,
Rattling an ancient sistrum at his head:
  'Speakst thou of Syrian princes? Traitor base!
Mine, Goddess! mine is all the hornèd race.
True, he had wit, to make their value rise;
From foolish Greeks to steal them, was as wise;
More glorious yet, from barbarous hands to keep,
When Sallee rovers chased him on the deep.   380
Then taught by Hermes, and divinely bold,
Down his own throat he risked the Grecian gold;
Received each demigod, with pious care,
Deep in his entrails—I revered them there,
I bought them, shrouded in that living shrine,
And, at their second birth, they issue mine.'

'Witness great Ammon! by whose horns I swore,'
Replied soft Annius, 'this our paunch before
Still bears them, faithful; and that thus I eat,
Is to refund the medals with the meat.   390
To prove me, Goddess! clear of all design,
Bid me with Pollio sup, as well as dine:
There all the learned shall at the labour stand,
And Douglas lend his soft, obstetric hand.'
    The Goddess smiling seemed to give consent;
So back to Pollio, hand in hand, they went.
    Then thick as locusts blackening all the ground,
A tribe, with weeds and shells fantastic crowned,
Each with some wondrous gift approached the power,
A nest, a toad, a fungus, or a flower.   400
But far the foremost, two, with earnest zeal,
And aspect ardent to the throne appeal.
    The first thus opened: 'Hear thy suppliant's call,
Great Queen, and common Mother of us all!
Fair from its humble bed I reared this flower,
Suckled, and cheered, with air, and sun, and shower,
Soft on the paper ruff its leaves I spread,
Bright with the gilded button tipped its head,
Then throned in glass, and named it CAROLINE:
Each maid cried, 'Charming!' and each youth,
        'Divine!'   410
Did nature's pencil ever blend such rays,
Such varied light in one promiscuous blaze?
Now prostrate! dead! behold that Caroline:
No maid cries, 'Charming!' and no youth, 'Divine!'
And lo the wretch! whose vile, whose insect lust
Laid this gay daughter of the spring in dust.
Oh punish him, or to th' Elysian shades
Dismiss my soul, where no carnation fades.'
    He ceased, and wept. With innocence of mien,
Th' accused stood forth, and thus addressed the
        Queen: 420
'Of all th' enamelled race, whose silvery wing
Waves to the tepid zephyrs of the spring,
Or swims along the fluid atmosphere,
Once brightest shined this child of heat and air.
I saw, and started from its vernal bower

The rising game, and chased from flower to flower.
It fled, I followed; now in hope, now pain;
It stopped, I stopped; it moved, I moved again.
At last it fixed, 'twas on what plant it pleased,
And where it fixed, the beauteous bird I seized: 430
Rose or carnation was below my care;
I meddle, Goddess! only in my sphere.
I tell the naked fact without disguise,
And, to excuse it, need but show the prize;
Whose spoils this paper offers to your eye,
Fair ev'n in death! this peerless *butterfly*.'
     'My sons!', she answered, 'both have done your
          parts:
Live happy both, and long promote our arts.
But hear a mother, when she recommends
To your fraternal care, our sleeping friends.   440
The common soul, of heaven's more frugal make,
Serves but to keep fools pert, and knaves awake:
A drowsy watchman, that just gives a knock,
And breaks our rest, to tell us what's o'clock.
Yet by some object every brain is stirred;
The dull may waken to a humming-bird;
The most recluse, discreetly opened, find
Congenial matter in the cockle-kind;
The mind, in metaphysics at a loss,
May wander in a wilderness of moss;   450
The head that turns at super-lunar things,
Poised with a tail, may steer on Wilkins' wings.
     O! would the sons of men once think their eyes
And reason given them but to study *flies!*
See nature in some partial narrow shape,
And let the author of the whole escape:
Learn but to trifle; or, who most observe,
To wonder at their maker, not to serve.'
     'Be that my task,' replies a gloomy clerk,
Sworn foe to mystery, yet divinely dark;   460
Whose pious hope aspires to see the day
When moral evidence shall quite decay,
And damns implicit faith, and holy lies,
Prompt to impose, and fond to dogmatize:
'Let others creep by timid steps, and slow,

On plain experience lay foundations low,
By common sense to common knowledge bred,
And last, to nature's cause through nature led.
All-seeing in thy mists, we want no guide,
Mother of arrogance, and source of pride!   470
We nobly take the high *priori* road,
And reason downward, till we doubt of God:
Make nature still encroach upon his plan:
And shove him off as far as e'er we can:
Thrust some mechanic cause into his place;
Or bind in matter, or diffuse in space.
Or, at one bound o'er-leaping all his laws,
Make God man's image, man the final cause,
Find virtue local, all relation scorn,
See all in *self*, and but for self be born: 480
Of nought so certain as our *reason* still,
Of nought so doubtful as of *soul* and *will*.
Oh hide the God still more! and make us see
Such as Lucretius drew, a God like thee:
Wrapped up in self, a God without a thought,
Regardless of our merit or default.
Or that bright image to our fancy draw,
Which Theocles in raptured vision saw,
While through poetic scenes the genius roves,
Or wanders wild in academic groves;   490
That NATURE our society adores,
Where Tindal dictates, and Silenus snores.'
    Roused at his name, up rose the boozy sire,
And shook from out his pipe the seeds of fire;
Then snapped his box, and stroked his belly down:
Rosy and reverend, though without a gown.
Bland and familiar to the throne he came,
Led up the youth, and called the Goddess *Dame*.
Then thus: 'From priestcraft happily set free,
Lo! every finished son returns to thee: 500
First slave to words, then vassal to a name,
Then dupe to party; child and man the same;
Bounded by nature, narrowed still by art,
A trifling head, and a contracted heart.
Thus bred, thus taught, how many have I seen,
Smiling on all, and smiled on by a queen.

Marked out for honours, honoured for their birth,
To thee the most rebellious things on earth:
Now to thy gentle shadow all are shrunk,
All melted down, in pension, or in punk!   510
So Kent, so Berkeley sneaked into the grave,
A monarch's half, and half a harlot's slave.
Poor Warwick nipped in folly's broadest bloom,
Who praises now? his chaplain on his tomb.
Then take them all, oh take them to thy breast!
Thy *Magus*, Goddess! shall perform the rest.'

    With that, a WIZARD OLD his *cup* extends;
Which whoso tastes, forgets his former friends,
Sire, ancestors, himself. One casts his eyes
Up to a *star*, and like Endymion dies: 520
A *feather* shooting from another's head,
Extracts his brain, and principle is fled,
Lost is his God, his country, everything;
And nothing left but homage to a king!
The vulgar herd turn off to roll with hogs,
To run with horses, or to hunt with dogs;
But, sad example! never to escape
Their infamy, still keep the human shape.

    But she, good Goddess, sent to every child
Firm impudence, or stupefaction mild;   530
And straight succeeded, leaving shame no room,
Cibberian forehead, or Cimmerian gloom.

    Kind self-conceit to some her glass applies,
Which no one looks in with another's eyes:
But as the flatterer or dependant paint,
Beholds himself a patriot, chief, or saint.

    On others interest her gay livery flings,
Interest, that waves on party-coloured wings:
Turned to the sun, she casts a thousand dyes,
And, as she turns, the colours fall or rise.   540

    Others the siren sisters warble round,
And empty heads console with empty sound.
No more, alas! the voice of Fame they hear,
The balm of Dulness trickling in their ear.
Great Cowper, Harcourt, Parker, Raymond, King,
Why all your toils? your sons have learned to sing.
How quick ambition hastes to ridicule!

The sire is made a peer, the son a fool.
   On some, a priest succinct in amice white
Attends; all flesh is nothing in his sight!   550
Beeves, at his touch, at once to jelly turn,
And the huge boar is shrunk into an urn:
The board with specious miracles he loads,
Turns hares to larks, and pigeons into toads.
Another (for in all what one can shine?)
Explains the *Sève* and *Verdeur* of the vine.
What cannot copious sacrifice atone?
Thy truffles, Perigord! thy hams, Bayonne!
With French libation, and Italian strain,
Wash Bladen white, and expiate Hays's stain.   560
Knight lifts the head, for what are crowds undone
To three essential partridges in one?
Gone every blush, and silent all reproach,
Contending princes mount them in their coach.
   Next bidding all draw near on bended knees,
The Queen confers her *titles* and *degrees*.
Her children first of more distinguished sort,
Who study Shakespeare at the Inns of Court,
Impale a glowworm, or vertù profess,
Shine in the dignity of F. R. S.   570
Some, deep freemasons, join the silent race
Worthy to fill Pythagoras's place:
Some botanists, or florists at the least,
Or issue members of an annual feast.
Nor passed the meanest unregarded, one
Rose a Gregorian, one a Gormogon.
The last, not least in honour or applause,
Isis and Cam made doctors of her laws.
   Then blessing all, 'Go children of my care!
To practice now from theory repair.   580
All my commands are easy, short, and full:
My sons! be proud, be selfish, and be dull.
Guard my prerogative, assert my throne:
This nod confirms each privilege your own.
The cap and switch be sacred to his Grace;
With staff and pumps the Marquis lead the race;
From stage to stage the licensed Earl may run,
Paired with his fellow-charioteer the sun;

The learned baron butterflies design,
Or draw to silk Arachne's subtle line;   590
The judge to dance his brother sergeant call;
The senator at cricket urge the ball;
The bishop stow (pontific luxury!)
An hundred souls of turkeys in a pie;
The sturdy squire to Gallic masters stoop,
And drown his lands and manors in a soup.
Others import yet nobler arts from France,
Teach kings to fiddle, and make senates dance.
Perhaps more high some daring son may soar,
Proud to my list to add one monarch more;   600
And nobly conscious, princes are but things
Born for first ministers, as slaves for kings,
Tyrant supreme! shall three estates command,
And MAKE ONE MIGHTY DUNCIAD OF THE LAND!'
    More she had spoke, but yawned—all nature
        nods:
What mortal can resist the yawn of gods?
Churches and chapels instantly it reached;
(St James's first, for leaden Gilbert preached)
Then catched the schools; the Hall scarce kept
        awake;
The Convocation gaped, but could not speak: 610
Lost was the nation's sense, nor could be found,
While the long solemn unison went round:
Wide, and more wide, it spread o'er all the realm;
Ev'n Palinurus nodded at the helm:
The vapour mild o'er each committee crept;
Unfinished treaties in each office slept;
And chiefless armies dozed out the campaign;
And navies yawned for orders on the main.
    O Muse! relate (for you can tell alone,
Wits have short memories, and dunces none)   620
Relate, who first, who last resigned to rest;
Whose heads she partly, whose completely blessed;
What charms could faction, what ambition lull,
The venal quiet, and entrance the dull;
Till drowned was sense, and shame, and right, and
        wrong—
O sing, and hush the nations with thy song!

*   *   *   *   *   *

In vain, in vain,—the all-composing hour
Resistless falls: the Muse obeys the power.
She comes! she comes! the sable throne behold
Of *Night* primeval, and of *Chaos* old!   630
Before her, Fancy's gilded clouds decay,
And all its varying rainbows die away.
Wit shoots in vain its momentary fires,
The meteor drops, and in a flash expires.
As one by one, at dread Medea's strain,
The sickening stars fade off th'ethereal plain;
As Argus' eyes by Hermes' wand oppressed,
Closed one by one to everlasting rest;
Thus at her felt approach, and secret might,
Art after Art goes out, and all is Night.   640
See skulking Truth to her old cavern fled,
Mountains of casuistry heaped o'er her head!
Philosophy, that leaned on heaven before,
Shrinks to her second cause, and is no more.
Physic of Metaphysic begs defence,
And Metaphysic calls for aid on Sense!
See Mystery to Mathematics fly!
In vain! they gaze, turn giddy, rave, and die.
Religion blushing veils her sacred fires,
And unawares Morality expires.   650
Nor *public* flame, nor *private*, dares to shine;
Nor *human* spark is left, nor glimpse *divine!*
Lo! thy dread empire, CHAOS! is restored;
Light dies before thy uncreating word:
Thy hand, great Anarch! lets the curtain fall;
And universal darkness buries all.

FINIS

Notes

Severe discipline has had to be exercised in an attempt to keep these notes
as short as possible. In particular: (1) A few persons are omitted who are
mentioned briefly in poems packed with names such as *The Dunciad*. Many
of these can be found in works of biographical reference: others will be
found in the biographical appendix to volumes of *TE*, e.g. v. 341–92. (2)
Biographic facts are supplied only where the text of the poem fails to make
complete sense without such information. (3) Straightforward references
to stock mythology, e.g. to Orpheus and his lyre, are not explained. (4)
Allusions to earlier poets, classical and native, are indicated where only a
strong local point is made, e.g. by heavy parody. Similarly, cross-references
to Pope's own poetry are not routinely signalized. Only minimal information
is given on bibliographical matters: the date of composition (where known)
and first publication are recorded. For fuller discussion of editorial prin-
ciples and choices, see the Introduction, pp. xix–xx.

ABBREVIATIONS

DNB	*Dictionary of National Biography*
Johnson	Samuel Johnson, *A Dictionary of the English Language* (1755)
OED	*Oxford English Dictionary*
P	Alexander Pope
TE	The Twickenham Edition of *The Poems of Alexander Pope*, ed. John Butt *et al.* (11 vols.; 1939–69)

1 *An Essay on Criticism.* Published in 1711; P gave different dates for
the year of composition, but in print generally stuck to 1709. Horace
was a prime model for the *Essay* although P also recalled Boileau's
Art poétique (1674) and English verse treatises of the Restoration era.
More generally he is indebted to a host of critics both ancient and
modern, ranging from Quintilian and Longinus to Dryden and the
recent French authorities such as Rapin and Le Bossu. P's aim lay
not so much in novelty of ideas as in the sparkle, compression, and
literary energy of their embodiment in poetry.

The three-part structure, as set out in a table of contents, was not
explicitly indicated until 1736. However, the broad pattern had been
clear all along: ll. 1–200 work towards establishing the primacy of the
ancients, most directly stated in ll. 181–200; ll. 201–559 anatomize
the faults of the moderns, whilst ll. 560–744 set out a programme of
reform and offer a brief history of criticism (one of the first attempted
at this level of discrimination). Underlying the various stages of the

argument are the disputes over artistic achievement, history, and the possibility of human progress which collectively made up the international 'battle of the books' or grand *querelle*, which had been raging for almost twenty years.

1 *Horace. Epistles*, vi. 67–8: 'If you know any more correct rules than these, share them frankly with me; if not, use these as I do.'

ll. 13–14. *Both must . . . write*. Playing with the tag *poeta nascitur, non fit*.

l. 26. *schools*. Academic pedantry.

ll. 27–8. *And some . . . sense*. Three crucial concepts are introduced, with the rich and complex words *wit* (intelligence, literary skill, inventiveness, creative zest); *nature* (order, universally accepted principles, the actual state of the world, but also innate reality, the unmediated truth of things); and *sense* (judgement, taste, good humour, and a feeling for proportion).

2 l. 34. *Maevius*. The proverbial type of an untalented poetaster, deriving his name from a real writer mentioned by Virgil and Horace.
in Apollo's spite. In contempt of the rules of good writing prescribed by the god of poetry, Apollo.

l. 43. *equivocal*. Spontaneous, because insects (which then included frogs and snakes) were believed to be hatched along the flooded banks of the Nile. The word also suggests 'of nondescript status' and 'of dubious parentage'.

l. 44. *tell*. Count.

l. 61. *art*. The realm of learning.

l. 67. *stoop*. Condescend to apply oneself to.

l. 69. *still*. Always.

3 l. 76. *informing*. Animating.

l. 77. *spirits*. Subtle fluids permeating the body through the bloodstream and directing the key functions of life (the old psychological explanation of human personality).

l. 84. *the Muse's steed*. Pegasus, the winged horse.

l. 86. *generous*. Mettlesome.

ll. 108–11. *So modern . . . fools*. Referring to the controversy surrounding the proposal for a public dispensary which underlay a famous mock-heroic poem, *The Dispensary* (1699) by P's friend Samuel Garth.

l. 109. *bills*. Prescriptions, but punning on modern sense of 'charges'.

4 l. 115. *receipts*. Recipes.

l. 120. *fable*. Plot.

l. 123. In a note P quoted some lines identifying Zoilus (the ancient critic who had been most severe on Homer) with Charles Perrault, who had opened up the campaign of the moderns with strictures on the most revered ancient, Homer (see headnote).

l. 129. *comment.* Commentary.　　*Mantuan Muse.* Virgil.

l. 130. *young Maro.* Virgil (P. Virgilius Maro).

l. 138. *the Stagyrite.* Aristotle (from his birthplace, Stagira in Macedonia).

l. 141. *declare.* Make clear.

l. 142. *happiness.* Spontaneous felicity or grace.

5　l. 168. *seizes.* Takes possession of (as by a legal order).

l. 170. *faults.* Pronounced 'fawtes' in P's day and thus a good rhyme.

ll. 183-4. *Secure . . . age.* The flames are those of fires such as that which destroyed the library of Alexandria; the envy that of malevolent critics like Zoilus; the wars those mounted by invading barbarians; and the age means 'the long reign of ignorance and superstition in the cloisters'.

l. 186. *consenting.* In concord.

l. 187. *joined.* 'Jined' was then the pronunciation.

6　l. 206. *recruits.* Supplies.

l. 208. *wants.* Is deficient.

l. 216. *Pierian spring.* A spring sacred to the muses, who were called the Pierides from a district on the slopes of Mt Olympus.

l. 220. *tempt.* Attempt.

l. 224. *science.* Knowledge.

7　ll. 247-8. *Thus when . . . Rome.* Referring to the cupola of St Peter's, Rome.

l. 261. *verbal critic.* Pedant, esp. of a philological cast, who concentrates on the textual letter rather than the spirit.

ll. 267-84. The story derives from a spurious continuation to *Don Quixote*, which had recently been translated into English.

l. 270. *Dennis.* John Dennis (1657-1734) is named on account of his pronounced emphasis on 'regularity' in dramatic composition. This was the start of a prolonged quarrel between P and Dennis.

l. 273. *nice.* Fastidious.

8　l. 276. *unities.* The prescribed limitations of time and place in the action of a play.

ll. 289-96. *Some . . . of art.* Aimed at the then unfashionable metaphysicals and other baroque writers of the seventeenth century.

l. 308. *upon content*. Without question.

9   l. 321. *clown*. Yokel.

l. 323. *court*. The appropriate forms to the three settings are respectively pastoral, satire, and epic.

l. 337. *numbers*. Versification.

l. 345. *open vowels*. A hiatus caused in this line by *though/oft, the/ear, the/open*.

10   l. 357. *length along*. Itself an Alexandrine or twelve-syllable line.

l. 361. *strength*. Represented by the work of Sir John Denham (1615–69) and suggesting forceful, concise language.   *sweetness*. Belongs to Edmund Waller (1606–87), equally renowned for the highly flavoured diction and skilful use of ornament in his verse.

l. 372. *Camilla*. A Volscian maiden warrior who figures in the *Aeneid*.

l. 374. *Timotheus*. A poet and musician from the Ionian city of Miletus (447–357 BC).

l. 376. *Libyan Jove*. Alexander the Great visited the oracle of Ammon at an oasis in the Libyan desert in 331 BC and was proclaimed the son of God.

l. 390. *turn*. A piece of embellished language, or a specially worked phrase.

11   l. 398. *blessing*. Recalling Matt. 5: 45: 'He maketh his sun to rise on the evil and the good.'

l. 400. *sublimes*. Either 'exalts' or synonymous with 'ripens' in l. 401.

l. 415. *quality*. Social eminence.

l. 419. *sonneteer*. A writer of trifles.

l. 428. *schismatics*. Stress on first syllable.

12   l. 440. *school-divines*. Scholastic theologians.

l. 441. *sentences*. Theological maxims.

l. 444. *Scotists and Thomists*. Referring to disputes between the thirteenth-century founders of distinct religious philosophies, Duns Scotus and St Thomas Aquinas.

l. 445 note. A frequent metonym in Augustan satire for the book trade and for unwanted literature.

l. 454. *fondly*. Foolishly.

l. 459. *parsons, critics, beaux*. Parsons such as Jeremy Collier, who assailed Dryden's 'immorality'; critics such as Gerald Langbaine, who disparaged his plays; and beaux such as George Villiers, Duke of Buckingham, who satirized him in *The Rehearsal*.

l. 463. *Milbournes*. Sir Richard Blackmore and Revd Luke Milbourne, who had criticized respectively Dryden's pretensions to wit and his abilities as a translator.

l. 465. *Zoilus*. Greek grammarian of the fourth century BC, who had filled nine books with animadversions on Homer, and had become the type of the carping critic.

14 l. 521. *sacred*. Accursed (Lat. *sacer*).

l. 536. *monarch*. Charles II.

l. 541. *mask*. A woman who wore a mask at the theatre, often suggesting a prostitute.

l. 544. *a foreign reign*. That of William III.

l. 545. *Socinus*. The founder of what came in England to take the form of Unitarianism, i.e. the rejection of the Trinity and denial of the divinity of Christ. Lelio Sozzini (1525–62) was an Italian theologian.

l. 552. *wit's Titans*. Deists, rebels against the truths of the Church.

l. 553. *licensed blasphemies*. The lapse of the Licensing Act in 1695 led to the appearance of heterodox works which would formerly have been censored.

15 l. 563. *candour*. Kindliness.

l. 580. *complacence*. Anxiety to please.

l. 585. *Appius*. Certainly intended to point to John Dennis, who had written an unsuccessful tragedy called *Appius and Virginia* (1709). Dennis was famous for his glaring gaze and for his fondness for the word 'tremendous'.

l. 591. *degrees*. These were freely bestowed by the two English universities on peers without any academic requirements.

16 l. 592. *satires*. Pronounced 'sate-ers'.

l. 601. *tops*. 'A top sleeps when it moves with such velocity . . . that its motion is imperceptible' (*OED*).

l. 617. *Durfey*. Thomas Durfey, a popular miscellaneous writer. (1653–1723).

l. 623. *Paul's church yard*. A headquarters of the book trade; all kinds of business meetings and stray assignations were held within the cathedral itself.

17 l. 648. *Maeonian Star*. Homer, whose birthplace was sometimes given as Lydia or Maeonia; hence his sobriquet Maeonides.

l. 665. *Dionysius*. Dionysius of Halicarnassus, a Greek critic who lived in Rome at the time of Augustus.

l. 667. *Petronius*. Petronius Arbiter (d. AD 65), Roman author of the *Satyricon*, noted for his polished manners and good taste.

18 l. 669. *Quintilian*. M. Fabius Quintilianus (*c.* AD 35–*c.*95), author of *Institutio Oratoria*, the major textbook of ancient rhetoric.

l. 675. *Longinus*. The hugely influential author of a treatise on the sublime, a Greek work of unknown date and origin.

l. 684. *her eagles*. The Roman standards in battle.

l. 686. *Rome*. Pronounced to rhyme with *doom*.

l. 693. *injured name*. P refers to the criticism Erasmus had received from his fellow members of the Roman Catholic Church.

l. 697. *Leo's golden days*. The high point of the Renaissance was thought to have been reached under Pope Leo X, who reigned 1513–21.

l. 705 note. The Renaissance Latin poet Vida had written an art of poetry which was one of P's models for the *Essay*.

20 *Windsor Forest*. First published in 1713. The work existed in one shape or form by 1707, and most of the second section (beginning at l. 290) probably dates from 1712. It foreshadows the Peace of Utrecht, ending the long Marlborough wars, which was signed on 11 Apr. 1713. But revision had started earlier and seemingly went on up to the time of publication. Even after this there were significant alterations introduced.

The work belongs to a tradition of topographical poetry using local detail to encode historical, political, and moral issues. The classic exemplar is Denham's *Cooper's Hill* (1642), whose setting is in fact very close to that of P's poem. A pervasive Georgic strain reminds us that P had moved from his *Pastorals* as Virgil had gone on from *Eclogues* to *Georgics*. Echoes of Spenser, Drayton, Milton, and William Camden are among the more noticeable strands of allusion. The work embraces 'the matter of England', and its political celebration of a Tory peace draws on many elements of traditional patriotic and celebratory verse.

Lansdowne. George Granville, Lord Lansdowne (1667–1735), a poet, a member of the Tory ministry, and a supporter of P for several years.

Virgil. Eclogues, vi. 9–12: 'My song is no self-appointed task; all the grove of our tamarisk shrubs shall sing of you, Varus, nor is any page more agreeable to Apollo than that which is heralded by the name of Varus.' The tamarisk was sacred to Apollo.

l. 1. *Windsor*. P had grown up at Binfield, in Windsor Forest, about ten miles from the town of Windsor. The castle had first been sited there by William I. The Order of the Garter had first been instituted by Edward III at Windsor on St George's Day in 1349, and the castle was remodelled under the supervision of William of Wykeham, to serve as a meeting-place for knights of the order.

l. 5. *Granville*. Lord Lansdowne (see note to dedication).

ll. 7–10. *The groves . . . fame*. Referring explicitly to the re-creation of Eden by Milton in *Paradise Lost*, Books IV–V, esp.

21 l. 14. *harmoniously confused*. Opening up the theme of *discors concordia*, a concept derived from Ovid, *Metamorphoses*, i. 433.

l. 21. *lawns*. Clearings.

l. 26. *desert*. 'Formerly applied . . . to any wild, uninhabited region, including forest' (*OED*).

l. 27. *tufted trees*. Trees in small clumps.

l. 31. *borne*. Referring to the oak-built ships which carried rich spices and other goods from the East, providing the foundations of Britain's overseas empire.

l. 37. *Pomona*. Goddess of fruits. (Pan is here the god of shepherds and flocks.)

l. 38. *enamelled ground*. Referring to the practice of enamelling a base coat on metals as a background for painting.

l. 42. *a Stuart*. Queen Anne, who was to die within a year from the appearance of the poem. As early as this, P is relating the beauties of Windsor to the harmonious arrangement of politics under the last Stuart monarch, and linking the quiet prosperity of the district to the beneficent peace brought about by the Tory ministry. Lines 42–90 describe the creation of royal hunting-grounds by the Normans and the destruction of the local environment and community this involved. By association this is extended to the unpopular Dutch invader of more recent times, William III.

l. 45 note. The 'forest laws' covered areas specifically excluded from the common law and subject to particularly severe restrictions.

22 l. 61. *Nimrod*. The 'mighty hunter' (Gen. 10: 9), who had come to be regarded as the type of a tyrant.

l. 65 note. P drew much of his materials on this from Camden's *Britannica*, which had been translated and re-edited in 1695, and was one of the key books of the age.

l. 66. *fanes*. Temples or shrines. P's imagination has leapt forward to the destruction of abbeys during the Reformation.

l. 71. *obscene*. Filthy, foul, disgusting.

ll. 79–80. *But see . . . a grave*. The burial of William I was delayed because a knight who held the patrimony of the chosen spot raised objections.

l. 81 note. Richard, the second son of William I, was killed by a stag whilst hunting in the New Forest.

23 ll. 83–4. *Lo Rufus . . . hart*. William II, nicknamed 'Rufus' was shot accidentally by Walter Tyrrel in 1100, once more during the chase in the New Forest. P recalls in this passage the death of William III in 1702, hastened if not caused by a hunting accident.

l. 90. *conscious*. Observing, witnessing.

ll. 91–2. *Fair Liberty . . . years*. Identifies liberty and prosperity with the rule of Anne.

ll. 93–4. *Ye vigorous . . . flood*. Refers to an abundance of healthy 'animal spirit', the forces which circulated in the blood, directing bodily exercise (as distinct from vital and natural spirits).

l. 101. *tainted*. 'Imbued with scent of an animal' (*OED*).

ll. 106–10. *When Albion . . . flies*. Recalling recent British military exploits, such as the capture of Gibraltar (1704).

24 l. 135. *genial*. Pleasantly warm, but also 'generative'.

l. 142. *Tyrian dye*. Crimson, as in the dye anciently made in Tyre (capital of Phoenicia).

l. 143. *volumes*. Coils of a serpent.

l. 147. *Fiery car*. Apollo's chariot, that is the sun, enters the constellation of Gemini around 21 May and then the constellation of the Crab around 22 June: thus midsummer begins under the astrological sign of Cancer.

l. 150. *opening*. 'Of hounds: [beginning] to cry when in pursuit of a scent' (*OED*).

l. 162. *a Queen*. P identifies Diana with Queen Anne.

25 l. 166. *Cynthus*. A mountain of the Ovidian *Metamorphoses*.

l. 176. *crescent*. i.e. the moon, Diana's emblem.   *zone*. girdle (epic diction).

l. 178. *fillet*. A headband or ribbon.

l. 186. *liquid*. Pure or transparent (Lat. *liquidus*).

26 l. 207 note. The Loddon flows into Thames not far from P's boyhood home at Binfield.

l. 221. *honours*. Adornments, that is leaves.

ll. 227–8. *Nor Po . . . strays*. The Eridanus, a river in classical mythology, was identified by Ovid with the Po; it is also the name of a constellation in the southern hemisphere whose shape was seen as that of a winding river.

27 l. 243. *exalts*. In alchemy, raises a substance to a higher power.

l. 244. *draws*. Extracts.

l. 246. *figured worlds*. As in a chart of the Zodiac.

l. 255. *kindred*. Possessing similar substance to that of the soul.

l. 257. *Scipio*. Scipio Africanus the elder (*c*.265–*c*.183 BC) retired to his estate in Campania after the successful outcome of the Second Punic War.

l. 258. *Atticus*. Pomponius Atticus (109–32 BC), the friend of Cicero, retired to Athens and held himself aloof from public events. Like Scipio, a type of the hero in retirement.

l. 264. *Cooper's Hill*. An eminence alongside the Thames near Egham, about five miles from Windsor, and celebrated in Denham's famous poem.

l. 272 note. The poet Abraham Cowley died at the Thames-side town of Chertsey in 1667.

ll. 273–4. *O early lost . . . led*. Cowley was only 49 at his death; his body was floated down the river by barge prior to his funeral at Westminster Abbey.

28 ll. 289–90. *To sing . . . star*. P suggests that his dedicatee Granville deserved to be made a knight of the Garter, just as he had recently been elevated to the peerage. The star refers to the insignia of the Garter.

l. 291 note. Surrey (*c*.1517–47) is mentioned specifically because of love poems supposed to have been written while he was imprisoned in Windsor Castle in 1537.

l. 297. *Geraldine*. Surrey's poetic mistress.

l. 298. *Myra*. The name Granville had used for his poetic mistress.

l. 300. *winding shore*. P follows the etymological hints of Camden's *Britannia*, where the name Windsor is derived from 'winding banks'.

l. 303 note. Edward III (b. 1312) had remodelled the castle and founded the Order of the Garter: see headnote. Other kings had either been born at Windsor or were buried there.

l. 305. *monarchs chained*. David II of Scotland and Jean le Bon of France, both held captive at Windsor during the reign of Edward III.   *Cressi*. The battle of Crécy in 1346, one of the major English victories in the Hundred Years War.

l. 306. *shield*. In 1340 Edward III 'assumed the title of king of France, and quartered the lilies of France with the leopards of France' (*DNB*). Another link in the chain of heraldic imagery and allusion.

l. 307. *Verrio's colours*. The Italian decorative artist Antonio Verrio (1639–1707) had been employed by Charles II to paint scenes of victories on the ceilings at Windsor.

l. 311. *Henry*. Henry VI, murdered near the end of the Wars of the Roses in 1471, and subsequently buried at Windsor, near to Edward IV, his adversary, who died in 1483 (see l. 314).

29 l. 316. *Belerium*. Land's End, in Cornwall.

ll. 319–20. *Make sacred . . . stone*. After his execution in 1649, Charles I had been buried at Windsor without ceremony.

l. 321. *fact*. Crime.

ll. 323–6. *She saw . . . scars*. P refers to the Great Plague in 1665, the Great Fire of 1666 consuming the 'domes' or buildings of London, and the struggles almost amounting to civil war in the reign of James II, culminating in the arrival of William III in 1689.   *dishonest*. Dishonourable.

l. 327. *Cease*. An allusion to the forthcoming Treaty of Utrecht, couched in the form of a parody of Gen. 1: 3.

ll. 329–54. There are many literary antecedents for this masque-like scene but the closest in many ways is an anonymous Latin poem, *De connubio*, which had been translated in Camden's *Britannia* (1695 edn.).

l. 332. Horns of a bull were a conventional attribute of river gods in iconography.

l. 336. *Augusta*. London (poetic).

l. 340. *Thame*. The marriage of the Thame and Isis to produce the infant Thames was a common poetic topos.

l. 343. *Cole*. The Colne, which flows south through the district west of London.

l. 345. *Vandalis*. The Wandle, which flows northwards through what is now south London.

l. 346. *gulphy*. Eddying.

l. 348. *blood*. Probably alluding to the battle of Otford (1016), which is mentioned by Camden in connection with the Darent.

30 l. 358. *Hermus*. A river in Lydia with sands, according to legend, covered in gold.

l. 359. *Nilus flows*. The Nile's seven mouths; its source was still unknown.

l. 363. *Volga's banks*. Referring to the course of the war between Charles XII of Sweden against Peter the Great of Russia; Charles had invaded Muscovy but had suffered defeat at Poltava in 1709.

l. 365. *Ganges*. Referring to Moghul wars in recent years.

l. 368. *Iber's sands*. The Ebro in Spain; P refers to the victories in the Iberian campaign in 1710.   *Ister*. The Danube. The reference is to Britain's greatest recent victory, at Blenheim in 1704.

l. 378 note. Queen Anne had promoted the building of fifty churches in London, but in the end no more than twelve were built.

l. 379. *two fair cities*. London and Westminster, situated on a sweeping bend in the Thames.

l. 380. *Whitehall*. Most of the historic Whitehall Palace had been burnt down in 1698. There were several plans for restoration, never implemented.

ll. 381–422. Pervasively drawing on Isa. 60.

l. 384. *once more*. As in the time of Elizabeth I.

l. 387. *her cross*. The red cross of St George: a possible Rosicrucian strand of allusion surfaces here.

l. 389. *tempt*. Risk or attempt.

31   l. 396. *gold*. The sun was thought to ripen precious metals in the earth.

l. 404. *side*. Recalling a famous recent event, when four Iroquois chiefs visited London in 1710.

l. 409. *freed Indians*. South American natives, liberated from the dominion of Spain.

l. 411. *race of kings*. The Incas.

l. 420. *wheel*. The wheel of torture.

l. 434. *sylvan strains*. Just as Virgil had concluded his *Georgics* with a recollection of the opening of the *Eclogues*, so P echoes the first line of his own *Pastorals*.

THE RAPE OF THE LOCK

32   The earlier two-canto version of this poem was probably written around Aug. or Sept. 1711. P's friend John Caryll had been staying with Lord Petre at Ingatestone, Essex, the assumed setting of the 'rape'. It was Caryll who brought the family quarrel to the attention of P, remarking that the Petres and the Fermors had lived 'long in great friendship before'. Caryll suggested that Pope should 'write a poem to make a jest of it, and laugh them together again'. The first version of the poem was published by Lintot in a miscellany on 20 May 1712. P then set about revising and expanding the poem, ostensibly to

safeguard Arabella's honour, in reality to fill out the literary resonances of his mock-epic. In its full form it appeared on 2 Mar. 1714.

The version in two cantos ran to no more than 334 lines, whereas the expanded poem contains 794 lines. Major additions include the entire machinery of sylphs and gnomes, starting from Belinda's dream at the outset. Also new are the description of the toilet in Canto I; the scene on the Thames in Canto II; the game of ombre in Canto III; the Cave of Spleen in Canto IV; and (from 1717) Clarissa's speech in Canto V, which was otherwise less disturbed.

The most immediate models for Pope's venture into mock-heroic were Boileau's *Le Lutrin* (1674–83), a satire in six cantos on ecclesiastical politics; and Samuel Garth's *Dispensary* (1699). Mock-heroic is a mode of satire by means at once of belittlement and aggrandizement. Epic action is scaled down, but trivial doings are accorded the dignity of inflated language. The *Rape* contains the plot of a full-dress epic in a comically reduced compass; equally it reduces a world of epic adventures to a domestic frame. Instead of the plains of Ilium, a young lady's boudoir; instead of the wine-dark Aegean stretching to the horizon, a short stretch of urban waterway (which is yet given the lyrical cognomen of 'the silver Thames'). Moreover, specific elements of the standard epic are parodied: the arming of the hero feminized into a make-up session (i. 121–48); the epic voyage as a boat-trip on the Thames (ii. 1–52); heroic sports transformed downwards into a fashionable card-game (iii. 25–100); gargantuan feats into an English tea-table (iii. 105–20); mortal combats into a domestic tiff (v. 75–112). Along with the appropriate changes in stylistic register, these inversions of epic expectation serve to achieve the main literary effect of the poem, that is to realize in narrative terms the proverbial idea of a storm in a teacup, hinted at in the two opening lines.

A brief identification suffices for the 'real' hero and heroine, since they were little more than the occasion for the poem. Belinda is based on Arabella Fermor (*c*.1689–1738), daughter of a well-established Catholic family settled in Oxfordshire. The Baron derives from Robert, seventh Baron Petre (1690–1713), member of one of the main English families of the Catholic faith, with a seat at Ingatestone, Essex. He married a different woman in 1712. Sir Plume is a caricature of Sir George Browne (d. 1730), a relative of the Fermors. The episode underlying the poem took place probably in 1711, quite likely at Ingatestone; Pope's informant was his friend John Caryll (*c*.1666–1736), a wealthy Catholic squire, who was a relative of the Petres and had been staying at Ingatestone that summer. Arabella married a Berkshire gentleman in 1714 or 1715 and lived an uneventful life thereafter.

The poem is one of the most fecund ever written in terms of literary allusion. As well as the parody of ancient epic (Homer and Virgil above all), there are numerous hints of Milton, Spenser, and many other English poets; Boileau and Garth are frequently enlisted, and incidental passages recall less obviously relevant poets such as Ovid and Dryden.

Mrs Arabella Fermor. Added with the expanded version in 1714. The dedication, though not openly insulting, is much less flattering than it appears.

machinery. The technical term in epic for the gods and supernatural forces influencing the action.

Rosicrucians. A kind of philosophy which grew up in the seventeenth and flourished in the eighteenth century, and which had been used as the basis of a light and erotic fantasy by the Abbé de Villars, *Le Comte de Gabalis* (1670).

four elements. The spirits belong respectively to the four substances once thought to constitute the universe, that is air, earth, water, and fire. A whole series of correspondences in Renaissance lore went with the different elements: thus there is a connection with times of day and with stages in life. Here, Canto I is dominated by the sylphs, by air, by morning, and by youth. Canto IV is pervaded by the gnomes, by earth, by evening, and by age and experience. Canto I is sanguine; Canto IV melancholy.

Canto I

Martial. Book II, Epigram 86: 'It is not for me, Belinda, to lay violent hands upon your hair, but it delights me to pay you the tribute you have entreated.'

33 l. 3. *I sing.* One of the marks of the epic proposition, which invoked the muses' assistance to the poet, was inversion of word-order and esp. putting the object at the head of the statement.

l. 9. *unexplored.* Undiscovered.

l. 10. *belle.* A recent importation from the French, underlying the name 'Belinda'.

l. 11. *little men.* 'Pope is stating the mock-heroic discrepancy; he is also referring to Lord Petre's short stature' (*TE*, ii. 45). He is also remembering his own puny size.

l. 18. *sound.* The recently introduced 'repeater' watch sounded a chime when the pendant was pressed in.

34 ll. 21–6. *'Twas he . . . to say.* In epic, gods often gave signals to mortals through apparitions during sleep.

l. 23. *birth-night beau.* A fashionable young man in the splendid court dress worn on royal birthdays.

l. 35. *know*. Suggesting the Annunciation: Luke 1: 26–38.

ll. 37–8. *Some secret . . . revealed*. Cf. Matt. 11: 25.

l. 44. *the Ring*. A small circular course in Hyde Park, used to parade fashionable coaches.

l. 45. *equipage*. 'A carriage and horses, with attendant footmen' (*OED*).

l. 46. *chair*. Sedan chair.

l. 56. *ombre*. See Canto III, l. 27.

l. 58. *elements*. The doctrine of the four elements underlies not just this passage but also much of the poem. It was a physical and psychological way of distinguishing between character types.

l. 59. *termagants*. A termagant was 'a bawling turbulent woman' (Johnson).

35 l. 62. *tea*. A good rhyme as the word was pronounced 'tay'.

ll. 69–70. *For spirits . . . please*. A parody of *Paradise Lost*, i. 423–4.

l. 73. *spark*. 'A lively, showy, gay man' (Johnson).

l. 89. *blush*. By means of using rouge.

l. 94. *impertinence*. 'Trifle: thing of no value' (Johnson).

l. 100. *moving toyshop*. The adjective means unstable or fickle; the noun refers to a shop where gewgaws and baubles were sold.

l. 101. *sword-knots*. Ribbons tied round the hilt of a sword.

36 l. 115. *Shock*. A shough was a shaggy-coated lapdog.

l. 121. *toilet*. Dressing-table. As well as the arming of an epic hero, the passage recalls Juno's dressing herself in *Iliad*, Book XIV.

37 l. 144. *eyes*. By the use of eye-drops to enlarge the pupils.

l. 148. *Betty*. A stock name for a maidservant.

Canto II
l. 4. *silver Thames*. In sober reality, the shores of the river were encrusted with coal-dust. In addition, the sewers of the city flowed directly into the Thames; it is to be hoped that Belinda embarked upstream from the Fleet Ditch.

l. 14. *shine on all alike*. Blasphemous suggestion of Matt. 5:45.

l. 20. *locks*. A sly allusion to the fact that 'it was the fashion some years ago [written 1721] for virgins to go bare-headed': a gloss on the proverb, 'All are not maidens that wear bare hair'.

38 l. 45. *prayer*. *Aeneid*, xi. 794–5.

l. 64. *dew*. Gossamer was popularly thought to be made by spiders from dried dew.

39 l. 99. *invention*. Creative skill.

l. 100. *furbelow*. 'A piece of stuff plaited and puckered together ...
on the petticoats or gowns of women' (Johnson).

l. 105. *Diana's law*. Chastity.

40 l. 113. *drops*. Pendant ear-rings.

l. 118. *petticoat*. Not then an undergarment so much as a skirt, made
visible by the pinning back of the gown; the whalebone hoops (l. 120)
went beneath the petticoat. Here the petticoat takes the place of the
shield in epic contexts.

l. 131. *styptics*. Astringent preparations, commonly made of alum.

l. 132. *rivelled*. To rivel was to 'contract into wrinkles and corrugations'
(Johnson).

l. 133. *Ixion*. For his temerity in trying to win the love of Hera, Zeus
punished Ixion by having him bound on a wheel which turned everlast-
ingly in the underworld.

Canto III

41 l. 4. *Hampton*. Hampton Court, standing on the banks of the Thames
some twenty miles by river from Westminster.

l. 7. *three realms*. England, Ireland, and Scotland.

l. 17. *snuff*. A recent craze among the fashionable.

l. 23. *th' Exchange*. Italicized in the original text, indicating not a
general reference but a specific allusion to the Royal Exchange, the
principal place for transacting business in the City of London.

l. 27. *ombre*. A three-handed card-game in which nine cards are dealt
to each player; it was the aim of each player to win a majority of the
nine tricks. Belinda is the 'ombre' who has the option of declaring
the trump suit.

l. 30. *sacred nine*. The nine Muses.

l. 32. *important*. 'Significant'.

l. 33. *matadore*. The highest-ranking cards in ombre (mentioned indi-
vidually in ll. 49–53).

42 l. 41. *succinct*. A comically elevated word for 'short'.

l. 46. *they were*. A blasphemous rephrasal of Gen. 1: 3.

l. 49. *Spadillio*. The ace of spades, the pre-eminent matadore.

l. 51. *Manillio*. The two of spades, another matadore.

l. 52. *verdant field*. The green cloth of the card-table seen as the site
of battle and as a heraldic display.

l. 53. *Basto*. The ace of clubs, also a matadore card.

l. 61. *Pam.* The knave of clubs in the game of loo (l. 62).

43 l. 92. *codille.* Defeat of the ombre, which would mean that Belinda must pay the entire stakes of the hand.

l. 94. *trick.* Punning on the term in cards and the sense of stratagem.

l. 107. *shining altars of Japan.* Japanned or lacquered tables.

l. 117. *coffee.* Coffee-houses were centres of political gossip and news-mongering.

44 ll. 122-4. *Fear . . . injured hair.* Ovid tells the story of a princess of Megara named Scylla. She was spurned by Minos and transformed into a bird.

l. 128. *two-edged weapon.* Scissors here, in mock-heroic diction.

l. 152. *unites again.* The reference in *Paradise Lost*, vi. 330-53, is to angels.

45 l. 164. *coach and six.* A splendid carriage drawn by three pairs of horses.

l. 165. *Atalantis.* P refers with heavy irony to *The New Atalantis*, by Delarivière Manley (1709), a popular *chronique scandaleuse*.

l. 174. *Troy.* According to legend, the walls of Troy had been built by Apollo and Neptune.

Canto IV
l. 1. *oppressed.* Parodies a passage in Book IV of the *Aeneid*.

l. 8. *manteau.* A loose outer garment which could be pinned back so as to reveal the petticoat beneath. Cynthia suggests the virgin goddess Diana.

ll. 11-88. An extended parody of the journey to the underworld which was a stock motif in epic, and in particular the shades visited by Aeneas in *Aeneid*, Book VI. The gnomes are the tutelary spirits of this dark underside of fashionable life, and the controlling idea is that of sexual repression.

l. 16. *Spleen.* A word whose meaning extends from melancholy and depression to bad temper or peevishness through to neurosis. In the old humours psychology, the organ was the seat of melancholia, since an excess of black bile (produced in this organ) would cause depressive tendencies. But in this passage P seems to be using the organ as a cover for the womb, presumed seat of hysteria.

l. 18. *vapour.* Punning on 'the vapours', a popular expression for depression.

46 l. 20. *east.* Like a moist climate (l. 18), a wind from the east was supposed to induce fits of melancholia.

l. 24. *side.* On the left, where the spleen is located.   *megrim.* 'A disorder of the head' (Johnson).

l. 25. *wait.* Wait on.

ll. 43–6. *Now glaring fiends . . . machines.* Effects drawn from the elaborate staging devices used in the popular theatre, esp. the 'pantomimes' which were currently all the rage. Machines also puns on epic machinery.

l. 43. *spires.* Spirals or coils.

l. 51. *pipkin.* Small pot made of earthenware.

47 l. 69. *citron-waters.* Brandy distilled with lemon-peel.

l. 71. *horns.* Those of the cuckold.

l. 77. *chagrin.* Another word which historically had implied 'melancholy' but was now coming to suggest merely vexation or bad temper.

l. 78. *half the world.* Men.

l. 82. *Ulysses.* In *Odyssey*, Book X.

l. 89. *Thalestris.* Queen of the Amazons.

l. 97. *Was it for this.* An epic formula.

48 l. 99. *paper durance.* Referring to curl-papers for the hair, held in place by thin strips of lead.

l. 109. *toast.* 'A celebrated woman whose health is often drunk' (Johnson).

l. 117. *Hyde Park Circus.* Same as the Ring (i. 44 above).

l. 118. *sound of Bow.* The mercantile city popularly identified with the region in earshot of St Mary le Bow, as opposed to the fashionable districts of Westminster.

l. 121. *Sir Plume.* Based on Sir George Browne (see headnote) but also a type-figure of the foppish man about town.

l. 124. *clouded cane.* 'A walking stick having an amber head with streaks of a darker colour'.

49 ll. 147–76. The basis for this speech is the lament by Achilles for his friend Patroclus in *Iliad*, Book XVIII.

l. 156. *bohea.* A superior variety of tea, very black in colour.

l. 161. *omens.* Another epic property.

l. 162. *patch-box.* A decorative container in which women kept the patches they wore on their face.

Canto V

50 ll. 1–6. *She said . . . in vain.* Parodying the story of Dido and Aeneas in *Aeneid*, Book IV.

l. 7. *Clarissa.* P's footnote refers to an episode in the *Iliad*, Book XII, which he had translated in 1709.

l. 20. *smallpox.* Lord Petre had died of this ever-present scourge in 1713, even before the five-canto edition had made its first appearance.

51 l. 37. *virago.* 'A female warrior, a woman with the qualities of a man' (Johnson).

l. 47. *Latona.* Daughter of the Titans, and mother of Apollo and Diana.

l. 53. *sconce.* 'A pensile candlestick' (Johnson).

ll. 62–3. *Dapperwit . . . Sir Fopling.* Names of fashionable society characters in plays by Wycherley and Etherege.

l. 65 *Maeander.* The Meander was a river with a serpentine course flowing into the Aegean from Phrygia.

52 l. 88. *bodkin.* 'A bodkin, which to Hamlet had been a stiletto, was more and more degenerating into an ornament for the head and a dressmaker's tool'.

53 l. 126. *Proculus.* Romulus was transported to heaven under the cover of a cloud; he was never seen again on earth, apart from a brief apparition before Julius Proculus. See Livy, Book I.

l. 127. *liquid.* Pure or transparent.

l. 129. *Berenice.* Wife of Ptolemy III of Egypt; she dedicated a lock of her hair to the gods when her husband embarked on war to ensure his safe return. It subsequently disappeared and the court astronomer devised a story that it had been transformed into a constellation to be known as *Coma Berenices.*

l. 133. *the Mall.* A fashionable walk in St James's Park, not yet a major thoroughfare.

l. 136. *Rosamonda's lake.* An ornamental pond in St James's Park, which was a noted trysting place for lovers.

l. 138. *Galileo's eyes.* Galileo had made large improvements in the telescope and enabled astronomy to take great strides.

l. 140. *Louis.* Louis XIV.

54 *Epistle to Miss Blount, on her leaving the Town after the Coronation.* Written probably in 1714; first published in *Works* (1717).

The coronation of George I took place on 20 Oct. 1714. The recipient is the elder of the Blount sisters, Teresa. The Blounts had to leave town immediately after the coronation; Martha had caught smallpox and missed the actual ceremony.

l. 1. *fond.* Tender-hearted.

l. 3. *roll a melting eye.* Language appropriate to romantic heroines.

l. 4. *spark.* 'A lively, showy, splendid, gay man' (Johnson).

l. 7. *Zephalinda.* Suggesting the extravagant world of the seventeenth-century French romance.

l. 11. *plain-work.* 'Needlework as distinguished from embroidery; the common practice of sewing or making linen garments' (Johnson).

l. 15. *bohea.* 'A species of tea, of higher colour, and more astringent taste, than green tea' (Johnson). The rhyme is *bohay/tay*.

l. 17. *Or o'er cold coffee . . . spoon.* A deliberately cacophonous line to emphasize boredom and routine.

l. 18. *dine exact at noon.* Unduly early hours for a fashionable lady.

l. 23. *rack.* Get the better of, torment.

l. 24. *whisk.* Whist (not the most fashionable game).

l. 26. *buss.* Kiss.

l. 32. *triumphs.* Punning on coronation ceremonies and conquests in love.

55 l. 38. *flirt.* 'A quick elastic motion' but also calling up the newer sense of 'a pert young hussey' (Johnson).

l. 46. *Parthenia.* This may refer to Martha Blount, who had adopted the fanciful name 'Parthenissa' in some of her letters.

l. 47. *Gay.* John Gay.

l. 48. *chairs.* Sedan-chairs.

Eloisa to Aberlard. First published in the *Works* (1717). P is imitating Ovid's *Heroides* or 'letters from heroines', twenty-one poems in elegiac verse, which had been popular in England since the Renaissance and had spawned native versions such as Drayton's *England's Heroical Epistles* (1597–9). The original letters of Abelard and Eloisa had appeared in Latin in 1616, but the immediate source for P was a version by John Hughes in 1713.

Peter Abelard (1079–1142), French theologian, fell in love with his pupil Heloise, who bore him a son, and was privately married to him. After this was discovered, Abelard was castrated and entered monastic life whilst Heloise took the veil. Abelard's retreat became the abbey of the Paraclete (a name for the Holy Spirit), near Troyes.

Argument. The liaison began in 1117, when Abelard was 38 and Heloise 17.

56 l. 16. *dictates.* Stress on first syllable, as always in P.

l. 20. *horrid.* Bristling.

57   l. 56. *excuse.* Do away with the need for.

　　l. 63. *attempering.* Moderating, soothing.

58   l. 104. *common.* Shared.

　　l. 126. *partial.* Fond.

59   l. 133. *these hallowed walls.* The Paraclete, where Heloise had become
　　sister after Abelard had moved to the Abbey of St Gildas in Brittany.

　　l. 142. *domes.* Structures, edifices.

61   l. 219. *spouse prepares the bridal ring.* Nuns as the bride of Christ wear
　　his ring.

　　l. 229. *all-conscious night.* Night when Heloise is made aware of all
　　her feelings and exposed to a sense of guilt.

62   l. 282. *dispute.* Bring contrary arguments to my attention.

　　l. 284. *idea of the skies.* Image or sentiment provoked by or connected
　　with the heavens.

63   l. 288. *fiends.* Diabolic spirits.

64   l. 343 note. The statement is true, but in 1817 both were reburied in
　　a single tomb at Père Lachaise in Paris.

　　l. 351. *mutual pity.* Pity for both of them.

　　l. 355. *relenting.* Warming.

65   *Elegy to the Memory of an Unfortunate Lady.* First published in the *Works*
　　(1717), and generally assumed to be written around the same year.
　　There was a long debate on the supposed identity of a 'real' lady, with
　　the most popular choice Mrs Elizabeth Weston (d. 1724), but modern
　　scholarship inclines to the view that no single individual is meant.

　　　P has several models, mostly Roman: Ovid's epistles and the elegies
　　of Tibullus helped to provide him with the 'plan' he considered neces-
　　sary in such poems.

　　l. 8. *a Roman's part.* Follow the acceptable Roman practice of suicide.

　　l. 9. *reversion.* A right of succession (esp. in property).

　　l. 14. *glorious fault.* The rebel angels, as in *Paradise Lost,* and the Titans
　　who waged war on Zeus, before they were flung into Hell—the fate
　　held out in P's time to suicides.

　　l. 35. *ball.* The earth as orb or emblem of justice.

66   l. 41. *Furies.* The three avenging goddesses or Erinyes.

　　l. 64. *green turf . . . breast.* Paraphrasing the familiar Roman inscription
　　on gravestones, *sit tibi terra levis.*

67   *Epitaph Intended for Sir Isaac Newton.* Newton died at the age of 84 on
　　20 Mar. 1727. P's epitaph was first published in 1735; it was probably

written not long before its first publication. A Latin inscription added may be rendered, 'Isaac Newton, whom time, nature, and heaven declare to be immortal, while this stone acknowledges his mortal being.' A different Latin inscription was in fact added to Newton's tomb at Westminster Abbey in 1731.

An Epistle to Richard Boyle, Earl of Burlington. Published on 13 Dec. 1731; composed 1730-1. A short prose 'argument' is omitted here. The poem was the first to appear of the four which were to comprise the *Epistles to Several Persons* or *Moral Essays*. The present poem was placed fourth in the sequence, also comprising the epistles to Cobham, to a lady, and Bathurst, when this grouping was first established in the *Works* (1735). However, it is clear that the sequence had not been properly defined when P published this first epistle in 1731. The dedicatee is the Earl of Burlington (1695-1753), architect and patron.

l. 7. *Topham.* A prominent antiquarian and collector (d. 1753).

l. 8. *Pembroke.* The Earl of Pembroke (1656-1733), politician and collector.

l. 9. *Hearne.* Thomas Hearne (1678-1735), the great medieval scholar.

l. 10. *Mead.* Dr Richard Mead (1673-1754).   *Sloane.* Sir Hans Sloane (1660-1753). Both notable as physicians and as collectors.

68 l. 15. *Sir Visto.* Suggesting one given to the fine contrived views treasured by landscape gardeners; it is possible P had Walpole in mind.

l. 18. *Ripley.* Thomas Ripley (1683-1758) worked for Walpole at Houghton.

l. 20. *Bubo.* Latin for an owl, suggesting stupidity; P may intend George Bubb Dodington (1691-1762).

l. 32. *dog-hole.* 'a mean habitation' (Johnson).

l. 34. *rustic.* Rusticated stone, i.e. left with an irregular surface.

l. 36 note. A window with an arch at the top and two narrower panes at the sides.

69 l. 46. *Le Nôtre.* Andre Le Nôtre (1613-1700) designed the gardens at Versailles for Louis XIV.

l. 57. *genius of the place.* Anglicizing *genius loci*, the presiding spirit guarding a favoured place.

l. 63. *intending.* Directing the gaze of the eyes.

l. 70. *Stowe.* P had first visited the house in 1724, after Bridgeman and Vanbrugh had completed the first phase of its elaborately planned garden.

l. 72. *Nero's terraces*. Referring to Nero's Golden House: see Suetonius, *Nero*, 31.

l. 73. *parterres*. Ornamental flower-beds laid out in a regular pattern.

70 l. 78. *hermitage*. Alluding to the installation of busts, including that of the theologian Samuel Clarke in the mock-rustic garden feature at Richmond Park which was known as the Hermitage; it was the private shrine of Queen Caroline.

l. 80. *espaliers*. A framework of stakes along which ornamental fruit-trees are trained.

l. 99. *Timon's villa*. The intense controversy which grew up around allegations that P was aiming at the Duke of Chandos and his house at Canons, near Edgware (now destroyed).

71 l. 123. *Amphitrite*. Sea-goddess, the wife of Neptune.

l. 124 note. Two of the most famous statues from the ancient world.

l. 126. *Nilus*. The Nile, as commemorated in the standard way by an urn representing the river-god.

72 l. 136. *Aldus*. Aldo Manutio (1450–1515), Venetian printer famous for Aldine classics.   *Du Suëil*. Augustin Deseuil (1673–1746), French cleric and bookbinder.

l. 146. *Verrio*. Antonio Verrio (1630–1707), Italian decorative painter, who came to England in 1671 and worked mainly on royal commissions.   *Laguerre*. Louis Laguerre (1663–1721), French decorative artist, came to England *c.*1684.

l. 155. *genial*. Punning on various senses of the word listed in *OED*: 'pertaining to a feast; festive'; 'cheering, enlivening'; 'pleasantly warm, mild'; 'natural'.

73 l. 160. *Sancho's dread doctor*. From *Don Quixote*, ii. 47, where a doctor whisks away dishes set before Sancho Panza without giving him a chance to eat.

l. 174. *slope*. An artificially constructed bank in landscape gardening.

l. 176. *Ceres*. Goddess of agriculture.

l. 178. *Bathurst*. See p. 197.   *Boyle*. Burlington's family name.

l. 190. *country*. 'A tract or district . . . owned by the same lord or proprietor' (*OED*).

l. 193. *Palladio*. Burlington had published designs by Palladio in 1730 and by Inigo Jones in 1727.

74 l. 195 note. P refers to the problems with some of the new 'Queen Anne' churches in London, damaged by subsidence and faulty workmanship; to the ineffective measures to remedy a breach of the Thames at Dagenham in 1707; and to the political wranglings over

the proposed second London bridge at Westminster, not completed until after P's death.

l. 200. *mole*. Breakwater.

An Epistle to Allen Lord Bathurst. First published on 15 Jan. 1733. The process of composition probably goes back to 1730. A short prose 'argument' is omitted here.

The addressee is P's long-time friend, Allen Lord Bathurst (1684–1775), politician and patron.

l. 1. *doctors*. The learned.

l. 3. *Momus*. The god of satire and derision.

75 l. 20. *Ward . . . Chartres*. John Ward (d.1755), a crooked politician; Peter Walter (1664–1746), a rapacious broker; and Francis Charteris (1675–1732), a libertine. In his note P quotes a savage epitaph by Dr Arbuthnot, attributing to Charteris 'insatiable avarice' and 'matchless impudence'.

76 l. 34. *saps*. Undermines.

l. 39. *supply*. Recourse.

l. 41. *imped*. From a word used in falconry, meaning 'to strengthen or improve the flight' of a bird (*OED*).

77 l. 45. *sibyls*. The Roman sibyls inscribed their prophecies on leaves, left outside their cave. P's note refers to the *Aeneid*, Book VI, involving the Cumaean sibyl.

l. 51. *Rome*. Home of the Pretender's court.

l. 53. *confound*. 'Confuse . . . the brain with liquor' (*OED*).

l. 54. *water all the quorum*. Bribe the justices of the peace.

l. 62. *Worldly*. Edward Wortley Montagu (1681–1761), the mean and self-contained husband (by now estranged) of Lady Mary Wortley Montagu.

l. 65. *Colepepper*. A nonentity (1668–1740), only remembered for P's mention.

l. 67. *White's*. The gaming club in St James's Street, London.

78 l. 73. *Adonis*. A type of the fop, but P may be thinking of his regular adversary Lord Hervey (1696–1743), courtier.

l. 76. *quadrille*. The most fashionable card-game.

l. 82. *Turner*. Richard 'Plum' Turner, a Turkey merchant (d. 1733).

l. 84. *Wharton*. Philip, Duke of Wharton (1698–1731).

l. 85. *Hopkins*. John Hopkins (*c*.1663–1732), a notoriously grasping financier.

l. 86. *vigour*. Sexual prowess.   *Japhet*. Japhet Crook (1662–1734); the events described in P's note took place in 1731.

l. 87. *Hippia*. One with the 'hips' or neurotic depression.

79 l. 91. *Harpax*. Robber (Greek).

l. 96. *cat*. P's note indicates the Duchess of Richmond (1647–1702), who allegedly made a bequest to her cats.

l. 100. *Bond*. Denis Bond (1676–1747): according to a parliamentary inquiry, he had said to his fellow directors of the Charitable Corporation, 'Damn the poor, let us go into the City where we may get money.' He had already been expelled from the House of Commons.

l. 101. *Sir Gilbert*. Heathcote (1652–1733), a leading City magnate famous for his meanness.

l. 103. *Blunt*. See l. 133 for Sir John Blunt.

l. 107. *pelf*. Riches.

l. 117. *South-Sea Year*. 1720, when the South Sea Bubble burst and thousands of investors and annuitants were ruined. The directors of the company were prosecuted for their corrupt management.

80 ll. 119–20. *Phryne . . . excise*. The name Phryne is taken from that of a Greek courtesan; it is probably applied here to Walpole's mistress Molly Skerret.

l. 122. *plum*. Slang for £100,000; one who had assets of this size would be equivalent to the later millionaire.

l. 123. *Peter*. Peter Walter (see l. 20).

l. 127. *crown of Poland*. This was elective and had several times been offered to the highest bidder; it had become vacant in 1733 when Augustus II died.

l. 128. *Gage*. Joseph Gage (1677–1753) had attempted to buy the Polish crown in 1719 on the profits he had made from the Mississippi scheme. He gained a monopoly right to work the gold mines in Austria from the King of Spain. His wife, formerly Lady Mary Herbert, had previously sought a royal consort: her mother, the Marchioness of Powis, was allegedly the illegitimate daughter of James II.

l. 133. *Blunt*. Sir John Blunt (1667–1733), Director of the South Sea Company. He was seen, with some justice, as the very linchpin of the South Sea swindle.

81 l. 139. *statesman and patriot*. Government and Opposition.

l. 140. *box*. In the theatre.

l. 141. *job*. Use their office corruptly.   *bite*. Cheat.

l. 142. *pack*. Shuffle fraudulently.

l. 144. Referring to the historic victories in the reign of Edward III, notably Crécy, and of Anne, notably Blenheim.

l. 145. *scrivener*. Blunt had been apprenticed to a scrivener, or money-lender, in Holborn.

ll. 161–2. Quoted from *Essay on Man*, ii. 165–6 (adapted), ii. 205–6 (adapted).

l. 167. *change*. The Royal Exchange, centre of financial dealing.

82 l. 183. *pulse*. Peas and beans.

l. 187. *Chartreux*. The Carthusian monastery, used as an emblem of austere living.

l. 196. *eat*. Pronounced 'ate'.

l. 203. *hecatombs*. Large public sacrifices of animals (literally one hundred oxen).

l. 208. *that great house*. That of the Hanoverians.

83 l. 214. *train-bands*. A form of civic militia.   *burns a Pope*. Ritual burning of the Pope in effigy was a standard feature of anti-Catholic protest in P's youth.

l. 235. *ambergris*. A secretion of the sperm-whale, used in making perfume.

l. 243. *Oxford*. P's note identifies his friend the second Earl, Edward Harley (1689–1741).

84 l. 250. *Man of Ross*. John Kyrle, a philanthropist from Ross-on-Wye, Herefordshire.

l. 251. *Vaga*. The River Wye.

l. 267. *portioned*. With a marriage portion bestowed on them.

l. 282. *stars*. The insignia of the chivalric orders, specifically those of knighthood.

85 l. 296. *buckle*. 'The state of the hair crisped and curled by being kept long in the same state' (Johnson).   *Parian stone*. Stone from the island of Paros, a white marble famed for its long-lasting qualities.

l. 301. *flock-bed*. One stuffed with scraps of cloth rather than the feathers used in superior circles.

l. 303. *George and garter*. Insignia of the Order of the Garter, including an emblem of St George.

l. 305 note. George Villiers, Duke of Buckingham (1628–87), playwright and politician. The account of his death here is fanciful.

l. 308 note. The event took place in 1668.

86 l. 315. *Cutler*. Sir John Cutler (*c.*1608–93), a parsimonious City gran-dee who may also be the basis of Old Cotta above (l. 178).

l. 342. *Balaam*. The name is biblical (Num. 22: 21–35 tells the story of Balaam and his ass), but otherwise there is no direct link.

87 l. 358. *chirping*. *OED* quotes a slang expression, '*chirping-merry*, very pleasant over a glass of good liquor'.

l. 362. *factor*. A junior official of the East India Company. *gem.* Thomas Pitt, ancestor of the great Pitt dynasty, bought the famous Pitt diamond while governor of Madras.

l. 364. *bit*. Cheated.

l. 378. *lucky hit*. A stock phrase, for a stroke of any kind, here a financial coup.

l. 384. *catched*. Just beginning to be an informal past tense, if not yet quite a vulgarism.

88 l. 388. *St James's air*. The salubrious atmosphere of the West End, as opposed to the busy city of London.

l. 394. *St Stephen*. A metonym for Parliament.

l. 397. *Coningsby*. Thomas, Lord Coningsby (1656–1729), politician: he is in effect used as a stock figure of the hypocritical Whig and Hanoverian.

The First Satire of the Second Book of Horace Imitated. First published on 15 Feb. 1733. Written with unusual speed during a spell of ill-health in the previous month. In early editions the Latin text was printed oppo-site the English version, so that well-equipped readers (always a min-ority) could compare the respective wordings. A short 'advertisement' is omitted here.

Fortescue. William Fortescue (1687–1749) had served as Walpole's secretary, and he later became a senior judge. P consulted Fortescue for advice in his capacity as a private lawyer; they had known each other for some twenty years.

l. 3. *complaisant*. Polite, courteous.

ll. 3–4. *Peter . . . Chartres*. Peter Walter and Francis Charteris, whom he had named in the *Epistle to Bathurst*.

l. 6. *Lord Fanny*. Lord Hervey.

l. 8. *counsel*. William Fortescue, who was a barrister.

89 l. 18. *lettuce*. Believed to act as a bromide.

l. 19. *Celsus*. Aulus Cornelius Celsus, who wrote eight influential works on medicine in the first century AD.

l. 20. *hartshorn.* Sal volatile or ammonium carbonate, used not as smelling-salts to revive a patient but as a sedative.

l. 21. *Caesar.* George II.

l. 22. *bays.* The post of laureate.

l. 23. *Sir Richard.* Blackmore (1654–1729), poet.

l. 24. *Brunswick.* The house of Brunswick (the royal family).

l. 27. *Budgell.* Eustace Budgell (1686–1737) had written a poem, celebrating the King's exploits at the battle of Oudenarde in 1708, when he led a cavalry charge and had his horse shot from under him.

l. 30. *Carolina.* Perhaps not the Queen but her somewhat unattractive daughter Caroline.

l. 31. *Amelia.* Another daughter of the King and Queen.   *the nine.* The Muses.

l. 34. *twice a year.* The Poet Laureate had to produce official odes at the New Year and on the King's birthday.

l. 38. *quadrille.* Referring back to *Epistle to Bathurst*, l. 38; the joke is that blasphemy should be reserved for such trivial pursuits.

l. 40. *Peter.* Peter Walter.

l. 42. *Timon.* See *Epistle to Burlington*, l. 99.   *Balaam.* See *Epistle to Bathurst*, l. 342.

l. 44. *Bond.* See *Epistle to Bathurst*, l. 100.   *Harpax.* See *Epistle to Bathurst*, l. 92.

l. 46. *Scarsdale.* The fourth Earl (1682–1736). A minor politician.
        Darty. Charles Dartiquenave (1664–1737), an epicure and friend of the Scriblerus group.

90 l. 47. *Ridotta.* A woman addicted to socializing.

l. 49. *Fox.* The brothers Stephen and Henry Fox; the latter was to become a prominent politician. Stephen was a close friend of Lord Hervey.   *Hockley Hole.* A bear-garden in north London.

l. 52. *Shippen.* William Shippen (1673–1743), Tory politician.

l. 71. *Hectors.* Rowdies and street-brawlers.

l. 72. *supercargoes.* Cargo-superintendents, reputed to gain corrupt wealth.   *directors.* South Sea Managers.

l. 75. *Fleury.* The leading minister of France, Cardinal Fleury (1653–1743).

l. 80. *burden.* Refrain.

l. 82. *Page.* The notorious judge: see p. 212.

l. 83. *Sappho.* Lady Mary Wortley Montagu (1689–1762), woman of letters, whom P at first loved and later came to hate. The reference is to her campaign for inoculation against smallpox.

91 l. 89. *Walter*. Peter Walter.

l. 100. *Lee*. The dramatist Nathaniel Lee (1653–92), who had been lodged in Bethlehem Hospital ('Bedlam') from 1684 to 1689.
Budgell. He was believed to have taken his own life by drowning after the accusation of embezzlement.

l. 103. *plums*. In effect, millionaires.

l. 104. *testers*. Sixpences ('club' means collect together).

l. 108. *star*. That of knighthood.

l. 112. *Louis*. Louis XIV, Boileau's patron.

l. 113. *pimp and friar*. Dryden, whilst Poet Laureate to Charles II, had created the character of an immoral priest in *The Spanish Friar* (1680).

l. 127. *St John*. Lord Bolingbroke.

92 l. 129. *Iberian lines*. The Earl of Peterborough (1658–1735) P's close friend, who had become famous in the Peninsular campaign.

l. 130. *quincunx*. Four trees planted at the corners of a square, with a fifth at the middle point.

l. 145. *Richard*. P refers to the case of a poet named Collingbourne during the reign of Richard III. He was a Wiltshire gentleman, hanged at Tower Hill in 1484 for a rhyme satirizing the King and his counsellors.

ll. 147–8. *quart. . . . quint. Eliz.* Early acts against libel and sedition, including 3/4 Edward VI, c. 15; 1 Elizabeth I, c. 6; and 5 Elizabeth I, c. 15.

l. 153. *Sir Robert*. Walpole.

93 *Epistle to Dr Arbuthnot*. First published on 2 Jan. 1735; P acknowledged that the poem had been spliced together from existing fragments, some written many years before. However, the act of assemblage and the forging of a coherent poem took place in 1734.
  On 17 July 1734 P's long-time friend, the former royal physician John Arbuthnot, wrote to P disclosing that his own illness was terminal. On 25 Aug. P told Arbuthnot that he intended to address to his friend 'one of my epistles, written by piecemeal many years, and which I have now made haste to put together'. Arbuthnot died on 27 Feb. 1735.

rank and fortune. P refers to Lady Mary Wortley Montagu and Lord Hervey.

l. 1. *John*. P's servant and gardener, John Serle.

l. 3. *dog-star*. Sirius, which appears in the sky in northern latitudes in

August; this was always the time of year when poetry recitations were held in Rome.

l. 8. *grot*. P's famous grotto at Twickenham, with a view towards the nearby Thames.

94 l. 12. *sabbath day*. Debtors were immune from arrest on Sundays, as they were in the Mint (l. 13), a sanctuary in Southwark.

l. 15. *parson*. Revd Laurence Eusden, the previous Poet Laureate (1688–1730): P's phrase 'bemused in beer' is more than a pun and a rhyme, since Eusden was notoriously bibulous.

l. 18. *engross*. Copy out legal documents.

l. 23. *Arthur*. The corrupt politician Arthur Moore (1666–1730), an adventurer and company promoter.

l. 25. *Cornus*. From *cornu* (Lat.) a horn; that is, cuckolded.

l. 29. *drop*. Patent medicine.

l. 41. *high*. Up in a garret.   *Drury Lane*. Then a street with some dubious associations, including squalid courts where criminals and prostitutes flourished.

l. 43. *term*. The legal and publishing season.

95 l. 53. *Curll*. One of P's most regular adversaries, the bookseller Edmund Curll (1683–1747).

l. 62. *Lintot*. Another bookseller, Bernard Lintot (1675–1736).

l. 66. *go snacks*. Share: proverbial.

l. 72 note. The most famous source for the story of Midas is Ovid, *Metamorphoses*, Book XI.

96 l. 85. *Codrus*. The type of a bad poet, from references by Virgil and Juvenal.

l. 97. *Colley*. Cibber.

l. 98. *Henley*. John 'Orator' Henley, who had delivered a sermon on butchers in 1729.   *Freemasons*. Moore Smythe was a freemason.

l. 99. *Bavius*. A bad poet, derived from one who is mentioned by Horace and Virgil.

l. 100. *one bishop*. Ambrose Philips had acted as secretary to Hugh Boulter, Archbishop of Armagh.

l. 106. *slaver*. Saliva.

l. 113. *Letters*. By a complicated subterfuge P had arranged it so that Curll published an 'unauthorized' edition of his letters in 1726.

l. 117. *Ammon's great son*. Alexander the Great; P is alluding to his own deformity.

l. 122. *Maro*. Virgil, from his cognomen.

97 l. 135. *Granville*. George Granville, Baron Lansdowne.

l. 136. *Walsh*. William Walsh (1663–1708), poet and critic.

l. 137. *Garth*. The poet and physician Sir Samuel Garth (1661–1719).

l. 139. *Talbot, Somers, Sheffield*. Literary patrons: the Duke of Shrewsbury, John, Baron Somers, and P's friend the Duke of Buckingham.

l. 140. *Rochester*. Francis Atterbury (1662–1732), Bishop of Rochester.

l. 141. *St John*. Henry St John, Viscount Bolingbroke (1678–1751), politician and close friend of P.

l. 146. *Burnets, Oldmixons, and Cookes*. Miscellaneous writers, all mentioned in *The Dunciad*.

l. 149. *Fanny*. Pointing to Lord Hervey; the name derived from Fannius, a poetaster mentioned by Horace as *ineptus* (vapid).

l. 151. *Gildon*. Charles Gildon (1665–1724).

l. 153. *Dennis*. The critic John Dennis, one of P's sturdiest opponents.

98 l. 158. *kissed the rod*. Proverbial.

l. 163. *ribalds*. Abusive and scurrilous louts.

l. 164. *Bentley ... piddling Tibbalds*. Linking the classical scholar Richard Bentley and the Shakespearian editor Lewis Theobald, hero of the first version of *The Dunciad*.

l. 179. *pilfered pastorals*. P alleged that Philips's pastorals were a tissue of plagiarisms.

l. 182. *hard-bound*. Constipated.

l. 190. *Tate*. Nahum Tate, best known for his improved *King Lear*, poet and dramatist (1652–1715).

l. 193. *one*. Atticus is a portrait of Addison, built up from a number of earlier versions.

99 l. 209. *Cato*. Cato the younger (95–46 BC), famous for his austere patriotism and his high-principled suicide at Utica, which forms the subject of Addison's successful tragedy *Cato* (1713).

l. 211. *templars*. Young law students, noted for their desire to shine as literary pundits.

l. 214. *Atticus*. The name is taken from Cicero's friend and correspondent T. Pomponius Atticus (109–32 BC), a patron and promoter of literature.

l. 215. *rubric*. With red lettering on the title-page, which was displayed by booksellers as there were then no dust-jackets or cover designs.

l. 216. *claps*. Posters.

l. 222. *birthday song*. The Poet Laureate's chief duty was to compose a birthday ode for the monarch every year.

l. 230. *Bufo*. A toad in Latin, here suggesting a patron who enjoys the flattery of toadying authors; it may point to George Bubb Dodington or else to Lord Halifax.   *Castalian*. Relating to the spring sacred to the Muses on Mount Parnassus.

100 l. 260. *Queensberry*. The Duke and Duchess of Queensberry were Gay's most loyal supporters, esp. after the banning of his follow-up to *The Beggar's Opera*, entitled *Polly*, 1728.

101 l. 280. *Sir Will*. Possibly Sir William Yonge, a loquacious supporter of Walpole.   *Bubo*. Probably Bubb Dodington.

l. 305. *Sporus*. Derived from the catamite of the emperor Nero (Suetonius, *Nero*, 28). The character attacks Lord Hervey.

102 l. 306. *ass's milk*. Given to invalids and convalescents; taken by Hervey but also by P himself.

l. 309. *bug*. Bedbug.

l. 310. *painted child*. Hervey used cosmetics to disguise his extreme pallor.

l. 318. *prompter*. Walpole.   *puppet*. Hervey himself.

l. 319. *Eve*. Queen Caroline.

l. 324. *now master up, now miss*. Hervey was probably bisexual.

l. 330. *rabbins*. Rabbis.

l. 341. *stooped*. Swooped, like a falcon.

l. 343. *stood*. Withstood.

103 l. 353. *pictured shape*. P was often depicted in attacks as an ape or some kind of deformed monster.

l. 355. *friend in exile*. Atterbury.

l. 363. *Japhet*. Japhet Crook: see *Epistle to Bathurst*, l. 86.

l. 365. *knight of the post*. One who made a living by giving false evidence. A knight of the shire was the MP for a county.

l. 371. *his distress*. When Dennis fell on hard times at the end of his life, P gave him assistance, including a prologue written for a benefit performance.

104 l. 375. *Welsted*. The writer Leonard Welsted, also featured in *The Dunciad*.

l. 378. *Budgell*. Eustace Budgell was convicted of forging a will.

l. 380. *two Curlls*. The real Curll and Hervey.

l. 381 note. P is wrong in several particulars, including the age of his father at his death (71).

l. 383. *sin to call our neighbour fool*. Recalling the Sermon on the Mount (Matt. 5: 22).

l. 391. *Bestia*. Possibly indicating Marlborough; the name is taken from a corrupt Roman consul in the late second century BC.

105 l. 397. *oath*. By early Hanoverian legislation, Catholics were required to take oaths of loyalty; if they refused, they were excluded from public office.

l. 410. *lenient*. Gentle, caring.

l. 417. *Queen*. Arbuthnot had been physician to Queen Anne 1705–14.

106 *An Epistle to a Lady*. First published in Feb. 1735. Composition seems to date from about 1732. The lady of the title is Martha Blount (1690–1763), P's closest woman friend.

l. 7. *Arcadia's Countess*. A great lady such as the Countess of Pembroke who was frequently painted in different guises. The allusion is to Philip Sidney's *Arcadia* (1590), linked in its full title to Sidney's sister Mary, Countess of Pembroke.

l. 8. *Pastora*. Suggests the lady is depicted as a shepherdess.

l. 9. *Fannia*. Based on a notorious Roman adulteress.

l. 12. *Magdalen*. Mary Magdalene, who wiped the feet of Jesus with her hair (John 11: 2).

l. 16. *romantic*. Excessive, hyperbolic.

l. 18. *trick her off*. Sketch roughly.

l. 20. *Cynthia*. The moon-goddess, symbolizing instability.

l. 21. *Rufa*. Red-haired (Lat.), then associated with sexual promiscuity.

107 ll. 24–6. *Sappho's diamonds … an evening mask*. Sappho is probably P's code-word for his familiar target Lady Mary Wortley Montagu.

l. 31. *nice*. Genteel, refined.

l. 37. *Papillia*. Taken from the Latin for butterfly.

l. 45. *Calypso*. Goddess of the *Odyssey*, who at the start of the poem has detained the hero on her island for seven years.

l. 54. *wash*. A lotion or cleansing cosmetic.

l. 57. *trim*. Get-up, pose.

108 l. 63. *Taylor*. The great devotional writer, Bishop Jeremy Taylor.
Book of Martyrs. John Foxe's martyrology, first published in 1563.

l. 64. *citron*. Brandy flavoured with lemon-peel.   *Chartres*. The notorious rake and rogue Francis Charteris: see p. 197.

l. 70. *punk*. Prostitute.

l. 73. *fault*. Pronounced 'fawt'.

l. 78. *Tallboy*. A booby squire.   *Charles*. A footman.

l. 79. *Helluo*. A glutton.

l. 80. *hautgout*. Applied to food 'with a strong relish or strong scent' (Johnson).

l. 83. *Philomedé*. The character of Philomedé is possibly based on Henrietta, daughter and heiress of the Duke and Duchess of Marlborough.

l. 92. *Rosamonda's bowl*. Referring to 'fair Rosamond' Clifford (d. ?1176), mistress of Henry II. Legend recounts that Queen Eleanor of Aquitaine forced her to drink from a poisoned bowl.

109 l. 101. *Simo*. A simian character.

l. 110. *ratafee*. Cherry-brandy.

l. 115. *Atossa*. Taken from the Persian queen, daughter of Cyrus.

110 l. 142. *cheat*. Pronounced 'chate'.

l. 155. *do the knack*. Bring off the effect. The word 'equal' means uniform.

111 l. 182. *Queen*. Queen Caroline.

l. 184. *ball*. The orb of royalty.

l. 193. *Queensberry*. The beautiful and eccentric Duchess of Queensberry.

l. 198. *Parson Hale*. P's neighbour, the pioneer physiologist Revd Stephen Hales (1677–1761).

112 l. 239. *hags*. Witches.

l. 241. *round and round*. As in the carriage-ride at the Ring (l. 251) in Hyde Park.

l. 249. *friend*. P addresses Martha Blount directly.

113 l. 257. *temper*. Equanimity.

l. 266. *tickets*. Lottery tickets.   *codille*. The losing hand at ombre.

l. 267. *smallpox*. Martha had herself suffered from the disease in her youth.

l. 283. *year*. Martha was about 49 when the poem first appeared. P borrows the manner of Swift's poems to Stella.

l. 285. *ascendant*. In the sky and so astrologically dominant.

114 l. 289. *wit and gold refines*. The sun-god Apollo presided over poetry and also 'ripened' gold in the ground.

Epilogue to the Satires: Dialogue I. Published separately on 16 May 1738, it was grouped with the second dialogue (published two months later) in the *Works* (1739) under the title *Epilogue to the Satires*.

l. 1 note. The source is Horace, *Satires*, II. iii. 1–4.

l. 8. '*Tories . . . a Tory*'. Adapted from *Second Satire of the First Book*, l. 68.

l. 10. '*To laugh at fools . . . trust in Peter*'. Adapted from *Second Satire of the First Book*, l. 40. Peter Walter, once more.

l. 11. *nice*. Discreet.

l. 12 note. Any owlish commentator, but perhaps George Bubb Dodington in particular.

l. 13. *Sir Billy*. Sir William Yonge (1693–1755).

l. 14. *Blunt*. See *Epistle to Bathurst*, l. 133.   *Huggins*. (d.1745), corrupt Warden of Fleet Prison.

l. 15. *Sappho*. Lady Mary Wortley Montagu.

115 l. 18 note. A facetious reference to one of the most contentious political issues of the day, which actually brought about the War of Jenkins' Ear in 1739.

l. 22 *Screen*. A nickname for Walpole, also known as Screenmaster-General. He was thought to have allowed the ministerial agents of the South Sea affair to escape, and to have shielded allies from parliamentary inquiry.

l. 34. *what he thinks mankind*. Walpole was widely identified with the maxim, 'Every man has his price', but this was a distortion of the view he actually expressed.

l. 39 note. Sir Joseph Jekyll, who opposed the Government in a crucial division in 1735.   *Old Whig*. One of the ancient breed of 'honest' Revolution Whigs, contrasted with the new men who had come to power under Walpole.

l. 40. *wig*. Full-bottomed wigs had gone out of fashion in favour of the shorter tie-wigs, but Jekyll, aptly perhaps for a senior judge, clung on to the older style.

l. 42. *Lord Chamberlains*. By the theatrical Licensing Act of 1737, all new plays had to be submitted to the Lord Chamberlain for censorship, a practice which survived until 1968.

116 l. 47 note. George Lyttelton (1709–73), one of P's closest allies now and a leader of the opposition centred on the Prince of Wales.

l. 50. *Lord Fanny*. Hervey.

l. 51 note. *Sejanus, Wolsey*. Walpole's enemies were said to find 'an odious parallel in Wolsey's rise from humble beginnings and in his engrossment of power, wealth and honours'.   *Fleury*. André de Fleury (1653–1743), cardinal and chief minister of France.

l. 66. *Henley ... Osborne*. John 'Orator' Henley and James Pitt ('Mother Osborne'), opposition writers.

l. 69 note. Referring to a speech of condolence on the death of the Queen in 1737, addressed to the King by Henry Fox, but perhaps written by Hervey, who used it in a Latin epitaph on the Queen.

117 l. 75. *Middleton and Bland*. Conyers Middleton, author of a life of Cicero, and Henry Bland, headmaster of Eton, who are suggested as the true authors of the Latin epitaph.

l. 82. *All parts performed ... children blessed*. 'Contemporary gossip reported that the Queen had died without taking the last sacrament and without being reconciled to the Prince of Wales' (*TE*, iv. 304).

l. 84. *gazetteer*. Official Government spokesman in the press, or merely a hack journalist paid to put the party line.

l. 92. *Selkirk ... De la Ware*. The Earl of Selkirk and Earl De La Warr: see *Dialogue II*, l. 61.

l. 98. *nepenthe*. A herb that dulls sorrow and induces oblivion.

l. 102. *All tears ... all eyes*. Alluding to Isa. 25: 8.

l. 104. *lose a question*. Suffer defeat in Parliament.   *job*. A corruptly organized deal.

118 l. 108. *gracious Prince*. A coded message, expressing Opposition hopes of a glorious future under the Prince of Wales, who was in fact to predecease his father.

l. 115. *Cibber's son*. The actor Theophilus Cibber.

l. 116. *Rich*. John Rich (1692–1761), theatre manager.

l. 119. *Ward*. John Ward, the MP expelled for forgery: see *Epistle to Bathurst*, l. 20.

l. 120. *Japhet*. Japhet Crook, also a forger: see *Epistle to Bathurst*, l. 86.   *his Grace*. The Archbishop of Canterbury, William Wake, who had helped to suppress a will left by George I.

l. 121. *Bond*. Denis Bond: see *Epistle to Bathurst*, l. 100.   *Peter*. Peter Walter.

l. 123. *Blount*. Charles Blount (1654–93), deistical writer, who committed suicide in unclear circumstances.

l. 124. *Passeran*. The Count of Passerano (1698–1737), Italian free-thinker, was arrested in 1732 for publishing his book in favour of the right to suicide. He was also reviled as a homosexual.

l. 130 note. The first Gin Act of 1736 attempted to put a stop to the gin trade by prohibitive duties, but it proved unenforceable. The Opposition contested its passage through Parliament.

l. 131. *Foster.* James Foster (1697–1753), an anabaptist preacher.

l. 133. *Quaker's wife.* Mary Drummond (d. 1777) became famous for preaching to large congregations in London in 1735.

l. 134 note. Llandaff was one of the poorest seats for a bishop to occupy, worth barely £200 at the start of the century. Its current incumbent was John Harris (1680–1738).

119 l. 135. *Allen.* P's great friend, the Bath philanthropist Ralph Allen (1693–1764).

l. 138. *Virtue.* Implies the political probity of the Opposition, against the corruption ('vice') of the Government.

l. 149. *scarlet head.* Suggesting the Whore of Babylon: Rev. 17, 18.

l. 150. *carted.* Prostitutes were drawn through the streets on a cart as part of their punishment.

l. 154. *flag inverted.* A sign of dishonour.

l. 157. *pagod.* Idol.

120 *Epilogue to the Satires: Dialogue II.* First published 18 July 1738, two months after the first dialogue, under the title *One Thousand Seven Hundred Thirty Eight, Dialogue II.* Then joined to its predecessor in the *Works* under the present title.

l. 1. *Paxton.* Nicholas Paxton, the Treasury Solicitor, who oversaw the regulation of the press and conducted government prosecutions.

l. 6. *amain.* At full speed.

l. 7. *Invention.* Imagination.

l. 11 note. James Guthrie succeeded the poet Thomas Purney as Ordinary, or chaplain, of Newgate Prison. It was part of his role to publish penitent deathbed confessions by the condemned criminals.

l. 15. *souze.* Swoop like a hawk.

l. 17. *hall.* Westminster Hall, symbolic of justice.

l. 20. See *Dialogue I*, l. 112.

l. 22. *the poisoning dame.* Probably referring to *First Satire of the Second Book*, l. 81.

l. 29. *royal harts.* A hart royal was a stag 'that has been chased by a royal personage' (*OED*); it might then be 'proclaimed', i.e. an order issued that none should pursue it any more.

121 l. 39. *Wild.* The thief-taker Jonathan Wild (1683–1725), the great criminal boss of London.

l. 41. *drench*. Duck at a pump in the street.

l. 49. *directors*. Still a word with baneful South Sea overtones; indicates leaders of the large city institutions such as the East India Company.   *plums*. £100,000.

l. 57. *Peter*. Peter Walter.

l. 61. *Selkirk*. Charles Douglas, Earl of Selkirk (1663–1739) a Scottish peer.

122 l. 65 note. *Scarborough*. When this note was written, Scarborough was dead, having committed suicide in 1740.

l. 67. *Kent*. The architect William Kent, who laid out the gardens at Esher.   *Pelham*. Henry Pelham (1694–1754), Prime Minister from 1746 to his death.

ll. 71–2. *Secker ... Rundle ... Benson*. Three prelates, Thomas Secker, Thomas Rundle, and Martin Benson.

l. 73. *Berkeley*. The philosopher George Berkeley (1685–1753), a friend of Swift.

l. 77. *Somers ... Halifax*. Somers and Halifax were the leading patrons of their time, and both took an interest in the young P's work.

ll. 79–80. *Shrewsbury ... Carleton ... Stanhope*. Shrewsbury, Henry Boyle (Lord Carleton) and James Stanhope, leading politicians earlier in the century.

ll. 82–9. *Atterbury's softer hour ... and his own*. Atterbury had been imprisoned in the Tower of London before his exile. He had died in 1732; the remaining names form a roll-call of Opposition heroes and a pantheon of P's private heroes among statesmen.

123 l. 99. *Man of Ross*. John Kyrle: see *Epistle to Bathurst*, l. 250. John Barnard, Lord Mayor of London (1685–1764).

l. 110. *stoop*. Swoop.

l. 111. *number*. Lat. *numerus*, the (undistinguished) many.

l. 116. *Louis*. Louis XIV and his father's powerful minister, Cardinal Richelieu.

l. 117. *young Ammon*. Alexander the Great.

124 l. 120. *one honest line. Aeneid*, viii. 670 ('Secretos pios, his dantem iura Catonem'), which P read as a tribute to the republican hero Cato the younger.

l. 129. *Arnall*. The Government hack William Arnall.

l. 130. *Polwarth*. Henry Hume, Lord Polwarth (1708–94); he had a distinguished career in national politics and was one of P's executors.

l. 137. *Verres*. See *Dialogue I*, l. 51. Verres, from the corrupt governor of Sicily attacked by Cicero, had become another Opposition nickname for Walpole.

l. 142. *pretend*. Take upon himself, presume.

l. 150. *Turenne*. Vicomte de Turenne (1611–75), Marshal of France.

125 l. 159. *Page*. The brutal Judge Francis Page (1661–1741).

l. 160. *bard*. P's note refers to a poem by George Bubb Dodington, addressed to Walpole in 1726.

l. 172. *Westphaly*. Westphalia, the German region noted for producing ham.

ll. 185–6. *Japhet ... Chartres*. Japhet Crook, the forger, and Colonel Francis Charteris.

l. 187. *Pindus*. A mountain in Thessaly, home of the Muses.

126 l. 191. *gin*. Referring again to the agitation over the Gin Act: see *Dialogue I*, l. 130.

l. 192. *in*. In office.

l. 194. *on his brows*. The horns of the cuckold.

l. 218. *tardy Hall*. Westminster Hall, centre of the obstructive system of justice.

127 l. 227. *Gazette*. The *London Gazette*, the official record of government.   *address*. Official address from the Lords or Commons to the monarch.

l. 230. *Waller's wreath*. Waller had mourned the death of Cromwell in a poem published in 1659.

l. 231. *feather to a star*. Boileau's *Ode* had made a star of the French King's hat-plume, as a comet portending disaster to his enemies.

l. 237 note. John Anstis (1669–1744), herald.

l. 238. *other stars than * and ***. The stars may indicate George and Frederick, the King and Prince of Wales.

l. 239. *Mordington*. A particularly anonymous Earl.   *Stair*. John Dalrymple, second Earl, soldier and diplomat.

l. 241. *Digby*. Lord Digby (1662–1752), father of P's friend Robert Digby.

128 l. 252. *that cause*. Liberty.

Epigram Engraved on the Collar of a Dog. Written around 1736 or 1737; first published in 1738. The dog in question was apparently one of the puppies of P's own bitch, Bounce, and was presented to Frederick, Prince of Wales (the focus of opposition to the court) in 1736. The year 1737 was the year of the irrevocable break between the Prince and his father, King George II. The Prince had lived at Kew House since 1732.

THE DUNCIAD

129 The history of *The Dunciad* is exceedingly complicated, as regards both composition and publication. For purposes of clarity, four stages may be identified: (1) The original work in three books, published on 18 May 1728. (2) The poem garnished with an extensive prose apparatus and many blanks filled in with real names: this was known as *The Dunciad Variorum*, and published on 10 Apr. 1729. (3) A fourth book, added on 20 Mar. 1742, entitled *The New Dunciad*. (4) The complete four-book version, published on 29 Oct. 1743. In this, the king of the dunces became Colley Cibber, in place of Lewis Theobald.

All the voluminous preliminaries and appendices have been omitted, including (1) An 'Advertisement to the Reader', attributed to Warburton but probably P's own. (2) 'Testimonies of Authors', a satirical conspectus of the views of his victims and adversaries. (3) Various appendices, including a list of attacks on P prior to the appearance of *The Dunciad*; an advertisement (preface) to the new fourth book in 1742; a short notice in the press from 1730; a 'Parallel of the Characters of Mr Dryden and Mr Pope', drawn from contemporary sources; a 'Declaration' by the author of the authenticity of the poem, in mock-legal form; an index to the 'matters' of the poem. Other preliminaries include a satire on Bentley, probably written by Warburton.

P had been amassing materials to discountenance his enemies for many years, but *The Dunciad* itself took shape only in the later 1720s. During Swift's visit to England in 1726, the project seems to have gained momentum. One spur to action had been the appearance of *Shakespeare Restored* by Lewis Theobald in 1726, a work whose assault on P's credentials as an editor led to the enthronement of Theobald as the original king of the dunces. The coronation of George II gave P new opportunities and may have influenced the choice of a Lord Mayor's installation as the setting.

The annotation in this edition has had to be strictly limited in order to avoid swamping the volume. (See above, p. 175.) Only sustained and significant literary allusions are glossed, most notably those to P's epic predecessors.

Ovid. From *Metamorphoses*, xi. 58–60: 'But Phoebus is at hand to freeze the monster as it reappears to bite, and fixes its mouth in a rictus with gaping jaws.'

Book I

l. 1. *Mighty Mother.* Magna mater, sometimes confused with other maternal deities.

l. 2. *Smithfield muses*. P suggests that the low entertainments of the fairground, traditionally held like Bartholomew Fair in the less salubrious environs of the City, have now invaded the West End.

l. 6. *Dunce the first*. Unmistakably pointing to the succession of George II to his father in 1727.

l. 10. *Thunderer*. Jove (epic diction).

130 l. 20. *Dean*. Swift is celebrated as Dean of St Patrick's, and author of the *Drapier's Letters* and the *Bickerstaff Papers*, as well as *Gulliver's Travels*.

l. 25. *Boeotia*. The district north of Athens which became, unfairly, proverbial for the stupidity of its inhabitants.

ll. 29–30. *Close to those walls . . . Monro would take her down*. Bedlam, or Bethlehem Hospital, stood on the northern fringe of the historic City. James Monroe was physician to the hospital.

l. 39. *miscellanies*. Poetic anthologies (stress on first syllable).

l. 42. *Journals, Medleys, Merc'ries, Magazines*. Titles used by journals: the first 'magazine' in the modern sense dates from 1731.

l. 44. *Grub Street*. A real location near Bedlam and Moorfields which had become synonymous with indigent hack writers.

l. 46. *virtues*. The four traditionally recognized cardinal virtues.

l. 50. *who thirst for scribbling sake*. Recalling Matt. 5: 6 (righteousness, rather than scribbling).

l. 57. *Jacob*. Jacob Tonson.   *third day*. The benefit night for dramatists.

131 l. 74. *Zembla*. The Arctic land Novaya Zemlya.   *Barca*. In the desert region of Libya (modern El Marj).

l. 85. *when ** rich and grave*. In the original version of the poem, the name of Sir George Thorold, Lord Mayor in 1719, had been spelt out.

l. 91. *shrieves*. Sheriffs.

132 l. 101. *Bruin*. Bears were supposed to lick their young into shape.

l. 108. *Bays*. Cibber, who was adorned with laurel by virtue of his office.

l. 126. *sooterkins*. Small animals which according to folklore were born to Dutchwomen huddled over their stoves. By extension, abortive literary productions.

133 l. 144. *jakes*. Privy.

l. 145. *Gothic*. Of the dark ages, medieval (pejorative).   *Rome*. Pronounced 'room'.

l. 168. *butt and bays*. The Poet Laureate was entitled to a cask of wine annually, along with his imaginary laurels. But the phrase wonderfully suggests a low tavern.

134 l. 202. *box*. Dice-box.

l. 203. *White's*. The gaming club in St James's Street.

l. 209. *Curtius*. Marcus Curtius, a defender of Rome.

l. 211. *Rome's ancient geese*. The Romans were warned by geese of the approach of the enemy when the Gauls attacked the Capitol in 390 BC, allowing Manlius Capitolinus to resist the assault.

l. 222. *Hockley Hole*. A bear-baiting centre in Clerkenwell, north of London.

135 l. 224. *fiddle*. Jester.

l. 234. *mundungus*. Strong tobacco of poor quality.

ll. 250–3. *the Cid . . . dear Nonjuror claims*. Cibber's plays and play-doctorings.

l. 256. *Ilion*. The destruction of Troy as described by Virgil in *Aeneid*, Book II.

136 l. 281. *'scape*. By benefit of clergy.

ll. 289–91. *her bird . . . on his crown*. A blasphemous parody of the descent of the dove after Christ's baptism (Matt. 3: 16).

l. 298. *fool of quality*. Perhaps Lord Hervey, who may also be the 'aide de camp' in l. 305.

137 l. 306. *points*. Sharp turns of wit.

l. 307. *Billingsgate*. Coarse and abusive language, appropriate to the Thames-side fish-market.

l. 312. *nursing-mother*. A relevant verse in Isa. 49: 23 had been used in Stuart coronation services.

l. 330. *King Log*. In Aesop's fable, Jove first sends a useless lump of wood down to the frogs who had asked for a king; when they are still dissatisfied, he sends down a stork which devours them. The meaning is that the wooden George I may be succeeded by a rapacious George II.

Book II

l. 4. *showers*. Of eggs and rotten fruit.

138 l. 14. *scarlet hats*. Those of cardinals.

l. 16. *seven hills*. The Septimontium, seven elevated parts of Rome on which the ancient city was built.

l. 21. *bags*. Bag-wigs, with the back-hair of the wig in a pouch.

l. 22. *crapes*. Of the clerical order.   *garters*. Of the knightly order.

l. 24. *hacks*. Hackney carriages.

l. 27. *that area*. Around St Mary le Strand, the first of the new Queen Anne churches, built by James Gibbs 1714–17. A maypole had stood on the site, and though it was pulled down under the Commonwealth, it was replaced and the last one set up as recently as 1713. The church stood on a spot where the Strand was then joined by small streets leading out of the raffish Covent Garden area. The 'saints of Drury Lane' (l. 30) are prostitutes who populated the district. Jacob Tonson's shop stood opposite Catherine Street, about a hundred yards west of the church.

l. 31. *stationers*. The book trade in general.

l. 37. *adust*. Dark and gloomy.

139 l. 50. *More*. James Moore Smythe (1702–34), minor author.

l. 72. *cates*. Provisions, dainties.

l. 78. *vaticide*. Murderer of poets (by mangling their works, etc.).

l. 82. *the Bible ... the Pope's Arms*. Curll's shop had been opposite Catherine Street (see l. 27), but he later moved to Covent Garden and the Pope's Head in nearby Rose Street. Lintot's shop was near Temple Bar, some two hundred yards further east along the Strand.

140 l. 92. *Ichor*. The fluid supposed to flow in the veins of the gods.

l. 98. *black grottos*. Coal wharves which lay at the foot of Milford Lane, which ran south from the Strand between St Mary's and the western end of the Temple.

l. 100. *link-boys*. Boys who carried torches in the streets to light the way.

l. 103. *sympathetic*. Acting by an occult affinity.

l. 107. *vindicates*. Lays claim to (as victor).

141 l. 128. *empty Joseph*. The word Joseph could mean a loose upper-coat.

l. 135. *hapless Monsieur*. Nicolas-François Rémond: a lover of Lady Mary Wortley Montagu.

l. 146. *confessors*. Those who proclaim the faith (stress on first syllable).

l. 147. *Defoe*. He was put in the pillory in 1703 on account of the ill-managed irony of *The Shortest Way with the Dissenters*. He did not actually lose his ears.

l. 155. *labours*. Travail.

142 l. 171. *lettered post*. A post used as a billboard to advertise books.

l. 181. *horns*. Associated with river-gods (like that of Eridanus, sometimes identified with the Po, but also the river into which Phaethon was cast by Jove's thunderbolt), and with cuckolds.

l. 184. *burn*. P's note suggests that Curll's 'condition' was venereal infection.

143 l. 218. *only tender part*. Paris shot Achilles in his vulnerable heel and killed him.

l. 238. *Norton*. Defoe's son Benjamin Norton Defoe. *brangling*. Wrangling.

l. 240. *snipsnap*. Sharp repartee.

l. 242. *major, minor, and conclusion quick*. Referring to the term of a syllogism in formal logic.

144 l. 251. *Sir Gilbert*. Heathcote.

l. 255. *enthusiast*. Here, a canting, fanatical preacher belonging to a radical religious sect.

ll. 261-8. Rufus's hall is Westminster Hall, which went back to the time of William II (Rufus). Hungerford Market lay on the river side of the Strand at its western end, on the site now occupied by Charing Cross station.

l. 269. *Bridewell*. The house of correction for vagrant women and prostitutes, located near the junction of the Thames and Fleet Ditch.

l. 271. *disemboguing*. Discharging, into a larger current.

l. 281. *pig*. Ingot.

l. 287. *lighter*. Thames barge.

145 l. 295. *. Probably Aaron Hill, a dramatist and poet who attempted to form a friendship with P despite various clashes.

l. 311. *Niobe*. According to myth, her seven sons and seven daughters were killed by Apollo and Diana; Niobe wept for them until she was turned into stone.

l. 312. *Mother Osborne*. In reality James Pitt.

146 ll. 333-4. *Lutetia ... Nigrina ... Merdamante*. Names suggesting dirt and dung: Lutetia was the Latin name for Paris, from its muddy location.

l. 336. *Hylas*. The page of Hercules, drawn down into a spring by water-nymphs enamoured of his beauty.

l. 341. *Alpheus*. A Greek river which rose in Greece, near the Grecian town Pisa, flowed through the sea and came up in the fountain of Arethusa in Sicily.

l. 346. *from Paul's to Aldgate*. i.e. from St Paul's cathedral to the eastern gate of the city at Aldgate.

l. 350. *surcingle*. A girdle round a priest's cassock.

l. 353. *confess*. Make confession to.

l. 354. *flamen*. Priest.

l. 358. *Heaven's Swiss*. Mercenaries, as in the proverbial phrase, 'Law, logic and the Switzers fight for anybody'.

l. 359. *Lud's famed gates*. Ludgate, where Fleet Street enters the ancient walled city: Lud was a legendary British king.

147 l. 374. *Ulysses' ear . . . Argus' eye*. Ulysses filled the ears of his men with wax to ensure that they resisted the call of the Sirens; Argus was a herdsman with eyes all over his body, which rendered him perpetually awake.

l. 379. *sophs*. Sophomores, students.   *templars*. Students of law at the Temple.

l. 385. *mum*. A beer of German origin.

l. 398. *Arthur*. Blackmore had written epics on *Prince Arthur* and *King Arthur*.

l. 400. *Christ's no kingdom*. Bishop Benjamin Hoadley had set off the so-called Bangorian controversy with a sermon in 1717, denying the secular authority of the Church.

l. 409. *nutation*. Nodding.

148 l. 416. *front*. Forehead, but also impudence.

l. 420. *bulks*. Framework projecting from the shopfront, supposed to be the appropriate sleeping-place for a destitute poet.

l. 424. *round-house*. Gaol.

l. 425. *sink*. Sewer.

l. 427. *neighbouring Fleet*. The Fleet Prison stood by the Ditch, just north of Ludgate.

Book III

l. 4. *Cimmerian*. Cimmeria was a fabulous land on the outermost edge of the world, shrouded in perpetual mists.

l. 6. *refined from reason*. (1) Ostensibly, minds made specially acute by the power of reason; (2) ironically, minds too 'fine' to be penetrated by an idea.

l. 11. *chemist's flame*. In the alchemical still.

ll. 13–14. *on fancy's easy wing . . . th'Elysian shade*. A descent into the underworld, modelled particularly on *Aeneid*, Book VI.

149 l. 18. *Castalia's streams*. The spring sacred to the Muses on Parnassus,

but the whole line suggests the unwashed woman devotee of the Muses found elsewhere in P.

l. 26. *proof.* Invulnerability (as of armour).

l. 37. *band.* Collar.

l. 51. *thrid.* Thread.

150 l. 54. *owl's ivy.* The ivy of poetic honour inappropriately linked to the solemn fatuity of the owl.

l. 70. *burning line.* The Equator.

l. 74. *science.* Knowledge.

l. 85. *Hyperborean.* Belonging to the extreme north.

l. 87. *Maeotis.* The Sea of Azov adjoining the Crimea. The Tanais or Don enters the sea on its northern shore.

l. 91. *Alaric.* King of the Visigoths, who sacked Rome in AD 410.

l. 92. *Genseric.* King of the Vandals who pillaged Rome in AD 455.
Attila. King of the Huns (*c.* AD 410-453), known as 'scourge of God'.

l. 93. *Ostrogoths.* Eastern Goths.   *Latium.* Italy.

l. 94. *Visigoths.* Western Goths.

151 l. 105. *Livy.* Born at Patuvium (Padua).

l. 106. *Virgilius.* St Virgilius, the Irish-born Bishop of Salzburg (*c.* AD 700-784), condemned for asserting the existence of antipodean lands.

l. 107. *cirque.* The Colosseum.

l. 112. *Phidias . . . Apelles.* The greatest sculptor and painter, respectively, of antiquity.

l. 115. *linsey-wolsey.* Confused, indeterminate.

l. 131. *Berecynthia.* The *magna mater*, Cybele, a goddess of nature (see i. 1).

152 l. 142. *new Cibber.* The son of Colley, Theophilus Cibber.

l. 147. *gillhouse.* Tavern, drinking-house.

l. 160. *jacks.* Referring to the creaking of the turnspit used in cooking.

l. 162. *Break Priscian's head.* Break the rules of grammar (proverbial), from the fifth-century Latin grammarian.

l. 163. *larum.* 'Rush down with loud cries' (*OED*).

153 l. 179. *yon pair.* Probably Thomas Burnet and George Duckett.

l. 187. *myster wight.* Seemingly 'uncouth man'.

l. 195. *type.* Symbol.

l. 196. *pot.* Tankard.

154 l. 233. *sorcerer*. The passage refers to theatrical spectacles which became popular in the 1720s. Theobald had also contributed with a play called *The Rape of Proserpine* (1727), but Rich was the acknowledged master of the stage effects described here.

l. 243. *Cynthia*. Symbolizing the moon.

l. 254. *sarsenet*. A fine soft silk used for dresses.

155 l. 264. *Rides in the whirlwind, and directs the storm*. A parody of the famous line in Addison's *Campaign* (1705), l. 292.

l. 276. *Foreseen*. By Settle as City Poet, when he had been in charge of the pageantry for the Lord Mayor's Day show.

l. 278. *Bow's stupendous bells*. Bow bells, i.e. those of St Mary le Bow in Cheapside, traditionally defining the true 'city' by the range within which they could be heard.

l. 291. *carted*. Dragged through the street in a cart as a form of punishment.

156 l. 299. *booths*. The primitive theatrical stalls at a fair.

l. 301. *opera*. Italian opera had become highly fashionable in the 1720s.

l. 315. *Semele*. Semele was consumed by lightning when Jove made love to her, but her unborn child was rescued: this was Dionysus.

l. 324. *Midas*. King Midas of Phrygia showed his folly by judging Pan superior to Apollo in a contest of flute-playing.

l. 327. *new Whitehall*. Whitehall Palace in fact was never rebuilt after being destroyed by fire in 1698.

l. 328. *Boyle*. The Earl of Burlington.

l. 331. *Hibernian politics*. Swift had been preoccupied by Irish affairs since the time of the *Drapier's Letters* in 1724.

l. 336. *Westminster*. The school.

l. 337. *Isis' elders*. Oxford dons.

157 l. 340. *ivory gate*. According to Homer (*Odyssey*, Book XIX), there were two gates of dreams, one ivory (the source of false dreams) and one of horn (the source of true dreams). The passage from Virgil in the note renders the same idea.

Book IV

l. 3. *darkness visible*. See *Paradise Lost*, i. 63.

l. 9. *dog-star*. See *Epistle to Arbuthnot*, l. 3.

l. 21. *science*. Learning.

l. 22. *wit*. Imagination, creativity.

158 l. 28. *Chicane in furs, and casuistry in lawn*. i.e. legal manœuvring by

the ermine-clad judges, and sophistical reasoning by the lawn-clad bishops.

l. 31. *Mathesis*. Mathematics.

l. 41. *Thalia*. Muse of comedy.

l. 66. *Briareus*. One of the Hekatoncheires, sons of Uranus and Gaia, giants with a hundred hands.

159 l. 93. *bow the knee to Baal*. Proverbial from Rom. 11: 4, for worshipping false gods.

l. 96. *head*. A bust.

l. 103. *Narcissus*. Probably P's favourite target Lord Hervey, with his pallor and the fulsome praise he received from Dr Conyers Middleton.

l. 105. *Montalto*. Sir Thomas Hanmer, a high-bred politician who became Speaker of the Commons and then attempted a showy edition of Shakespeare in 1743–4.

160 l. 121. *Medea*. She restored Jason's father Aeson to Youth by boiling him in a cauldron with magic herbs.

l. 139. *spectre*. That of the famous Dr Richard Busby (1605–95), the strict and long-serving Master of Westminster School.

l. 141. *beavered brow*. Wearing a hat of beaver fur.

l. 144. *Winton*. Winchester College.

161 l. 180. *Council*. Privy Council.

162 l. 187. *Cam and Isis*. Cambridge and Oxford universities.

l. 198. *Crousaz*. Jean-Pierre de Crousaz, Swiss philosopher who had attacked the *Essay on Man*.   *Burgersdyck*. Francis Burgersdyck, professor of philosophy at Leiden.

l. 200. *Margaret and Clare Hall*. i.e. St John's and Clare Colleges at Cambridge.

l. 206. *Walker*. Dr Richard Walker, Vice-Master to Bentley at Trinity.

l. 217. *like Saul*. 1 Sam. 9: 2: 'from his shoulders and upward [Saul] was higher than any of his people'.

l. 222. *to C or K*. There is a hidden joke here because P has converted Cibber's name from a soft c to a hard c.

163 l. 226. *Manilius*. Bentley had edited the minor Latin writer in 1739.   *Solinus*. Obscure Latin compiler of the third century.

l. 237. *Kuster*. Ludolph Kuster (1670–1716), whom Bentley had assisted in an edition of the compiler Suidas.   *Burman*. Pieter Burmann (1688–1741), Dutch scholar who published some of Bentley's emendations.   *Wasse*. Joseph Wasse (1672–1738), classical scholar, who helped Kuster in his edition of Suidas.

l. 243. *head of many a house*. i.e. college principal in the universities.

164 l. 272. *governor*. Tutor on the Grand Tour.

l. 278. *opening*. Beginning to cry.

l. 283. *sacred*. Protected.

l. 298. *Bourbon*. The King of France.

165 l. 322. *turned air*. Turned into nothing more than operatic arias.

l. 328. *not undone*. Not arrested, because once elected for a borough he would be immune from arrest for debt.

l. 347. *Annius*. Possibly based on the ninth Earl of Pembroke, known as the architect earl.

166 l. 364. *Mahomet*. Mohammed was fabled to have caused a pigeon to take grains from his ear, under the pretence that he was receiving messages from God.

l. 366. *Lares*. Domestic possessions.

l. 367. *Phoebe*. A goddess sometimes associated with Diana, and thus with chastity.

l. 370. *Niger*. Another Roman emperor who reigned only for a year, with consequently few coins from his reign surviving.

l. 374. *sistrum*. An ancient Egyptian musical instrument, used in the rituals of the Egyptian Club, whose doings P evidently followed.

l. 380. *Sallee rovers*. The notorious Moorish pirates who swept the waters of the Mediterranean and North Atlantic.

167 l. 398. *tribe*. Antiquarians and virtuosi who formed cabinets of curiosities (not unlike the contents of P's own grotto).

l. 421. *th'enamelled race*. Butterflies.

168 l. 452. *Wilkins' wings*. Dr John Wilkins (1614–72), the prominent Royal Society figure, whose projects included a voyage to the moon.

l. 459. *clerk*. Clergyman.

l. 460. *mystery*. Revelation.

l. 463. *implicit faith*. 'Faith in spiritual matters, not independently arrived at by the individual, but involved in or subordinate to the general belief of the Church' (*OED*).

169 l. 479. *local*. Peculiar, not universal.

l. 484. *as Lucretius drew*. i.e. a god with no concern for or relevance to human beings, as expressed in the poem *De rerum natura*.

l. 488. *Theocles*. P refers to Shaftesbury's *Characteristics* (1711), including a 'rhapsody' entitled *The Moralists* uttered by one Theocles.

170 l. 511. *Kent, so Berkeley*. Apparently suggesting that the courtiers the

Duke of Kent and the Earl of Berkeley owed their posts to corruption involving a royal mistress.

l. 516. *Magus*. Oriental magician or sorcerer.

l. 520. *star*. Of knighthood.

l. 521. *feather*. Worn by Knights of the Garter in their headdress.

171   l. 549. *succinct in amice white*. Girdled in white linen resembling clerical garb. The passage parodies the transubstantiation of the host during the Eucharist.

l. 561. *crowds undone*. By the South Sea Bubble, which Knight helped to bring about as cashier of the Company.

l. 585. *cap and switch*. Belonging to a jockey ('switch' is a whip).

l. 586. *staff and pumps*. Belonging to running footmen.

172   l. 593. *bishop*. Based on William Talbot, Bishop of Durham.

l. 602. *first ministers*. Prime Ministers, and esp. Walpole.

l. 603. *three estates*. Lords spiritual, lords temporal, and Commons.

l. 609. *Hall*. Westminster Hall, centre of the judicial system.

l. 610. *Convocation*. The assembly of clergy which had been prorogued in 1717 and did not meet for another century.

l. 614. *Palinurus*. The helmsman of Aeneas, who fell into the ocean after dropping asleep (*Aeneid*, Books V–VI). Here representing Walpole as a leader not alert to the threat posed by foreign powers.

173   l. 635. *Medea*. As a priestess of Hecate she had supernatural powers and was able to bring down the constellations from the sky.

l. 637. *Argus' eyes by Hermes' wand oppressed*. Hermes slew Argus, the monster with a hundred eyes, with the help of his caduceus.

l. 656. *buries all*. The reading had been 'covers all' in the first version of the poem.

Further Reading

EDITIONS

J. Butt *et al.* (eds.), *The Twickenham Edition of the Poems of Alexander Pope* (11 vols.; London, 1939–69).

The Prose Works of Alexander Pope, vol. i, ed. N. Ault (Oxford, 1936); vol. ii, ed. R. Cowler (Oxford, 1986).

G. Sherburn (ed.), *The Correspondence of Alexander Pope* (5 vols.; Oxford, 1956).

BIOGRAPHY

M. Mack, *Alexander Pope: A Life* (London, 1985).

G. Sherburn, *The Early Career of Alexander Pope* (Oxford, 1934).

J. Spence, *Observations, Anecdotes, and Characters of Books and Men*, ed. J. M. Osborn (2 vols.; Oxford, 1966).

CRITICISM

Aids to Study

J. Barnard (ed.), *Pope: The Critical Heritage* (London, 1973).

M. Mack (ed.), *Essential Articles for the Study of Alexander Pope* (Hamden, Conn., 1968).

—— (ed.), *The Last and Greatest Art: Some Unpublished Poetical Manuscripts of Alexander Pope* (Newark, Del., 1984).

General Criticism

R. A. Brower, *Alexander Pope: The Poetry of Allusion* (Oxford, 1959).

H. Erskine-Hill, *The Social Milieu of Alexander Pope* (London, 1985).

M. Mack, *The Garden and the City* (Toronto, 1969).

—— *Collected in Himself: Essays Critical, Biographical and Bibliographical on Pope and some of his Contemporaries* (London, 1982).

G. S. Rousseau and P. Rogers (eds.), *The Enduring Monument: Alexander Pope Tercentenary Essays* (Cambridge, 1988).

Style

P. M. Spacks, *An Argument of Images: The Poetry of Alexander Pope* (Cambridge, Mass., 1971).

G. Tillotson, *On the Poetry of Pope*, 2nd edn. (Oxford, 1950).

Feminist Approaches

V. Rumbold, *Women's Place in Pope's World* (Cambridge, 1989).

Special Topics

M. R. Brownell, *Alexander Pope and the Arts of Georgian England* (Oxford, 1978).

P. Martin, *Pursuing Innocent Pleasures: The Gardening World of Alexander Pope* (Hamden, Conn., 1983).

Criticism of Particular Works

J. S. Cunningham, *Pope: The Rape of the Lock* (London, 1961).

H. Erskine-Hill, *Pope: The Dunciad* (London, 1977).

A. Williams, *Pope's 'Dunciad': A Study of its Meaning* (London, 1955).

M. Leranbaum, *Alexander Pope's 'Opus Magnum' 1729–1744* (Oxford, 1977), esp. for the *Essay on Man*.

A. D. Nuttall, *Pope's 'Essay on Man'* (London, 1984).

P. Dixon, *The World of Pope's Satires* (London, 1968).

F. Stack, *Pope and Horace* (Cambridge, 1985).

Index of Titles

Index of First Lines

The Oxford World's Classics Website

www.worldsclassics.co.uk

- Information about new titles
- Explore the full range of Oxford World's Classics
- Links to other literary sites and the main OUP webpage
- Imaginative competitions, with bookish prizes
- Peruse *Compass*, the Oxford World's Classics magazine
- Articles by editors
- Extracts from Introductions
- A forum for discussion and feedback on the series
- Special information for teachers and lecturers

www.worldsclassics.co.uk

American Literature

British and Irish Literature

Children's Literature

Classics and Ancient Literature

Colonial Literature

Eastern Literature

European Literature

History

Medieval Literature

Oxford English Drama

Poetry

Philosophy

Politics

Religion

The Oxford Shakespeare

A complete list of Oxford Paperbacks, including Oxford World's Classics, OPUS, Past Masters, Oxford Authors, Oxford Shakespeare, Oxford Drama, and Oxford Paperback Reference, is available in the UK from the Academic Division Publicity Department, Oxford University Press, Great Clarendon Street, Oxford OX2 6DP.

In the USA, complete lists are available from the Paperbacks Marketing Manager, Oxford University Press, 198 Madison Avenue, New York, NY 10016.

Oxford Paperbacks are available from all good bookshops. In case of difficulty, customers in the UK can order direct from Oxford University Press Bookshop, Freepost, 116 High Street, Oxford OX1 4BR, enclosing full payment. Please add 10 per cent of published price for postage and packing.

ALEXANDER POPE
SELECTED POETRY

ALEXANDER POPE was born in London in 1688. His elderly parents moved to Binfield in Windsor Forest around 1700 because of anti-Catholic laws. From early boyhood Pope suffered from a tubercular disease which retarded his growth and left him a lifelong invalid. A precocious poet, his first published work was the set of four pastorals published in 1709. A succession of brilliant poems followed, including *An Essay on Criticism* (1711), *Windsor Forest* (1713), and the five-canto version of *The Rape of the Lock*. Pope then embarked on a translation of the *Iliad* (1715–20), which together with the *Odyssey* (1725–6) left him financially secure. His position as the major living English poet was confirmed by the appearance of his *Works* in 1717. There followed a break in creative activity, during which Pope edited Shakespeare (1725). However, the appearance of the first *Dunciad* (1728) marked the beginning of a brilliant new phase, including the imitations of Horace, the *Essay on Man*, and the epistles to various friends. In 1742 Pope added a new fourth book to *The Dunciad*, and the complete work was published in 1743. Pope spent the last twenty-five years of his life at his villa in Twickenham, devoting much of his time to his celebrated garden and grotto. He died in 1744.

PAT ROGERS, DeBartolo Professor in the Liberal Arts at the University of South Florida, has written books on Pope, Swift, Johnson, Defoe, and Fielding, as well as general works such as *Grub Street* (1972), *The Augustan Vision* (1974), and *Literature and Popular Culture in Eighteenth-Century England* (1985). He is the editor of *The Oxford Illustrated History of English Literature* and has edited a selection of Pope's poetry and prose for The Oxford Authors Series as well as introducing Boswell's *Life of Johnson* for Oxford World's Classics. His most recent book is *The Samuel Johnson Encyclopedia* (1996).

OXFORD WORLD'S CLASSICS

For almost 100 years Oxford World's Classics have brought readers closer to the world's great literature. Now with over 700 titles—from the 4,000-year-old myths of Mesopotamia to the twentieth century's greatest novels—the series makes available lesser-known as well as celebrated writing.

The pocket-sized hardbacks of the early years contained introductions by Virginia Woolf, T. S. Eliot, Graham Greene, and other literary figures which enriched the experience of reading. Today the series is recognized for its fine scholarship and reliability in texts that span world literature, drama and poetry, religion, philosophy and politics. Each edition includes perceptive commentary and essential background information to meet the changing needs of readers.